The MAILBOX®

Science

MAILBOX® MAGAZINE

Grades 4–6

Great science activities and reproducibles
from the 1998–2003 issues of
The Mailbox® magazine

Life Science
- Cells
- The Heart
- Plants
- Ecosystems
- Genes

Earth Science
- Weathering and Erosion
- Storms
- Water
- Earthquakes
- Space

Physical Science
- Physics
- Chemistry
- Light
- Sound
- Energy

Plus 15 more science topics!

Editorial Team: Becky S. Andrews, Kimberley Bruck, Karen P. Shelton, Diane Badden, Thad H. McLaurin, Sharon Murphy, Karen A. Brudnak, Sarah Hamblet, Hope Rodgers, Dorothy C. McKinney

Production Team: Lori Z. Henry, Pam Crane, Rebecca Saunders, Jennifer Tipton Cappoen, Chris Curry, Sarah Foreman, Theresa Lewis Goode, Clint Moore, Greg D. Rieves, Barry Slate, Donna K. Teal, Zane Williard, Tazmen Carlisle, Marsha Heim, Lynette Dickerson, Mark Rainey

Manufactured in The United States
10 9 8 7 6 5 4 3 2 1

Table of Contents

Life Science

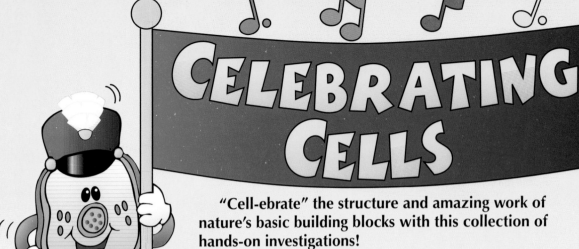

CELEBRATING CELLS

"Cell-ebrate" the structure and amazing work of nature's basic building blocks with this collection of hands-on investigations!

by Debi Kilmartin, Thomas M. Ryan Intermediate School, Hickory Corners, MI

WHAT'S MY SHAPE?

Topic: Shapes of cells

Invite students to take microscopic looks at the shapes of cells with this interesting investigation. In advance, gather for each group of four students, a copy of the chart on page 7, a microscope and the cell specimens and materials listed below and on the chart (or commercially prepared slides of similar specimens). Help students make temporary slides according to the directions provided.

Next, enlarge a copy of the chart to post on the board. Then divide students into groups of four. Have group members discuss what they think a cell of each specimen in the chart might look like and then draw that shape in their charts. In addition, have a member of each group draw that shape in the chart on the board. Then have groups view the slides and add actual drawings to their charts and to the one on the board. When students have completed their work, ask if the actual cell shapes matched their predictions. Conclude by having students discuss why different cells might be shaped the way they are.

Group Member Names:		
Cell Shapes		
	Prediction	Actual View
onion skin		
human skin (from under a fingernail)		
piece of thread		
piece of butterfly (or moth) wing		
human hair		

Making a Temporary Slide

Materials: slides and coverslips, tweezers, eyedropper, water, specimens

1. Place the specimen in the center of the slide.

2. Cover it with a drop of water.

3. Holding a coverslip by its side edges, place the bottom edge on the slide near the water drop.

4. Carefully lower the coverslip onto the specimen.

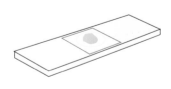

(Clean the slides and coverslips in warm water that contains a little dish detergent. Handle each slide by its sides. To dry a slide, stand it up at an angle on a dry paper towel. Let its upper end rest against a clean jar. Then soak the slide in rubbing alcohol to sterilize it. Allow the slide to dry completely before storing it.)

SIZE IS RELATIVE!

Topic: Size of cells

Help students understand the relative size of a cell with this measurement activity. Ask students to guess how big the average cell might be. List their answers on the board. Then share that the diameter of an average cell is about $^1/_{1,000}$ of an inch, much too small to be seen by the naked eye. Next, hold up a marble and suggest that it be used to represent a cell. Ask students, "How many times bigger do you think this marble is than the average cell?" Write students' guesses on the board. Then follow these steps to demonstrate how to find the marble's diameter:

1. Wrap a string around the marble and mark the length.
2. Using a ruler, measure from the end of the string to the mark.
3. Using a calculator, divide the measured circumference by 3.14 (π) to find the diameter *(about $^1/_2$ inch for an average-sized marble).*

Point out that the marble's diameter is actually 500 times that of an average cell! Provide groups of students with other round objects (such as Ping-Pong balls, tennis balls, or Oreo cookies), string, rulers, and calculators. Then have them practice finding the objects' diameters.

I'm really tiny... only about $^1/_{1,000}$ of an inch big!

HELPFUL WEB SITES

(current as of March 2006)

- **www.cellsalive.com**
  Visit this site for lots of links loaded with great visuals and animations.
- **www.eurekascience.com**
  This site is recommended by the National Science Teacher's Association. For an animated story about cells, visit the "I Can Do That" page. Then click on "Cells."

DIVING INTO CELLS

Topic: Cell structure

Dive into a study of the parts of a cell with this fun research and writing activity! First, have students use books and other resources, such as the Web sites shown, to research the structure and functions of plant and animal cells. Have students discuss their findings with the class. Then challenge pairs of students to use their research to help them write a story about their adventures scuba diving through a plant or animal cell. Have the pairs include dialogue that describes each structure they encounter. After each twosome shares its story, have each student complete a copy of page 8 as directed.

plant cell | animal cell

cell wall
mitochondrion
cell membrane
cytoplasm
vacuole
nucleus
endoplasmic reticulum
chloroplast

POINTING OUT THE DIFFERENCES

Topic: Differences between plant and animal cells

Challenge students to discover the major differences between plant and animal cells with this art project! Enlarge a copy of the cell diagrams on page 9 and then display it. Make one copy of page 9 for each small group of students. Also gather various art materials such as colorful paper, pipe cleaners, yarn, buttons, stickers, beads, and packing-foam pieces.

Next, tell students that they will be creating models of structures that make up plant and animal cells. Help the class read the list of cell structures on their copy of page 9. Then divide students into groups of four. Have the groups take turns choosing structures until all of the structures have been selected. Then provide the art materials and have each group create models of its structures. Explain that a group must make two copies of a model if a particular structure is found in both types of cells. When the models are finished, have the groups attach the structures in their correct positions on the display.

FATTEN UP THOSE CELLS!
Topic: Osmosis

Cells carry on many processes. One that's essential for survival is *osmosis*. During osmosis water moves from an area of greater concentration to one of lesser concentration. When water is taken into a cell, the cell swells. Have pairs of students observe this process of osmosis with a simple activity. Give each pair a lima bean seed, a tape measure, and a nine-ounce clear plastic cup half full of water. Have each pair measure and record the length and circumference of its bean and then drop it into the cup. Over the next three days, direct students to observe and measure the beans. At the end of the three days, discuss with students what happened *(the bean seeds swelled)*. Explain that because the bean seeds were dry inside, the water in the cup moved into the seed through its cell membrane. Conclude by having students think of other ways to observe osmosis *(wilted plants or lettuce, raisins plumping in water)*.

Levels of Organization

Cells—*Students*

Tissues—*Classes*

Organs—*Grade Levels*

Organ Systems—*Schools*

Organism—*School District*

GOIN' WITH THE FLOW
Topic: A cell's role in an organism

How is a cell like a worker in a toy factory? Find out with this thought-provoking activity. Tell students that the work of cells in multicellular organisms is often divided, meaning that each cell has a different job to do to keep the organism alive. Relate this to a toy factory where some workers assemble toys and others package them. Have students discuss what might happen in the packaging department if the assembly department stopped working. Next, display the list shown (leaving out the italicized parts). Explain the list as follows:

In organisms, cells (the lowest level) make up tissues, and tissues form organs. Organs form organ systems, and organ systems join together to make an organism (the highest level).

Have students discuss what might happen to an organism if one of its organs stops working. Then help students understand the different levels of organization within an organism by adding the italicized parts to the flow chart. Explain as follows:

In a school, students make up a class. Classes form grade levels. Grade levels make up schools, and schools join together to make up a school district.

Conclude by having pairs of students write and illustrate similar analogies to share with the class.

DEMONSTRATING DIFFUSION
Topic: Diffusion

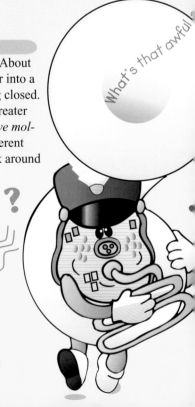

Help students understand cell diffusion with an activity that puts their sense of smell to the test! About 15 to 20 minutes before beginning the activity, use an eyedropper to insert four milliliters of vinegar into a regular-sized balloon. Blow up the balloon and place it inside a large brown paper bag. Fold the bag closed. Then explain to students that *diffusion* is a process that allows molecules to move from an area of greater concentration to one of lesser concentration. Ask students how diffusion is like osmosis *(both involve molecules moving from areas of greater concentration to ones of lesser concentration)* and how it's different *(osmosis involves only water, while diffusion involves all types of molecules)*. During this time, walk around the room carrying the bag. Soon students will detect its vinegary smell! When they do, remove the balloon and admit that you placed vinegar in it. Relate the balloon and its "skin" to a cell and its membrane. Point out that molecules (the vinegar) move through a cell's membrane (the balloon's skin) from an area of greater concentration (inside the balloon) to one of lesser concentration (outside the balloon). Conclude by having students answer the questions below.

- How did the smell from inside the balloon reach your nose? *The vinegar molecules moved from an area of greater concentration (inside the balloon) to one of lesser concentration (outside the balloon).*
- Where were the vinegar molecules more concentrated? *inside the balloon*
- Why did the vinegar molecules move out of the balloon? *to reach an area of lesser concentration*

Group Member Names:		
Cell Shapes		
	Prediction	Actual View
onion skin		
human skin (from under a fingernail)		
piece of thread		
piece of butterfly (or moth) wing		
human hair		

Group Member Names:		
Cell Shapes		
	Prediction	Actual View
onion skin		
human skin (from under a fingernail)		
piece of thread		
piece of butterfly (or moth) wing		
human hair		

©The Mailbox® • *Science* • TEC60859

Note to the teacher: Use with "What's My Shape?" on page 4.

SEEING A MALL IN A DIFFERENT WAY

What does a cell have in common with your favorite shopping mall? Plenty—if you think creatively! Find out by following the directions below.

Directions: Read the functions of the cell structures in the chart below. Then read the list of mall structures and their functions at the bottom of the page. In the chart, write each mall structure next to a cell structure that has a similar function. The first one has been done for you.

	Cell Structure	Cell Function	Mall Structure
1.	cell wall	outermost part in plants, provides support and protection	outside walls
2.	cell membrane	protects, controls movement of substances through it	
3.	cytoplasm	area of movement	
4.	nucleus	regulates and controls cell activities	
5.	nuclear membrane	protects nucleus, lets materials in or out	
6.	chromosomes	direct activities of cell	
7.	endoplasmic reticulum	transportation system	
8.	ribosomes	produce proteins	
9.	mitochondria	supply energy	
10.	vacuole	stores water and food	
11.	chloroplasts	produce food	

 (**Parking Lot**)

outside walls (provide shape, protection, support)

mall food court (produces food)

water tank and pipes (store water)

mall office (regulates and controls activities)

supply carts (transport merchandise)

mall office director (directs activities)

mall entrance (provides passage into and out of mall)

mall office walls and door (protect office, let workers in and out)

electrical system (supplies electrical energy)

hallways (areas for moving people and supplies)

vendors (produce supplies, goods)

Bonus Box: Can you think of two more ways that a mall and a cell are alike? Write your answers on the back of this page.

©The Mailbox® • *Science* • TEC60859 • Key p. 158

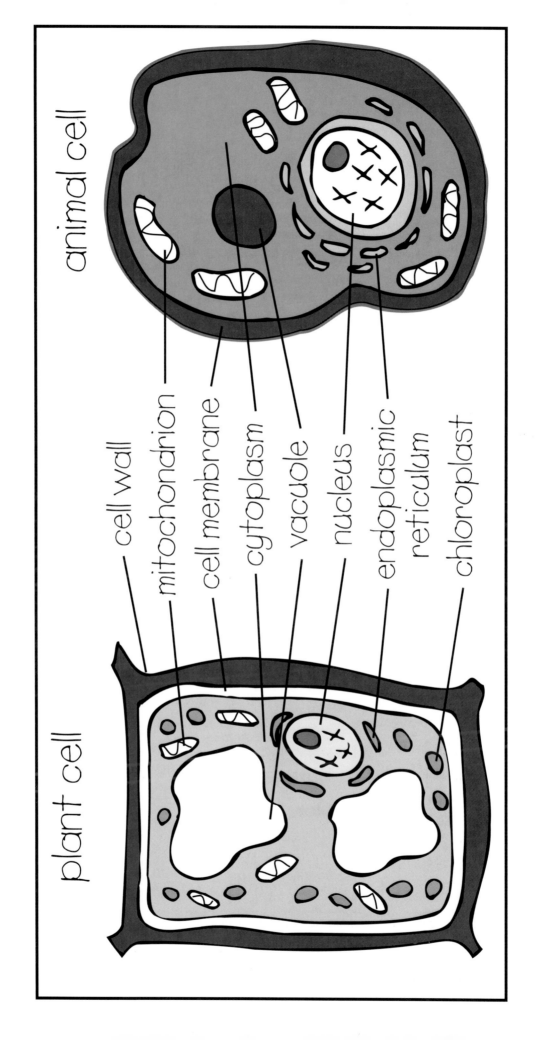

Cell Diagrams
Use with "Pointing Out the Differences" on page 5.

©The Mailbox® • Science • TEC60859

9

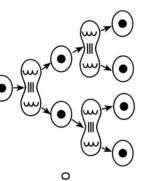

DIVIDE AND MULTIPLY!

Every living thing—from tiny microbes to enormous elephants—is made up of cells. Plants and animals have *lots* of them. How do they get so many? By cell division! One cell divides to form 2 cells, 2 cells divide to form 4 cells, and so on. Why do cells divide? To help organisms grow or to replace dead cells.

Some cells reproduce faster than others. But suppose that all cells divided once each day. How many cells would be formed in 1 week? 2 weeks? 30 days? Grab a calculator and follow the steps below to find out!

Step 1: Predict the number of cells formed from 1 cell in 1 week: _____ 2 weeks: _____ 30 days: _____

Step 2: Use your calculator to find the number of cells formed in 1 week. Record your answers in the chart.

Cells formed in 1 week: _____

Day	1	2	3	4	5	6	7
Number of Cells							

Step 3: Find the number of cells formed in 2 weeks. Use your answer from Day 7 above to help you continue your calculations. Record your answers in the chart.

Cells formed in 2 weeks: _____

Day	8	9	10	11	12	13	14
Number of Cells							

Step 4: Look back at your answers in the charts in Steps 2 and 3. Can you find a pattern? What is it? _____ . Starting with your answer from Day 14, use the pattern to find the number of cells formed in 30 days. Record your answers in the chart. Note that the number of cells formed in 3 weeks has been filled in for you. Warning! Your calculator won't be much help from Day 27 on (too many digits to handle)!

Day	15	16	17	18	19	20	21
Number of Cells							2,097,152

Day	22	23	24	25	26	27	28	29	30
Number of Cells									

Cells formed in 30 days: _____

Bonus Box: How many cells would be produced in 1 week if a cell divided *twice a day*?

Lub-Dub, Lub-Dub!

Creative Activities for Teaching About the Heart

February is the perfect time to celebrate a hardworking body organ: the heart. Use the following activities to help students appreciate this tireless muscle that works 24–7 for a lifetime!

An Unforgettable Journey
Concept: the route of blood through the body

Make the concept of how blood flows through the body easier for students to grasp with this simulation. In advance, make the signs shown in the diagram. Tape the signs and strips of red and blue bulletin board paper onto the floor of your school's gym as indicated. Add the arrows with marker. Then cut three large red paper circles and three blue ones. Tape each red circle back-to-back to a blue circle.

When the diagram is ready, have three students stand in the heart's blue section, each holding a paper circle to represent a blood cell. Direct the students to hold their circles with the blue sides facing out to represent oxygen-depleted blood. Instruct the students to follow the path to the lungs, where they will drop off carbon dioxide and pick up oxygen. As students leave the lungs, have them flip their circles to red to represent oxygen-rich blood and walk to the heart's red section. Next, have the trio leave the heart and follow the path of the arteries. Explain that arteries branch off into smaller blood vessels throughout the body until they join the veins at the capillaries, where oxygen and nutrients are released and waste products are collected. As students pass through the capillaries, have them flip their circles to blue and follow the path of the veins back to the heart's blue section. Announce that real blood cells make this trip in about a minute. Then repeat the process with additional threesomes until everyone has taken the circulatory journey. *adapted from an idea by Jan Drehmel Parkview Elementary, Chippewa Falls, WI*

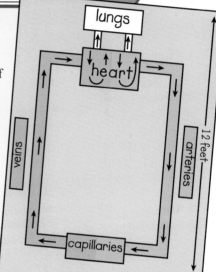

H = 8 squat thrusts

E = 5 push-ups

A = 1 deep knee bend

R = 18 jumping jacks

T = 20 sit-ups

Hearty Exercises
Concept: comparing resting and working pulse rates

How much harder does the heart pump when exercising than resting? Have students find out with this heart-healthy investigation. First, have each student find her resting heart rate by following the steps shown. (Have a stopwatch or watch with a second hand available.) Next, have the student spell the word *HEART* vertically on her paper. Beside the *H*, have her list an exercise she could do eight times, since *H* is the eighth letter of the alphabet. Direct her to complete the list as shown.

When students have finished their lists, direct each child to perform her first exercise. Then have her stop, calculate her heart rate, and record it on her paper. After the student rests for five minutes, have her perform her second exercise. Instruct the student to continue exercising, stopping, calculating, and resting until she has completed all five exercises. Conclude by having each student compare her resting heart rate with the working heart rate she recorded after completing each exercise. Ask volunteers to share their data and suggest which exercises might make their hearts stronger if done regularly.

To find your heart rate:
1. Press your fingertips under your jaw. Count the beats for 15 seconds.
2. Multiply the number of beats by four to find the beats per minute.
3. Record the beats per minute on your paper.

THE GENES SCENE
Groovy Activities on Genes and Heredity

Looking for activities to help students understand the basic concepts of heredity? Then try the following custom-made activities on for size. They're sure to be a perfect fit!

by Dr. Barbara B. Leonard, Winston-Salem, NC

Sports Star or Couch Potato?
Topic: Inherited versus acquired characteristics

Start your study with an activity that helps students think about the difference between inherited and acquired traits. First, explain that *heredity* is the passing on of biological attributes from one generation to the next. Then share the scenarios shown with students. Ask, "Which traits do you think Burt inherited from his parents? Which ones has he acquired because of his environment?" Repeat the discussion with Jeanie's scenario. Help students understand that as powerful as genes are, they don't completely control who we are. For example, a person may have inherited the potential to play the piano. But if he never takes lessons or practices, that potential may not be realized. After the discussion, ask each student to meet with a partner to talk about these questions:

- What are some traits you think you inherited from your parents?
- What traits do you think you have acquired from your environment?

Scenarios

- Burt Kromosome has a muscular build like his dad, a former professional football player. Burt roughhouses with his dad and can beat him at hand wrestling. But he'd rather sit on the couch watching TV and munching on potato chips. Burt could stand to lose some weight, but he says he'll never be out of shape.
- Jeanie Gene's mother teaches French and Spanish. Jeanie makes top grades in both languages, but she has trouble with math. Her parents hired a tutor, and now she makes the honor roll at school.

> I'm tall like my dad, but I have my mom's hair and eyes!

A Jumble of Genes
Topic: What makes us unique

Encourage students to consider what makes them unique with this thought-provoking activity. Bring in photos of your family. Have students examine the photos for physical traits that might have been passed down from parent to child, such as hair color, facial features, and height. Explain to students that, like you, they have inherited certain traits from their parents and grandparents. If you have siblings in the photos, have students compare your physical characteristics with theirs. Ask, "If siblings have the same parents, why don't they always look exactly alike?" Then explain that each person's mixture of about 50,000 genes differs slightly from everyone else's. Go over the definitions of *gene* and *chromosome* shown. Then conclude the activity by having each student list ways she is like and different from each of her parents.

gene: a section of a chromosome that is often associated with a certain characteristic or group of characteristics, such as hair color

chromosome: the structure on which genes are located, found in cells of all organisms

Clothespin Chromosomes
Topic: Structure of a chromosome

Help students visualize a chromosome's structure with this model-making activity. First, display enlarged versions of the posters shown. Explain to students that the drawings represent three specific human chromosomes. Point out the chromosomes' rod shapes and the pattern of dark bars that resemble bar codes. Then explain that the bands represent the genes that influence physical traits.

Next, provide each student with a spring-loaded wooden clothespin and a marker. Direct each student to mark both sides of the clothespin with the bands of one chromosome, adding the corresponding number (see the illustration). Have students clip their completed models to the matching posters or keep them as reminders of a chromosome's structure. For diagrams of other chromosomes, check out the Genome Database at http://www.gdb.org *(current as of March 2006)*.

X for Girls, Y for Boys
Topic: Determining a baby's sex

What are the chances that a baby will be a boy? 50%, 80%, 30%? Answer that puzzling question with an experiment students will flip over! First, review with students that humans have 23 pairs of chromosomes. One chromosome in each pair comes from the mother and the other from the father. The 23rd pair determines a baby's sex. How? A mother will always pass along an X chromosome. But a father can pass along either an X chromosome (producing a girl) or a Y chromosome (producing a boy). Because males produce an equal number of X and Y chromosomes, the chances that a baby will be a boy is 50%.

After this introduction, divide the class into pairs. Display tables similar to the ones shown. Have each twosome copy the tables on paper. Then give each pair a penny to use in conducting the probability test on the right. Conclude by helping students average their data to see if the percentage of tossing tails is close to 50%.

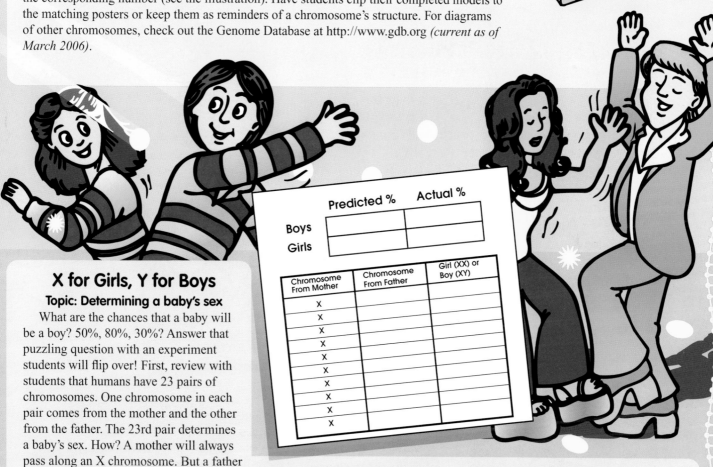

	Predicted %	Actual %
Boys		
Girls		

Chromosome From Mother	Chromosome From Father	Girl (XX) or Boy (XY)
X		
X		
X		
X		
X		
X		
X		
X		
X		
X		

Probability Test:
Heads represents the X chromosome (a girl), and tails represents the Y chromosome (a boy).
1. Predict the percentage of ten coin flips that could be heads (girls). Record your prediction.
2. Predict the percentage of ten coin flips that could be tails (boys). Record your prediction. If necessary, adjust your predictions so that the total percentage for heads and tails equals 100%.
3. Take turns flipping the coin five times each. Record the outcome of each flip (X or Y) in the father's column of the chart.
4. Record the baby's sex (XX or XY) in the girl/boy column to show how the chromosomes from the mother and father combine.
5. Find the actual percentage of boys. To do this, divide the total number of Ys in the father's column by ten (the total number of flips) and multiply the quotient by 100. Record your answer in the chart.
6. To find the actual percentage of girls, divide the total number of Xs in the father's column by ten and multiply the quotient by 100. Record your answer.

What Genes Are You Wearing?
Topic: Dominant and recessive genes

Tackle the topic of dominant and recessive genes with this fun-to-do partner activity. First, share with students that if each parent carries two different factors for a trait, then one is *dominant* and the other *recessive*. Provide each student with a copy of the checklist shown that leaves out the italicized words. Discuss with students the physical expression of each trait (see the illustrations). Then pair students. Have each student complete a checklist by circling the expressions his partner exhibits. When the twosomes are finished, combine the class's results by making tally marks in a chart you've drawn on the board. Have students guess the dominant and recessive traits. Then share the answers. Explain that only one dominant gene has to be inherited for that trait to have the potential of being expressed. If no dominant gene is inherited, then the recessive gene is expressed. For example, if T = tongue roller and t = nonroller, a person who *can* roll his tongue has either TT or Tt genes. If the person *cannot* roll his tongue, he has tt genes. Encourage students to take home extra copies of the checklist to complete with other family members.

Checklist for _____	
Expressed Trait	**Physical Expression of Trait**
Earlobe Shape	Free *(dominant)* or Attached *(recessive)*
Forehead Hairline	Widow's Peak *(dominant)* or Straight *(recessive)*
Tongue Rolling	Roller *(dominant)* or Nonroller *(recessive)*
Middigit Finger Hair	Hair *(dominant)* or No Hair *(recessive)*
Thumb	Straight *(dominant)* or Hitchhiker *(recessive)*
Dimples in Cheek	Dimples *(dominant)* or No Dimples *(recessive)*

Mendel's Genes
Topic: Dominant and recessive genes

For another nifty experiment on dominant and recessive genes, place on a table five containers, each labeled with one of the following: flower color, pod color, seed color, seed shape, or plant height. Give each group of five students one copy of the gene cards at the top of page 15. Have group members cut the cards apart, color them, and place them in the appropriate containers. Next, give each student a copy of page 16 to complete as directed. Afterward, have each group share its drawings with the class and note whether any plants exhibited some of the same traits or gene combinations.

Genetic Disease Detectives
Topic: Genetic diseases

Challenge students to investigate inherited genetic diseases with this research activity. Give each student a copy of the case sheet at the bottom of page 15 to help him research one of the topics below. Have the student search science books, encyclopedias, and Web sites such as those listed. Then schedule time for students to present their findings to the class.

Genetic Diseases: cystic fibrosis, sickle cell anemia, muscular dystrophy, hemophilia A, Huntington disease, Tay-Sachs disease, hemochromatosis, Gaucher's disease

Web Sites *(current as of March 2006)*:
Cystic Fibrosis Foundation: www.cff.org
The American Sickle Cell Anemia Association: www.ascaa.org
Muscular Dystrophy Association: www.mdausa.org
Taryn's World (a Web site for children with genetic diseases):
www.tarynsworld.org/taryn/index.htm

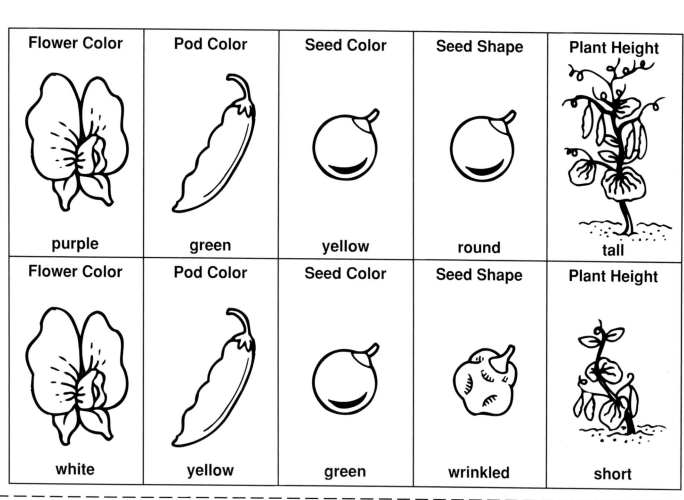

Flower Color	Pod Color	Seed Color	Seed Shape	Plant Height
purple	green	yellow	round	tall

Flower Color	Pod Color	Seed Color	Seed Shape	Plant Height
white	yellow	green	wrinkled	short

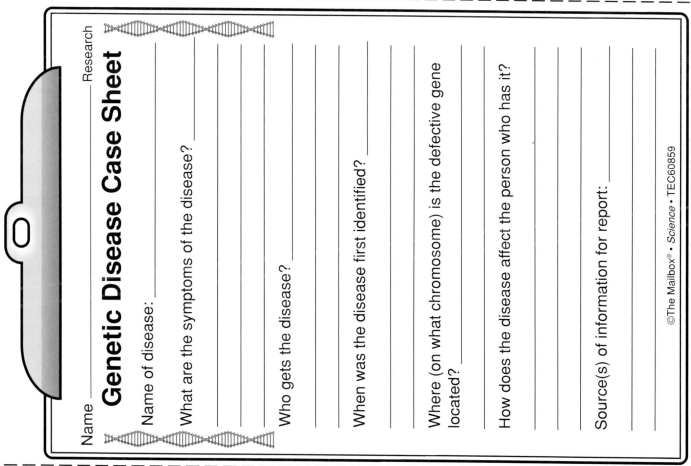

Name _____

Research

Genetic Disease Case Sheet

Name of disease: _____

What are the symptoms of the disease? _____

Who gets the disease? _____

When was the disease first identified? _____

Where (on what chromosome) is the defective gene located? _____

How does the disease affect the person who has it? _____

Source(s) of information for report: _____

©The Mailbox® • Science • TEC60859

Note to the teacher: Use the gene cards at the top of the page with "Mendel's Genes" on page 14. Use the case sheet with "Genetic Disease Detectives" on page 14.

Name ____________________

Mendel's Genes

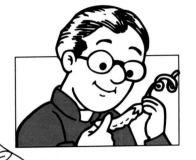

Gregor Mendel, an Austrian monk born in 1822, helped explain how heredity works. He studied pea plants that he grew in a monastery garden. By doing this, he was able to identify several plant traits and trace how they were passed from parent plants to their offspring. Follow the directions below to "grow" your own pea plant!

Directions:

1. Choose a trait: flower color, pod color, seed color, seed shape, or plant height. Choose a trait that is different from those selected by others in your group.
2. Draw two gene cards from the container labeled with your trait.
3. Check the table of pea traits to see if the characteristics on your cards represent dominant or recessive genes. Record each characteristic in the chart below, using a capital letter to represent a dominant gene and a lowercase letter for a recessive gene.
4. Gather data about the remaining traits from your group and record it in the chart below.
5. Determine the physical traits that your plant will express. (Remember: If at least one of the genes is dominant, that is the trait that will be expressed. If neither gene is dominant, the recessive trait will be expressed.) Compare answers with your group mates to see if they match.
6. Draw a picture of your plant. Make sure it expresses all of the physical traits listed in the chart.

Pea Traits

Trait	**Dominant Characteristic**	**Recessive Characteristic**
Flower color	purple *(P)*	white *(p)*
Pod color	green *(G)*	yellow *(g)*
Seed color	yellow *(Y)*	green *(y)*
Seed shape	round *(R)*	wrinkled *(r)*
Plant height	tall *(T)*	short *(t)*

Trait	**Gene for Plant 1**	**Gene for Plant 2**	**Expressed Physical Trait**
Flower color			
Pod color			
Seed color			
Seed shape			
Plant height			

Plant Drawing

 Note to the teacher: Use with "Mendel's Genes" on page 14.

Dishin' Up Good Nutrition!

Healthy eating habits and kids don't tend to go together, do they? But they can when you serve students these fun-to-do activities and reproducibles on nutrition!

by Lisa Waller Rogers

Split Pea Soup? Yuck!

Ask kids if they've ever had to eat a yucky food, and you'll hear a horror story from everybody! Introduce your nutrition unit with a picture book that features this dietary dilemma, *George and Martha* by James Marshall. Read aloud the first story in the book and invite students to share about times when they ate a yucky food. Then have them brainstorm two lists—"Foods Most Yummy" and "Foods Most Yucky"—while you list their responses on the board. Ask each child to vote on his favorite yummy food and least favorite yucky food; then have him graph the results of both polls. Finally have students compare the lists and graphs. Ask, "How are the foods in the yummy list different from those in the yucky list?" Help students understand that making healthful food choices keeps our bodies healthy.

Give Grains a Go!

Why is the bread, cereal, rice, and pasta group so important? Because its foods are our body's main source of energy. To motivate students to give grains a go, collect an empty pasta box for each child. Read aloud the poem "Pasta Parade" from *Food Fight: Poets Join the Fight Against Hunger With Poems to Favorite Foods* edited by Michael J. Rosen. With students, list kinds of pasta on the board. Next have each child use the words to write a poem about pasta on an index card. Direct him to glue the card to a pasta box. Place the boxes in a basket at your reading center. If desired, hold a pasta-tasting party using recipes from *Pretend Soup and Other Real Recipes: A Cookbook for Preschoolers & Up* by Mollie Katzen and Ann Henderson. Have small groups of students whip up batches of Noodle Pudding, Green Spaghetti, and Noodle Soup. Seconds, anyone?

Penne Pasta

A Poem About Penne

Peanut Butter

Veggie Bingo

Familiarize students with the variety of vegetables available—and their nutritional benefits—with this "veggie-rific" game! Give each student a copy of page 20. Discuss how to read the chart. Then ask students which veggies they have never heard of. Next have each child draw a 5 x 5 bingo grid on her paper and label the middle "free space." Have her write the name of a veggie from the list in each square.

To play, describe a vegetable from the chart. For example, "It's white, has about 60 calories, and contains 20 percent of the U.S. RDA of vitamin C." *(onion)* Each student uses her chart to identify the veggie and then covers it on her card with a marker. Continue describing various vegetables. When a student has bingo, have her read the names of the covered veggies and give a nutrition fact about each one. If successful, let the student take your place as caller.

Fruit and Veggie Vendors

Sell students on neglected fruits and vegetables with this fun activity! Label a set of index cards with vegetables from page 20 (ones seldom eaten by kids) and the fruits listed below. Display the cards at a center with a variety of cookbooks. Challenge each child to select a card and complete the following tasks:

- Research your fruit or vegetable to find out its nutritional benefits.
- Draw a picture of your fruit or vegetable. If desired, personify the drawing.
- Find a recipe featuring your food. Prepare the recipe (with an adult's help) and sample it.
- Write a paragraph describing the recipe, your taste test, and the food's benefits.
- In a presentation, try to sell your fruit or veggie to the class.

Fruits: apricot, avocado, blackberry, blueberry, cherry, cranberry, currant, fig, kiwifruit, lime, mandarin, mango, nectarine, olive, papaya, persimmon, plum, pomegranate, raspberry, tangelo

I'm really quite tasty!

Life in the Fast (Food) Lane

Two food groups—the milk, yogurt, and cheese group and the meat, poultry, fish, dry bean, eggs, and nuts group—are essential in providing our bodies with protein. But many protein-rich foods are also high in fat. One example is the fast-food hamburger meal, which packs lots of protein but also a day's worth of fat, sodium, and calories.

To help students get the lowdown on fast-food nutrition, write the following on the board: calories = 2,000; sodium = less than 2,400 mg; fat = less than 65 g. Explain that each figure gives the approximate recommended daily value for children their age. Next divide the class into groups. Give each group a nutrition guide from a local fast-food restaurant and a copy of the half-page reproducible at the top of page 21. Have the group complete the reproducible as directed and share its work with the class. Discuss how this nutritional information might alter students' dining habits.

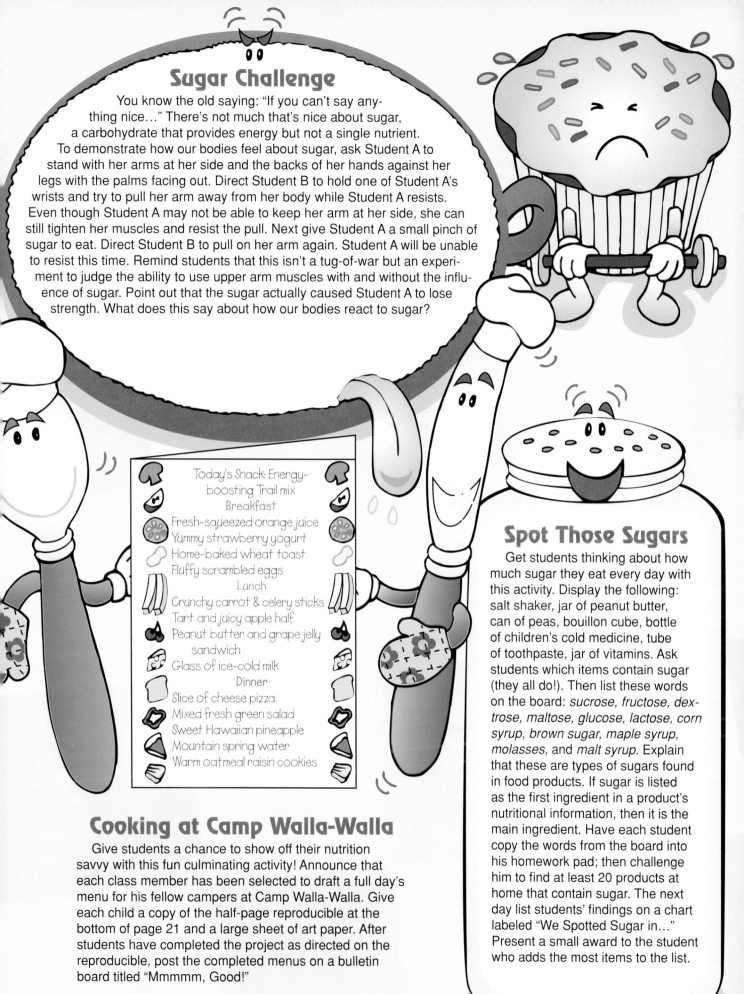

Sugar Challenge

You know the old saying: "If you can't say anything nice…" There's not much that's nice about sugar, a carbohydrate that provides energy but not a single nutrient. To demonstrate how our bodies feel about sugar, ask Student A to stand with her arms at her side and the backs of her hands against her legs with the palms facing out. Direct Student B to hold one of Student A's wrists and try to pull her arm away from her body while Student A resists. Even though Student A may not be able to keep her arm at her side, she can still tighten her muscles and resist the pull. Next give Student A a small pinch of sugar to eat. Direct Student B to pull on her arm again. Student A will be unable to resist this time. Remind students that this isn't a tug-of-war but an experiment to judge the ability to use upper arm muscles with and without the influence of sugar. Point out that the sugar actually caused Student A to lose strength. What does this say about how our bodies react to sugar?

Today's Snack: Energy-
boosting Trail mix
Breakfast
Fresh-squeezed orange juice
Yummy strawberry yogurt
Home-baked wheat toast
Fluffy scrambled eggs
Lunch
Crunchy carrot & celery sticks
Tart and juicy apple half
Peanut butter and grape jelly
sandwich
Glass of ice-cold milk
Dinner
Slice of cheese pizza
Mixed fresh green salad
Sweet Hawaiian pineapple
Mountain spring water
Warm oatmeal raisin cookies

Cooking at Camp Walla-Walla

Give students a chance to show off their nutrition savvy with this fun culminating activity! Announce that each class member has been selected to draft a full day's menu for his fellow campers at Camp Walla-Walla. Give each child a copy of the half-page reproducible at the bottom of page 21 and a large sheet of art paper. After students have completed the project as directed on the reproducible, post the completed menus on a bulletin board titled "Mmmmm, Good!"

Spot Those Sugars

Get students thinking about how much sugar they eat every day with this activity. Display the following: salt shaker, jar of peanut butter, can of peas, bouillon cube, bottle of children's cold medicine, tube of toothpaste, jar of vitamins. Ask students which items contain sugar (they all do!). Then list these words on the board: *sucrose, fructose, dextrose, maltose, glucose, lactose, corn syrup, brown sugar, maple syrup, molasses,* and *malt syrup.* Explain that these are types of sugars found in food products. If sugar is listed as the first ingredient in a product's nutritional information, then it is the main ingredient. Have each student copy the words from the board into his homework pad; then challenge him to find at least 20 products at home that contain sugar. The next day list students' findings on a chart labeled "We Spotted Sugar in…" Present a small award to the student who adds the most items to the list.

Very "Veggie-rific"!

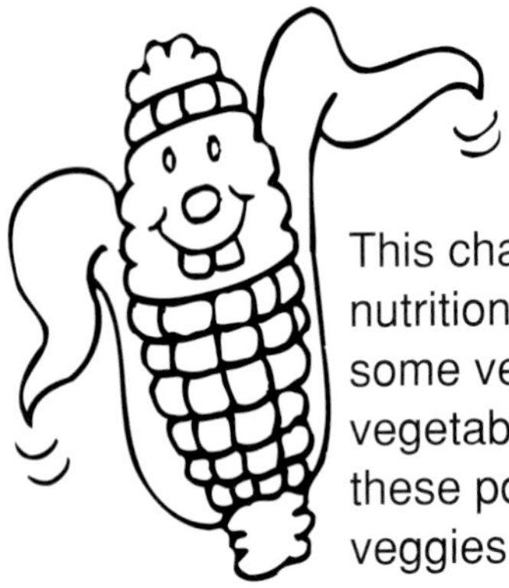

This chart shows the nutritional values for some very "veggie-rific" vegetables. Pile plenty of these positively palatable veggies on your plate!

	Total Calories	Protein (g)	Carbohydrates (g)	Total Fat (g)	Dietary Fiber (g)	Sodium (mg)	Vitamin A (% of U.S. RDA)	Vitamin C (% of U.S. RDA)	Calcium (% of U.S. RDA)	Iron (% of U.S. RDA)
Artichoke, 1 medium, cooked	75	5	17	0	12	140	3	25	7	11
Asparagus, 5 spears, raw	18	2	2	0	2	0	10	10	★	★
Beets, 2, cooked	31	1	7	0	2	49	★	9	★	3
Bell Pepper, 1 medium, raw	20	1	5	0	1	2	5	112	★	2
Broccoli, 1 cup chopped, raw	25	3	5	0	3	24	14	137	4	4
Brussels Sprouts, 1 cup, cooked	38	3	8	0	4	22	8	125	4	7
Cabbage, 1 cup shredded, raw	17	1	4	0	2	12	★	55	3	2
Carrot, 1 medium, raw	40	1	8	1	1	40	330	8	2	★
Cauliflower, 1 cup pieces, raw	18	2	3	0	2	45	★	110	2	2
Celery, 1 stalk, raw	6	0	2	0	1	35	★	5	★	★
Collard Greens, 1 cup, raw	11	1	3	0	1	7	12	14	★	★
Corn, Sweet, 1 ear, raw	75	3	17	1	1	15	5	10	★	3
Cucumber, 1/3 medium, raw	18	1	3	0	0	0	4	6	2	2
Eggplant, 1 cup cubed, raw	21	1	5	0	3	3	6	★	3	3
Green Beans, Snap, 3/4 cup cut, raw	14	1	2	0	3	2	8	4	4	★
Green Onions, 1/4 cup chopped, raw	7	0	1	0	0	0	3	20	★	5
Kale, 1 cup, raw	33	2	7	0	4	29	60	134	9	6
Leeks, 1 cup, raw	64	2	15	0	3	20	★	21	6	12
Lettuce, Iceberg, 1 cup shredded, raw	7	0	2	0	0	5	★	4	★	★
Lettuce, Leaf, 1 cup shredded, raw	10	1	2	0	1	5	11	17	4	4
Mushrooms, 5 medium, raw	25	3	3	0	0	0	★	2	★	★
Mustard Greens, 1 cup, raw	14	2	3	0	1	14	30	65	6	5
Okra, 8 pods, raw	27	2	6	0	2	4	5	23	5	2
Onion, 1 medium, raw	60	1	14	0	3	10	★	20	4	★
Parsley, 1/4 cup chopped, raw	10	1	2	0	1	12	16	45	4	10
Peas, Snow, 1 cup, raw	60	0	11	0	4	6	2	145	6	17
Potato, 1 medium baked in skin	220	5	51	0	5	16	★	44	2	25
Radishes, 7, raw	20	0	3	0	0	35	★	30	★	★
Sprouts, Alfalfa, 1 cup, raw	10	1	1	0	1	0	★	4.5	★	★
Spinach, 1 cup, raw	12	2	2	0	2	44	38	26	6	8
Squash, Yellow, 1 cup sliced, raw	25	1	5	0	2	3	4	18	3	3
Squash, Winter, 1 cup cubed, baked	18	2	4	0	1	4	4	20	2	3
Squash, Zucchini, 1 cup sliced, raw	136	3	36	0	7	10	11	44	11	13
Sweet Potato, 1 medium, baked	154	3	36	0	5	15	327	61	4	4
Tomato, 2 1/2" diameter, raw	26	1	6	0	2	11	8	39	★	3
Turnips, 1 medium, raw	23	0	5	0	2	57	★	30	3	★

★ less than 2%

Note to the teacher: Use with "Veggie Bingo" and "Fruit and Veggie Vendors" on page 18.

Things Are Cookin' at Camp Walla-Walla!

When you think of summer camp, do you think of fantastic food? Probably not. Well now's the time to change that! The director of Camp Walla-Walla has just asked you to plan a day's menu for your campmates. Follow these steps:

1 On a sheet of paper, brainstorm menu items for each of these meals: breakfast, lunch, dinner, campsite snack. These four meals must be delicious or the kids won't eat them; they must also be nutritious or the parents won't approve!

2 Look through your brainstormed list of menu items. Select the items you plan to include in each meal. Double-check to make sure your choices are nutritious.

3 On another sheet of paper, write each meal's menu. Use lots of colorful adjectives so that your campmates will be eager to dig in to your delicious cuisine! After you've written about your meals, have a classmate help you proofread your work.

4 Fold a sheet of art paper in half to make a menu. Open the menu. Use colorful markers and crayons to copy your meals in the menu. Add pictures too!

5 Illustrate the front of your Camp Walla-Walla menu. Include your name somewhere on the cover.

6 Share your menu with the class. Any mouths watering?

©The Mailbox® • *Science* • TEC60859

Note to the teacher: Use with "Cooking at Camp Walla-Walla" on page 19. Provide each student with a large sheet of art paper and markers or crayons.

Life in the Fast (Food) Lane

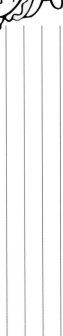

Name of restaurant: _____

For your restaurant, list the following in order:

The top four high-sodium foods:
1. _____
2. _____
3. _____
4. _____

The top four low-sodium foods:
1. _____
2. _____
3. _____
4. _____

The top four fatty foods:
1. _____
2. _____
3. _____
4. _____

The top four lowfat foods:
1. _____
2. _____
3. _____
4. _____

Answer these questions on the back or on another sheet of paper.
1. In terms of sodium and fat, what would be the worst meal to order at your restaurant?
2. What would be the healthiest meal to order?
3. If you could add something to the menu that was nutritious and tasty, what would it be?

©The Mailbox® • *Science* • TEC60859

Note to the teacher: Use with "Life in the Fast (Food) Lane" on page 18. Provide each student group with a nutrition guide available from a local fast-food restaurant.

Are You Supermarket Savvy?

Back in the 1950s, most supermarkets had about 3,000 products to sell. Now the average store sells about 8,000. Some even stock up to 20,000 items! A lot of thought goes into deciding where things get placed in a grocery store. And many of those decisions don't encourage you to buy nutritious foods. Become more supermarket savvy by visiting a store and answering these questions.

1. What areas do you see first when you enter the store? List several items you see displayed in these highly visible areas. _____

   _____

   Why do these items grab your attention? (Hint: look at the size of the lettering, the locations of the displays, the use of color, etc.) _____

   _____

2. People frequently come to the supermarket to buy milk. Where is the milk located?_____
   _____ Walk from the milk to the checkout line. What
   items do you pass that you might be tempted to buy?_____ __
   _____ Are they nutritious items?_____

3. List several items that are displayed at the ends of the aisles. _____

   _____

   Why do you think these items have been selected for these displays? _____

   _____

   Are they nutritious? _____

4. Find the mustard, pickles, relish, and ketchup. Are they located near each other? _____
   Why? _____
   Find another example of this type of grouping. _____

   _____

5. When shoppers buy something they didn't plan to buy, that's called *impulse shopping*. These items are often located right at the checkout line. List four items found near a checkout line in this store. _____
   Are the food items nutritious?_____ What other items did you see that might
   encourage impulse shopping? _____
   Where are they located? _____

   _____

   Bonus Box: On another sheet of paper, sketch a map of the store. Then study the map. Do you agree with this statement? "Shop only the outside aisles if you want a healthier diet." Explain your answer on the back of the map. Then staple the map to this page.

PICTURING PLANT AND ANIMAL ADAPTATIONS

How adaptable plants and animals can be! Some can adjust to extreme temperatures to survive in their environments. Others rely on growth tricks and poisons. Learn more about how plants and animals accomplish these amazing feats with the following ideas and reproducibles.

ideas by Linda Manwiller, Boyertown, PA

PLANTASIA'S PLANTS
Concept: Plant adaptations

Turn students into space-traveling botanists with this model-building and writing activity. Divide students into crews of three and share the following scenario: *You have been recruited to explore Plantasia, a planet that humans have never visited. Your assignment is to bring back a plant that could adapt to life on Earth.* Next, instruct each crew to plan a model of a plant from Plantasia. Allow students several days to collect materials. Then give each crew a sheet of poster board on which to construct and label its model. Also have the crew make a sensory chart about its plant on another piece of poster board as shown. Have the crews share their completed models and charts with the class. Follow up by having each student choose one of the prompts below and write about his crew's (or any other crew's) plant.

Writing Prompts
- Descriptive writing: Use the information in the sensory chart to write a detailed description of the plant. Include the plant's adaptations.
- Expository writing: Write a plan for taking care of the plant.
- Clarification writing: Compare and contrast the adaptations of the plant with a plant from your local area.
- Narrative writing: Write a story telling how you found the plant. Include the adaptations that enabled it to survive on Plantasia.
- Persuasive writing: Write a letter to persuade a group of U.S. scientists that the plant could survive on Earth. Focus on the adaptations that would enable it to live on Earth.

Sweetae Desertia				
Sight large, pink blossoms	Sound none	Taste sweet chewy	Touch cottony sticky	Smell sweet

Sweetae Desertia

huge flower in rainy season to gather water

hole for water storage

shallow roots to gather water

PLANT HALL OF FAME
Concept: Plant adaptations

Shine the spotlight on plants with unusual adaptations by putting them in a plant Hall of Fame! Pair students; then assign each pair a different plant to research from the list below. After each pair finds its plant's special adaptations, have the twosome draw a large picture of the plant on poster board and label it with the plant's name and its special parts and adaptations. Also have the pair list several questions that could be answered by studying its poster. After students share their posters, compile the questions and make copies; then display the posters in a hallway under a banner titled "Plant Hall of Fame." Invite students from other classes to answer the questions as they walk through your Hall of Fame.

yucca	barrel cactus	slime mold
tumbleweed	rafflesia	mimosa
Venus's-flytrap	mistletoe	creosote bush
pitcher plant	dodder	orchid
bladderwort	lichen	saguaro cactus
		mangrove

damages its host

parasite (grows and feeds on other plants)

sticky substance on seeds

dates back hundreds of years

Mistletoe

ANIMAL KINGDOM PASSPORT

Good traveling companions:
other male and female lions in the pride

The Secretary of Zoology?of the Animal Kingdom

hereby requests that the Animal Kingdom citizen named herein be allowed passage without delay or hindrance into desired area and be given all lawful aid and protection to which it is duly entitled.

Leah L. Lion
(signature of bearer)

NOT VALID UNTIL SIGNED

ANIMAL KINGDOM PASSPORT

Class: _Mammalia_
Order: _Carnivora_
Family: _Felidae_

Given Name: _Lion, Leah L._
Date of Birth: _8-14-94_
Habitat or Biome: _Savannas and semidesert areas of Africa_

ADAPTATIONS

Physical: _Large canine teeth, excellent sense of smell, very muscular, hooked claws, tawny color_

Behavioral: _Often hunts at night or with the pride, expert stalker_

PASSPORT, PLEASE!
Concept: Animal adaptations

Find out more about the adaptations of animals in your local area—or those living in a place students are currently studying—with this activity. On the board, list animals that live in your area. Discuss with students the adaptations these animals have had to make to survive. Next, explain that a passport is a document used for personal identification when traveling in foreign countries. Tell students that they will be creating passports for the animals listed. Then assign each student a different animal and give her a copy of page 26. Have students use encyclopedias and other reference materials to complete the page as directed. If desired, serve animal crackers while students work. Then use the completed passports to play the game on the right.

Steps to play Going Through Customs:

1. Have students form two lines so that each child faces a partner.
2. Designate the students in one line as immigration agents and those in the other line as animals traveling with passports.
3. Have each agent check his partner's passport for accuracy by asking the animal to provide the proper identification (name and special adaptations).
4. Direct each agent to move one place to his right to face a new partner. (Have the agent at the right end of the line move to the opposite end of the line). Repeat Step 3.
5. Continue until each agent has questioned five different animals. Then switch the lines' roles and play again.

BOOKS AND WEB SITES

Find out more about the amazing changes that some plants and animals make to survive with these great books and Web sites.

Plant books:
- *June 29, 1999* by David Wiesner

Animal books:
- *Rascal* by Sterling North
- *The Tarantula in My Purse and 172 Other Wild Pets* by Jean Craighead George

Plant and animal books:
- *Cactus Café: A Story of the Sonoran Desert* by Kathleen Weidner Zoehfeld
- *The Most Beautiful Roof in the World: Exploring the Rainforest Canopy* by Kathryn Lasky

Web sites *(current as of March 2006):*
- U.S. Fish & Wildlife Service: www.fws.gov/kids
- National Wildlife Federation: www.nwf.org/nwf/education
- Oakland Zoo (specific information about animal adaptations): www.oaklandzoo.org/atoz/atoz.html

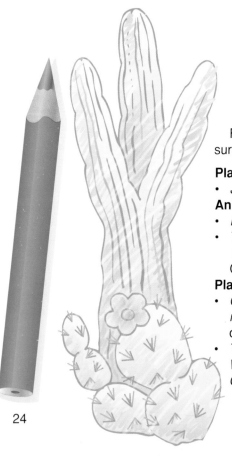

SUITCASE STUDY AIDS
Concept: Plant and animal adaptations

Help students review what they've learned about wildlife adaptations by making some handy graphic organizers. First, list types of animal adaptations on the board, such as body coverings, mouth parts, movement-related adaptations, protective coloration, protective resemblance, mimicry, migration, and hibernation. Discuss the terms with students. Repeat with types of plant adaptations, such as seed dispersal, tropisms, chemical emissions, leaves/needles/spines, and biological clocks. Then give each student a manila file folder. Have the student cut the folder on the fold and trim each half into a suitcase shape as shown. Direct the student to title one cutout "Fauna's Suitcase," divide it into six sections, and label each section with a different animal adaptation. Instruct him to label the other cutout "Flora's Suitcase," divide it into four sections, and label each section with a different plant adaptation. Finally, challenge the student to fill each section on his suitcases with two examples of animals or plants with that adaptation. After a sharing time, allow students to use their organizers to study with their buddies!

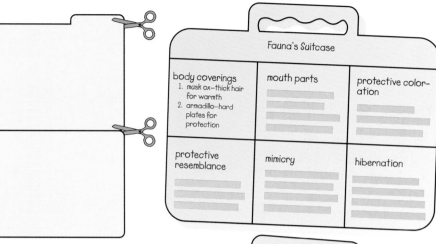

Fauna's Suitcase

| body coverings
1. musk ox–thick hair for warmth
2. armadillo–hard plates for protection | mouth parts | protective coloration |
| protective resemblance | mimicry | hibernation |

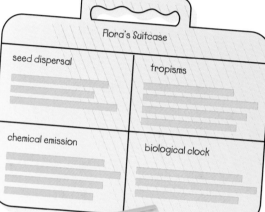

Flora's Suitcase

| seed dispersal | tropisms |
| chemical emission | biological clock |

AROUND THE WORLD WITH ANIMAL ADAPTATIONS
Concept: Animal adaptations within biomes

Use this small-group activity to give students a global perspective of how animals in different parts of the world adapt to their environments. Divide students into six groups and assign each group a different biome listed below. Give each group a sheet of chart paper and a different-colored marker. Have each group research its biome; then have the group use its marker to label the chart paper with the name of its biome and a brief description.

Next, have one group at a time share the description of its biome with the class. Help students understand the adaptations that would be necessary for animals to survive in that biome. Then place the labeled charts around the room and assign each group to a different biome. Instruct each group to use its colored marker to list on the chart animals (and their specific adaptations) that might live in that biome. After three minutes, signal the groups to rotate to the next biome and repeat the process. After the groups have visited every biome, have them return to their original charts and use reference materials to check the list of animals for accuracy. Conclude by having each group share its chart with the class. If desired, post the charts in the room so students can add examples during the unit.

grassland—a region covered with short or tall grass

Biomes
deciduous forest
desert
grassland
taiga
tropical rain forest
tundra

Passport, Please!

Agents in charge of admitting animals into the Animal Kingdom have an important job. They must make sure each animal that wants to live in a particular place can survive there. Help your animal get a passport into the Animal Kingdom by following the directions below.

Directions: Research your animal to help you fill in the information on the passport. Include a picture. Then cut out the passport along the solid lines and fold it down along the dotted line. On the front of the passport, draw a special insignia that represents the Animal Kingdom. On the back, list animals that would make good traveling companions for your animal.

The Secretary of Zoology of the Animal Kingdom

hereby requests that the Animal Kingdom

citizen named herein be allowed passage

without delay or hindrance into desired area and be

given all lawful aid and protection to which it is duly entitled.

_____
(signature of bearer)

NOT VALID UNTIL SIGNED

- -

ANIMAL KINGDOM PASSPORT

Class: _____

Order: _____

Family: _____

Given Name: _____

Date of Birth: _____

Habitat or Biome: _____

ADAPTATIONS

Physical: _____

_____

_____

Behavioral: _____

_____

_____

(picture)

Note to the teacher: Use with "Passport, Please!" on page 24. Students will need scissors, crayons or markers, and encyclopedias or other reference materials to complete the page.

Name _____

Scat It!

Dr. Sigmund Charles Anthony Tuttleberry, known as Dr. Scat, is a famous ornithologist. He has collected data to see if there is a relationship between a bird's wingspan and its body length. Use the data in the box to help him make a *scattergram* (a graph that shows paired data without connecting it with a line). Then answer the questions below.

Data Box

Bird	Approximate Wingspan	Approximate Body Length
caracara	50 in.	23 in.
golden eagle	84 in.	36 in.
magnificent frigate bird	84 in.	40 in.
gannet	72 in.	35 in.
marabou stork	113 in.	60 in.
common pigeon	24 in.	13 in.
Caspian tern	53 in.	20 in.
whooping crane	90 in.	60 in.

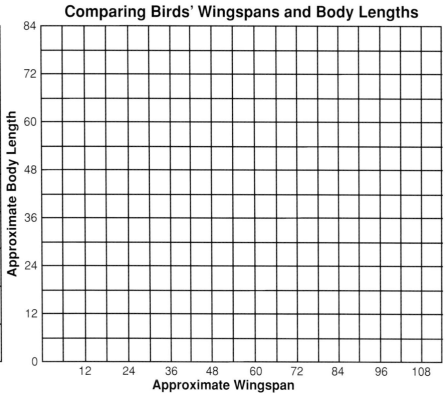

Comparing Birds' Wingspans and Body Lengths

1. Which bird has the greatest difference between wingspan and body length? _____

2. Which bird has the least difference between wingspan and body length? _____

3. List two pairs of birds that have about the same difference between body length and wingspan. _____

4. What is the difference between the longest and shortest wingspans? _____ Longest and shortest body lengths? _____

5. What is the average wingspan of the birds (to the nearest tenth of an inch)? _____

6. What is the average body length of the birds (to the nearest tenth of an inch)? _____

7. Does each column of data have a mode? _____ If so, what is it? _____

_____

8. What trend does this scattergram show? _____

_____

BONUS BOX: Change each measurement above to feet and inches. Then order the body lengths from least to greatest. Order the wingspans from greatest to least.

On the Go!

The adaptations of many plants and animals are related to how they move. Each ticket below tells how a particular plant or animal gets around. Write the name of each plant or animal from the suitcase below on the correct ticket. Use reference materials to help you.

1. has a flexible backbone that helps increase the length of its stride
_____

2. has muscles that squeeze an elastic material that helps it jump high into the air
_____

3. is the fastest flier in the insect world
_____

4. has seed pods that get caught in animal fur and on human clothing
_____

5. has seeds with miniature parachutes that help them float through the air
_____

6. has seeds with wings that let them spin and drop slowly toward the earth when blown by the wind
_____

7. swoops down through the air on its prey
_____

8. cruises in the air for many hours
_____

9. rolls across the land and scatters seeds
_____

10. moves with help from microscopic structures called *cilia*
_____

11. has body segments that extend and contract
_____

12. uses a form of jet propulsion
_____

Plants and Animals

flatworm	earthworm	squid
flea	maple	dragonfly
horse	peregrine falcon	cocklebur
swan	dandelion	tumbleweed

Bonus Box: List the following animals from fastest to slowest: African elephant, camel, cheetah, greyhound, hare. Write your answer on the back of this sheet.

Note to the teacher: Students will need encyclopedias or other reference materials to complete this page.

PLANT POWER!

What living things can withstand sweltering desert temperatures, frigid polar regions, salty ocean waters, and fiercely windy mountaintops? Green plants! Enter the amazingly powerful world of green plants with the following "plant-astic" activities and experiments!

ideas by Kristina Cassidy, Medina, OH

Plants Are... Everywhere!

Skills: Classification, research

Introduce your plant unit by giving students a quick WCFP (What Comes From Plants) quiz. On a table, display items that come from plants along with some that don't (see the suggested list). Direct each student to label the top of a sheet of paper with two columns: "From Plants" and "Not From Plants." Allow students to look at the objects and classify them. Then go over the answers together. Afterward, poll students to see if any classifications surprised them. Follow up by challenging groups of students to research which plant(s) produced each object listed in the "From Plants" column. Don't be surprised if students come up with "plant-y" of other items to add to the list!

From Plants:
chewing gum
aspirin
pencil
cotton ball
rubber band
wooden spoon
chocolate bar
cola drink
cotton or linen shirt
piece of paper
skin cream with aloe
shampoo
ink
dye
shaving cream
shoe polish
soap
rope

Not From Plants:
plastic bowl
plastic sandwich bag
woolen mitten
penny
plastic spoon
key
Slinky® toy
silverware
iron skillet
gold necklace or earring
mirror
aluminum foil
nylon comb
clear tape
seashell
marble
thumbtack
glass pitcher

This came from a plant?

SOAP

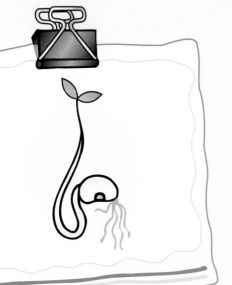

You Can't Fool a Plant...or Can You?

Skill: Using the scientific method

Can a plant's roots and stem be tricked about whether to grow up or down? To seek moisture, a plant's roots grow downward. Its stem grows upward toward the sunlight. But what would happen if a plant were turned upside down? Have students experiment to discover that no matter how a plant is turned, gravity and the plant's sensitive chemicals will make its roots grow down and its stem grow up. Give each student a copy of the experiment on page 32 and the materials listed on it. Hang the seed bags near a window—attached to a line, bulletin board, or other accessible place—so students can add water and turn the bags as directed. Students will learn that plants are both smart *and* powerful!

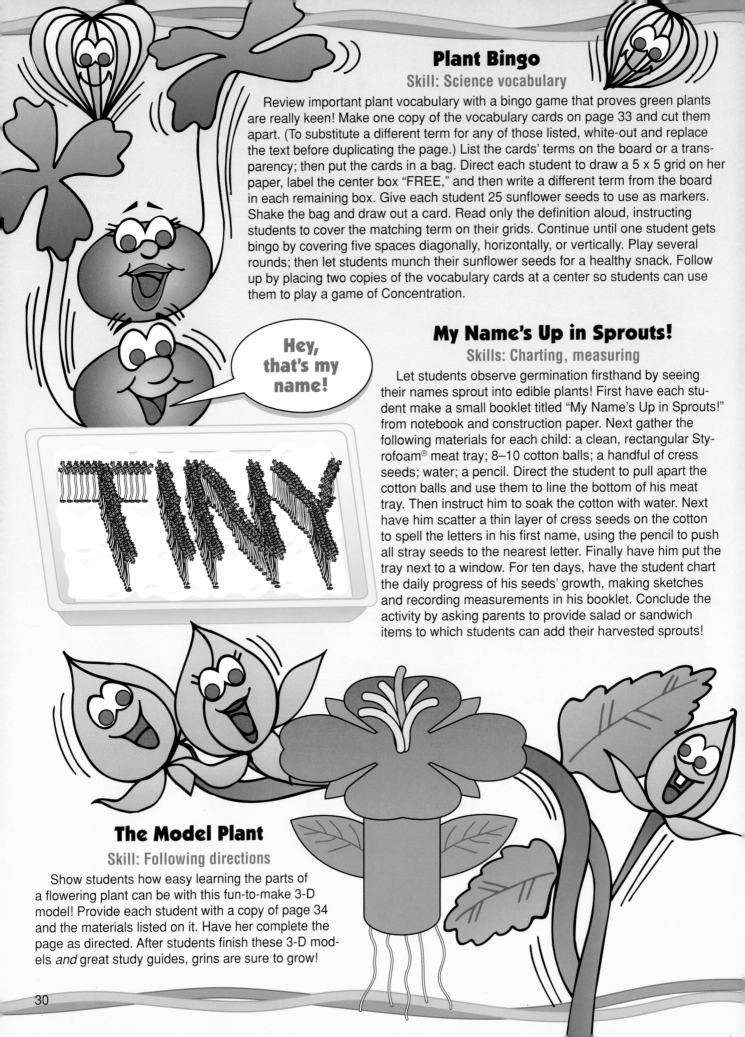

Plant Bingo
Skill: Science vocabulary

Review important plant vocabulary with a bingo game that proves green plants are really keen! Make one copy of the vocabulary cards on page 33 and cut them apart. (To substitute a different term for any of those listed, white-out and replace the text before duplicating the page.) List the cards' terms on the board or a transparency; then put the cards in a bag. Direct each student to draw a 5 x 5 grid on her paper, label the center box "FREE," and then write a different term from the board in each remaining box. Give each student 25 sunflower seeds to use as markers. Shake the bag and draw out a card. Read only the definition aloud, instructing students to cover the matching term on their grids. Continue until one student gets bingo by covering five spaces diagonally, horizontally, or vertically. Play several rounds; then let students munch their sunflower seeds for a healthy snack. Follow up by placing two copies of the vocabulary cards at a center so students can use them to play a game of Concentration.

Hey, that's my name!

My Name's Up in Sprouts!
Skills: Charting, measuring

Let students observe germination firsthand by seeing their names sprout into edible plants! First have each student make a small booklet titled "My Name's Up in Sprouts!" from notebook and construction paper. Next gather the following materials for each child: a clean, rectangular Styrofoam® meat tray; 8–10 cotton balls; a handful of cress seeds; water; a pencil. Direct the student to pull apart the cotton balls and use them to line the bottom of his meat tray. Then instruct him to soak the cotton with water. Next have him scatter a thin layer of cress seeds on the cotton to spell the letters in his first name, using the pencil to push all stray seeds to the nearest letter. Finally have him put the tray next to a window. For ten days, have the student chart the daily progress of his seeds' growth, making sketches and recording measurements in his booklet. Conclude the activity by asking parents to provide salad or sandwich items to which students can add their harvested sprouts!

The Model Plant
Skill: Following directions

Show students how easy learning the parts of a flowering plant can be with this fun-to-make 3-D model! Provide each student with a copy of page 34 and the materials listed on it. Have her complete the page as directed. After students finish these 3-D models *and* great study guides, grins are sure to grow!

Testing Seed Strength
Skills: Conducting an experiment, observing

Plants may not be able to move mountains, but watch students' surprise at what they can do! As they grow, plants can exert great pressure. To demonstrate this, give each group of students a packet of cress seeds, 24 cotton balls, three small plastic plates, water, and three paper circles that are the same size as the plates (one cut from copy paper, one from construction paper, and one from corrugated cardboard). Instruct the group to follow the directions below. Then explain that the growing tip of each plant is strong because it's filled with water. That's why you can sometimes see a plant strong enough to break through a small crack in a cement sidewalk. Your budding botanists will be so excited over their power-lifting plants that they'll want to redo the experiment using two pieces of cardboard, then three!

Directions:
1. Pull eight cotton balls apart slightly. Place them on a plate.
2. Repeat for the remaining plates.
3. Water the cotton on each plate thoroughly.
4. Sprinkle seeds over the cotton, dividing the seeds evenly among the three plates.
5. Cover one plate with the copy paper circle, the second plate with the construction paper circle, and the third plate with the cardboard circle.
6. Put the plates in a sunny spot.
7. Hypothesize whether the seeds, as they grow, will be able to lift each circle.
8. Check the plates daily. Record whether the circles are being lifted. Make sure the cotton stays moist.

You sure this isn't a spinach plant? It's strong!

Plants in Space?
Skills: Classifying plants, U.S. geography

Integrate social studies and language arts into your plant unit with Caldecott winner David Wiesner's book about a science project that produces unexpected results. Before reading *June 29, 1999* aloud to your class, post a sheet of chart paper on the board and give each child a reproducible U.S. map. Read the book aloud one time just for enjoyment; then reread it. As you read, have each student plot all the cities and states mentioned in the book on his map. In addition, ask students to help you record all the plants named in the book on the chart. After reading, have students classify the vegetables on the chart according to the plant parts they represent: stems, leaves, roots, flowers, or fruits. If desired, extend this activity with the following ideas.

- Have students predict what might happen if different items had been sent into the atmosphere. Then have students discuss the difference between writing fact and fantasy.
- Invite students to create different endings for Wiesner's book.
- Challenge students to write picture books that have fantasy themes, complete with powerful illustrations like Wiesner's.
- Discuss the interdependence of U.S. regions, as touched on in Wiesner's book.

Phyliss Grady Adcock, West Lake Elementary Apex, NC

The artichokes landed in Anchorage!

"Plant-astic" Resources

Dig your green thumb into the following books and Web sites *(current as of March 2006)* to learn more about the wonderful world of plants.

Web sites:
- University of Illinois Extension: www.urbanext.uiuc.edu/gpe A teachers' guide plus activities in which students help Detective LePlant find clues, do experiments, and solve problems about plants

Books:
- *Janice VanCleave's Plants: Mind-Boggling Experiments You Can Turn Into Science Fair Projects* by Janice Pratt VanCleave (John Wiley & Sons, 1997)
- *How Monkeys Make Chocolate: Foods and Medicines From the Rainforests* by Adrian Forsyth (Owl Communications, 1995)
- *3D Plant: Unique 3-D Color Photography That You Can Really See* by John Akeroyd (DK Publishing, 1998)

Can You Fool a Plant?

A plant's roots grow down and its stem grows up. But what happens if the plant is turned upside down? Will its roots still grow down and its stem grow up? Do this experiment to find out!

Purpose: To find out if a plant's roots will still grow down and its stem will still grow up if the plant is turned upside down

Hypothesis: Will a plant's roots still grow down and its stem grow up if the plant is turned upside down? _____

Materials: small plastic zippered bag, lima bean seed, paper towels, water

Procedure:

1. Wet the paper towels and place them in the plastic bag.
2. Put the seed between the paper towels and the bag so it can be seen. Zip the bag closed and hang it according to your teacher's directions.
3. Check the bag each day to see that the towels are still damp. Add water if needed.
4. After several days, look for a root to grow from one end of the seed and a stem from the other. When this happens, draw a picture in the left bag below showing how the sprouting seed looks.
5. Turn your bag upside down and hang it back in place. Be sure the roots are pointing up and the stem down.
6. Check the bag for several more days. Make sure the towels stay damp. Then draw a picture in the right bag below showing how the seed looks now.

Observations:

| After several days... | After several more days... |

1. In the left drawing, are the roots pointing up or down? _____ The stem? _____

2. In the right drawing, are the roots pointing up or down? _____ The stem? _____

Conclusions: Based on your observations, what can you say about the direction that a plant's roots and stem grow when the plant is turned upside down? _____

---

chlorophyll: the green pigment in plant cells	**petals:** leaflike structures that attract bees and other insects	**photosynthesis:** the food-making process of green plants	**seed:** a ripened ovule that contains a baby plant and its stored food	**spore:** a type of seed produced by a fungus
dicot: a plant that has two seed leaves	**root:** the part of a plant that absorbs water and nutrients and anchors the plant in the soil	**monocot:** a plant that has one seed leaf	**petiole:** the leaf's stalk	**phloem:** tubes that carry food from the leaves to the other parts of the plant
pistil: the female part of a flowering plant	**pollen:** the yellow dustlike powder produced by the male part of a flowering plant	**pollination:** the transfer of pollen from the male part of a flowering plant to the female part	**stamen:** the male part of a flowering plant	**taproot:** the primary root of a plant that grows downward and from which other roots grow
vein: a tubelike structure in a leaf that carries sap	**xylem:** tubes that carry water and minerals upward from the roots throughout the plant	**chloroplast:** the food-making part of a plant cell that contains chlorophyll	**conifers:** nonflowering plants that usually have cones and needle-shaped leaves	**cotyledon:** a leaf inside a seed that feeds a developing plant
cuticle: the waxy covering of most plants	**evergreen:** a plant with leaves that stay green all through the year	**germination:** the process of a seed beginning to grow	**leaf:** the main food-producing part of the plant	**sap:** a liquid that moves through a plant and contains water and minerals or food
sepal: the leaflike structure that surrounds and protects a flower before it opens	**stem:** the plant part that supports the leaves and flowers of a plant and transports water, minerals, and food	**seed coat:** a seed's protective outer layer	**sprout:** to start to grow	**stomata:** tiny holes, usually on the underside of a leaf, through which carbon dioxide, oxygen, and water vapor pass in and out of the leaf

Name_____ Project: flowering-plant model

The Model Plant

Follow the directions below to make a 3-D model showing all the parts of a flowering plant.

Materials: bathroom-tissue tube, five 3-inch lengths of string, 2 straws, two 9" x 12" sheets of construction paper (1 red, 1 green), two 15-inch pipe cleaners (1 green, 1 yellow), cornmeal, ruler, tape, scissors, pencil, glue

Directions:

Stem 1. Cut a 4½" x 6" piece from the green paper. Tape this piece in place around the tube.

Roots 2. Tape the lengths of string so they dangle from inside the tube's bottom.

Xylem and Phloem Tubes 3. Cut the straws the same length as the tube. Tape the straws inside along the tube's sides.

Sepals and Petals 4. Fold the remaining green paper in half. Cut out the sepals pattern below. Place the pattern on the green paper at the fold and trace. Then cut out your tracing.

5. Fold the red paper in fourths. Cut out the petal pattern below. Place the pattern on the red paper at the folds and trace. Then cut out your tracing.

6. Tape the sepals under the petals so the green leaves show between the petals. Fold the petals upward slightly so they appear to stand up.

Stamen and Pistil 7. Cut the yellow pipe cleaner into five 3-inch pieces. Cut a 3-inch length from the green pipe cleaner.

8. Make a small hole in the center of the petals and sepals. Push the pipe cleaner pieces through the hole so the green piece is surrounded by the yellow ones.

9. Twist the bottoms of the pipe cleaners together to hold them in place under the sepals.

10. Slightly bend the tops of the yellow pipe cleaners to make them fan out around the green one.

11. Tape the sepals and petals in place atop the cardboard stem.

Leaves 12. Cut two leaves from the scraps of green paper. Draw veins on the leaves. Then tape the leaves to the cardboard stem.

Pollen 13. Place a dab of glue at the end of each stamen (yellow pipe cleaner). Sprinkle the glue with cornmeal to represent pollen. (It's okay if some cornmeal winds up on the petals. That happens to real flowers, too!)

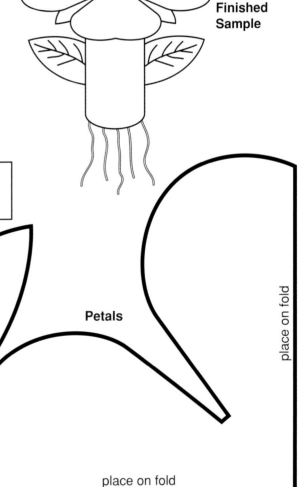

Finished Sample

Bonus Box: On the back of this sheet or on another sheet of paper, draw and label a diagram of your model. Include the function of each plant part.

Sepals place on fold

Petals place on fold

place on fold

©The Mailbox® • Science • TEC60859

34 **Note to the teacher:** Use with "The Model Plant" on page 30.

Taking a Look at Vertebrates

Amphibians, birds, fish, mammals, and reptiles…just how much do your students know about vertebrates? Sneak a peek at this fascinating group of animals with these exciting and fun-to-do activities!

ideas by Kimberly A. Minafo, Pomona, NY

Just a Drop in the Bucket

Concept: Size of vertebrate population

Begin your study of vertebrates by asking students to do a little population calculation! Prepare a 10 x 10 grid for each child. Also color four squares on an additional grid and mount it on construction paper as shown. On the back of the paper, write "Only about 4 percent of the animals on Earth are vertebrates."

After reviewing the five classes of vertebrates (fish, mammals, birds, reptiles, and amphibians), challenge the class to name 100 animals as you list them on the board. Have a reference book handy in case students get stuck. Place a check mark beside each vertebrate in the list. Have each student count the vertebrates listed. Then ask students to think about this question: Is this number greater than, less than, or equal to the percentage of animals in the world that actually are vertebrates? Give each child a blank grid; then direct him to color in squares on the grid to show what he thinks is the correct percentage. When students are finished, have them hold up their grids. Then display your mounted grid. Ask, "What could the four colored squares on this grid mean?" Then flip the paper to reveal the statement on the back. After students ooh and aah at this amazing statistic, invite them to speculate on why there are fewer vertebrates than invertebrates. Conclude by discussing how important vertebrates are to the food chain.

Only about 4 percent of the animals on Earth are vertebrates.

The Evidence Is In!

Concept: Characteristics of vertebrates

Turn students into "bone-a-fide" vertebrate experts with this reading and research activity. In advance, label resealable plastic bags with categories such as size, speed, feeding habits, adaptations, and parenting; then hang the bags on a bulletin board. Also cut out a large supply of construction paper bones and place them in a separate bag on the board. After a student reads an interesting fact about vertebrates, have her write it on a bone cutout (the fact on one side, the reference on the other side) and place it in the appropriate bag.

At the end of the unit, divide students into groups. Give each group a different bag of bones, glue, markers, and several sheets of construction paper. Challenge the group to sort its bones into subgroups and then display the resulting information as shown. Conclude by having each child summarize what she learned about her group's category on a large bone cutout. Provide time for students to share their bones with the class.

Animals' Activity Levels

Lions lie around for up to 21 hours a day!

Koalas sleep more than 14 hours a day!

Sea turtles have swimming frenzies for the first 24 to 48 hours of their lives!

Vampire bats can fly, run, jump, and hop!

35

Just Look at Those Legs!

Concept: Diversity of vertebrates

Help students understand the diversity within a class of vertebrates with this activity. Discuss with students that animal legs come in a variety of shapes and sizes and that the feet attached to those legs are even more diverse. Next, have each student research the legs and feet of any two different birds, reptiles, amphibians, or mammals. Then give students the materials listed and guide them through the steps below. When the projects have been completed (see the example), have each student write a paragraph comparing and contrasting the leg and foot structures of her two animals. Afterward, display students' projects side by side on the chalk tray or a table. Then take students on a virtual nature walk by having them share their information strips or summarize their paragraphs for the class.

Materials for each student: tissue paper roll, 4½" x 6" strip of white paper, 2½" square of white paper, markers, scissors, clear tape, six 1" x 9" paper strips (three each of two different colors)

Steps:

1. From the white square, cut a circle slightly larger than the tissue roll's opening. Notch the circle's edges and mold them around one end of the tissue roll. Tape the edges to the roll.
2. Wrap the white strip around the tissue roll and tape it in place.
3. Hold the tissue roll so that its covered end faces down. Then, on opposite sides of the roll, draw and label the leg and foot of each vertebrate researched.
4. On each set of colored strips, record three reasons why the leg and foot structures of each vertebrate are important to it.
5. Fold the labeled strips and place them inside the tissue roll.

My legs are very strong.

My sharp talons dig into my prey so I don't drop it.

The lower part of my legs is bare.

Bald Eagle

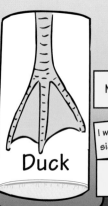

My feet help me swim well.

I waddle because my legs are set on the side and toward the rear of my body.

My feet are webbed.

Duck

Are You Qualified?

Concept: Characteristics and adaptations of vertebrates

Focus students' attention on the special abilities of vertebrates with this nifty research and writing project. First, gather facts about a vertebrate of interest to your students, such as the American alligator. Demonstrate for students how to use the facts to complete a resumé, such as the one shown. Afterward, have each student research a vertebrate of his choice, focusing on its special abilities and unique adaptations. Then have the student write a resumé for the vertebrate and share it with the class. For a fun extension, see "Vertebrates for Hire" on page 37.

RESUMÉ

Name: Albert E. Alligator

Nickname: Gator Breath

Class: Reptilia

Year of birth: 1985

Age: 16

Address: Rivers, ponds, lakes, and other wetland areas of the southeastern United States

Personal description: I am a male alligator, about 11 feet long and weighing 447 pounds. I have four short legs and am shaped like a large lizard. I have a powerful tail that you'd better watch out for! My skin is rough and scaly. I am a protected animal that eats fish, turtles, mammals, birds, and snakes. Sometimes, I even eat one of my own kind!

Job goal: I am looking for a job as a private investigator. I would be great at the job because with my dark, uniform color, I can lurk in murky waters and spy on suspected criminals. When confronted, I could use my large sweeping tail to knock my attacker down. Then I could either use my tail to keep him from getting away or threaten to bite him with my 80 teeth!

Vertebrates for Hire

Concept: Characteristics and adaptations of vertebrates

Follow up "Are You Qualified?" on page 36 with this creative-thinking activity. Arrange students' resumés around the perimeter of a bulletin board titled "Vertebrates for Hire!" Next, give each student an index card to label with a job for which his vertebrate might be suited (see the examples listed). After collecting the cards, use them to create a ballot that lists the different job titles as shown. Place a class supply of ballots in a plastic bag labeled "Blank Ballots" and attach it to the bulletin board along with another bag labeled "Completed Ballots." Also mount the job cards on the board. During free time, have students read the job titles, review the resumés, and complete the ballots. After each student has had a chance to vote, have groups of students tally the ballots. Discuss the results of the vote as a class.

Official Ballot

Directions: Write in the name of the vertebrate you think is most qualified for each job listed below. Explain why you voted for this vertebrate in the space provided.

Job	Most Qualified Vertebrate	Why I Voted for This Vertebrate
Treetop Duster	giraffe	It's tall enough to reach treetops.
Stone Overturner	African elephant	Its trunk can lift heavy objects.
College Mascot	American alligator	The alligator lives in Florida and is a mascot for a Florida college.
Flyswatter		

The Carnivore Café and Steak House
The Place Where Meat Eaters Meet!

If you're a meat-eating predator, you've come to the right place! Chef Bearclaw, himself a carnivore, has been with us for 11 years. We offer generous servings of our menu items because we know some of our carnivorous customers like big meals. For your convenience, you can even catch your own favorite animal right out back on our two-acre ranch and have Chef Bearclaw prepare it to your liking. If you're on the run, ask for one of our special take-out meals.

We allow all carnivores (even weasels) to eat at our establishment. But don't plan on having a long, leisurely dining experience. You see, some of our guests are so hungry they can't wait for their meals to be prepared. They just might [eat] you for dinner!

Hours: 1 P.M. to 3 A.M.

Dine at your own risk!

Grilled Gazelle
Marinated in Sahara sweet sauce and ready to eat in seconds so you don't have to wait! We take care of the horns and bones for you! Enough for a pride of lions to share! $237.99

Salmon à la Riverbed
Four salmon on a bed of river algae, sprinkled with extra crispy pieces of trout. Not too small, too hot, or too expensive. $49.99

Roadkill Delight
Our "Dead Deal of the Day" especially for hyenas! Ask your server for details. $9.99 or less

Mini Munchers
A bowl of bird, rabbit, and squirrel pieces, perfect for eagles and other carnivores! Free refills for just $5.99 more. $26.99

What's for Dinner?

Concept: Feeding habits of vertebrates

Investigate the feeding habits of vertebrates with this deliciously fun activity. Ask your media specialist to help you gather resources containing pictures of *carnivores* (meat-eating animals), *herbivores* (plant-eating animals), and *omnivores* (animals that eat both plants and meat). Also divide chart paper into three sections (carnivores, herbivores, and omnivores).

Next, divide students into three groups (one per section on the chart) and give each group its corresponding set of books. Direct each group to look through its books and call out names of vertebrates for you to list under each heading. Then challenge each group to research the eating habits of its assigned animal group. After the research has been completed, give each student markers and a 12" x 18" sheet of paper. Have him follow the directions below to create a menu that could tempt the palates of his assigned vertebrates. For fun, serve animal crackers for students to munch on as they share the meritorious menus!

Steps:
1. Fold the paper in half to make a menu.
2. On the front cover, write the name of your restaurant. Add a paragraph that introduces diners to the restaurant and explains the eating habits of vertebrates who might patronize the restaurant.
3. On the inside, list four to six different menu items with imaginative titles. List each item's main ingredients. Also mention which diners might enjoy the selections the most.

The Chordata Academy

It takes a backbone to be a student at the prestigious Chordata Academy! The school's board hires only the finest teachers. Also, headmaster Lionel Kingofbeasts takes great care in preparing class rosters so that students and teachers are perfectly matched. Help Lionel get this year's rosters ready by completing the list of student qualifications under each teacher's name (some may be used more than once).

The Chordata Academy
We welcome all vertebrates!

Qualifications:

warm-blooded	most have hair or fur	have scales
feed young with milk	live part of life in water,	breathe with gills or lungs
breathe with lungs	part on land	most bear live young
have feathers	live in water	have a beak or bill
cold-blooded	hatch from eggs	breathe mainly with gills

Instructor Aves Birdy's Class

- vertebrate
- _____
- _____
- _____
- _____
- _____

Lionel Kingofbeasts
Headmaster

Professor Reptilia's Class

- vertebrate
- _____
- _____
- _____
- _____

Mr. Mammalia's Class

- vertebrate
- _____
- _____
- _____
- _____
- _____

Dr. Amphibia's Class

- vertebrate
- _____
- _____
- _____

Ms. Four-Fish's Class

- vertebrate
- _____
- _____
- _____

Bonus Box: Design a school flag for Chordata Academy.

©The Mailbox® • *Science* • TEC60859 • Key p.158

Note to the teacher: To complete this page, students will need access to science books, encyclopedias, or other reference materials.

Mammal Nursery

For mammals that give birth to live young, the time during which the baby animal grows before being born is called *gestation*. Gestation times vary from animal to animal.

Directions: Many baby animals are in the Mammal Nursery below. Below each name is the baby's gestation period. Notice that some babies—like the rabbit—gestate in about a month, while a mother elephant waits nearly two years for her baby to be born! Have fun visiting the babies. Then use the gestation data to complete the bar graph at the right. (For this activity, one month equals 30 days.)

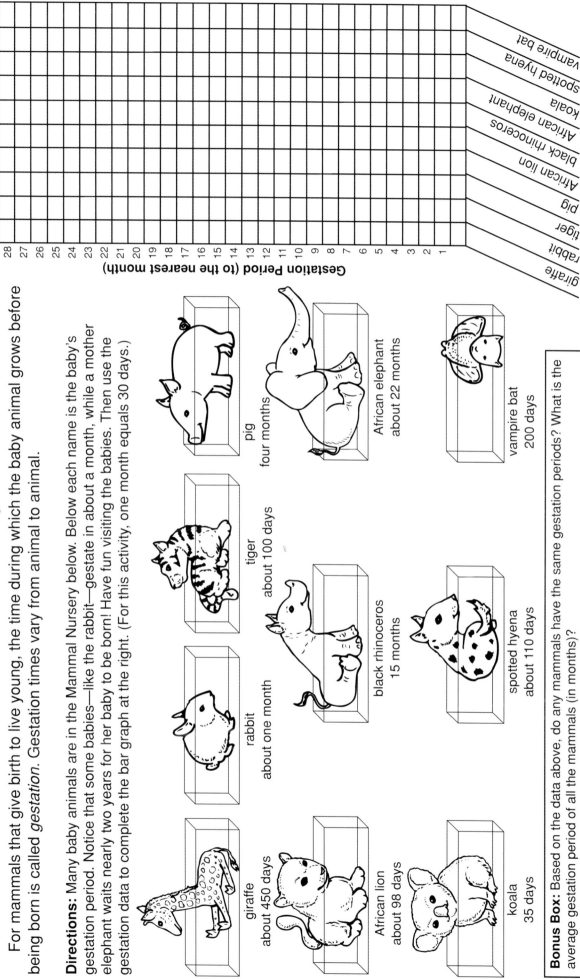

giraffe
about 450 days

rabbit
about one month

tiger
about 100 days

pig
four months

African lion
about 98 days

black rhinoceros
15 months

African elephant
about 22 months

koala
35 days

spotted hyena
about 110 days

vampire bat
200 days

Gestation Period (to the nearest month)

30 29 28 27 26 25 24 23 22 21 20 19 18 17 16 15 14 13 12 11 10 9 8 7 6 5 4 3 2 1

Mammal

giraffe · rabbit · tiger · pig · African lion · black rhinoceros · African elephant · koala · spotted hyena · vampire bat

Bonus Box: Based on the data above, do any mammals have the same gestation periods? What is the average gestation period of all the mammals (in months)?

Note to the teacher: If desired, provide students with colored pencils for completing the graph.

No Bones About It... Invertebrates Are Incredible!

Not having a backbone isn't as bad as it seems for some creatures. In fact, more than 95% of the world's animal population is spineless! Use the following hands-on activities and reproducibles to boost science-process skills and help students become "bone-a-fide" experts on invertebrates.

by Bonnie Pettifor

Invertebrates: 97, Vertebrates: 3

Begin this unit with a simple classification activity. Ask students to bring in safe items from home, such as plastic or stuffed toys, so that each team has at least 20 different objects. The next day divide the class into teams. Have each team study its items and then sort them into two groups by size, color, or any other categories. Explain to students that scientists have divided the animal kingdom into two main groups, one with backbones and the other without. The group with backbones, called *vertebrates,* makes up about 3% of all animals. The group without backbones, called *invertebrates,* makes up the other 97%. Since there is a great deal of difference between any two animals with backbones and any two without backbones, scientists have further divided both groups according to additional physical characteristics. Direct each team to subdivide one of its two groups into three subgroups and share its reasoning with the class. Use this activity again, with students bringing in different items, when studying a new group of living things.

Eight Fabulous Phyla

Introduce students to the animals that make up the eight largest phyla of invertebrates with this chart-making activity. Divide a large sheet of bulletin-board paper into eight columns, labeling it and listing examples as shown. Ask students to share what they know about each phylum. Add their comments to the chart. Next give each student a copy of the research activity on page 43 to complete as directed. As students learn more about invertebrates through their research, have them add information to (or delete information from) the class chart.

Sponges	Coelenterates	Flatworms	Roundworms	Segmented Worms	Mollus
sheepswool sponge	jellyfish	planarian	vinegar eel	clamworm	clam
sulfur sponge	sea anemone	fluke	hookworm	earthworm	squid
Venus's-flower-basket sponge	coral	tapeworm	trichina worm	leech	octopu

It's Always Wise to Have Sharper Eyes

Keen eyes are all future "invertebrate-ologists" need for this simple exercise on observation! Pass around an interesting seashell and a hand lens, giving no directions other than telling students to look at it. Once each child has examined the shell, put it away. Then ask each student to list every detail he can recall about the shell. (If desired, have students also make detailed drawings.) As students share their recollections, point out that careful observation—combined with accurate note taking and drawing—is vitally important when doing scientific investigations. For another activity that sharpens observation and data-recording skills, see the reproducible "Candy-Worm Dissection" on page 44.

To adapt this activity to any science unit, follow the same procedure as above. Simply substitute the shell for an object related to the new unit. Don't worry if students get wise to this method—simply reduce the time allowed for looking at the object!

Spineless Math

Strengthen students' graphing skills with this hands-on encounter with backyard creepy crawlies. For each small group, fill a large foam meat tray (donated by a local grocer) with the upper few inches of soil from under a rock, a log, or another object. Then guide the groups through these steps:

1. Spread out the soil on the tray.
2. Look for beetle larvae, earthworms, roundworms, slugs, pill bugs (also called roly-polies), centipedes, millipedes, ants, or other invertebrates in the soil.
3. Record the number of each invertebrate your group finds.
4. Make drawings of these invertebrates.
5. Record your group's observations about these invertebrates.
6. Use your group's data to create a bar graph of your findings.

Challenge all the groups to combine their data into a class graph. Post this graph above a terrarium set up by students for housing the invertebrates they found. Or return the animals to the area from which they were taken. For a great follow-up to this activity, see the reproducible on page 45 or "Bringing Up Baby" on this page.

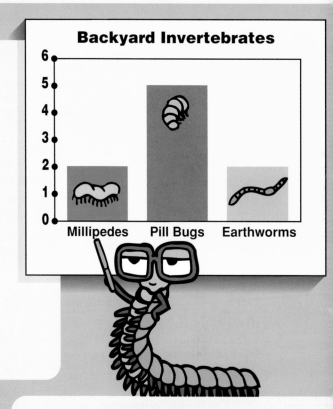

Backyard Invertebrates

Bringing Up Baby

Interested in keeping an invertebrate as a pet in the classroom? Most invertebrates—such as land or water snails, earthworms, lady beetles, and mealworms—require very little attention once their natural environment has been duplicated. In return they supply lots of fascinating entertainment for students. *And* putting the care of these invertebrates in the hands of students helps teach responsibility. Specimens can be collected from nature, or live invertebrates can be ordered from a biological supply company (see the box below). And guess what? No 2:00 A.M. feedings to worry about!

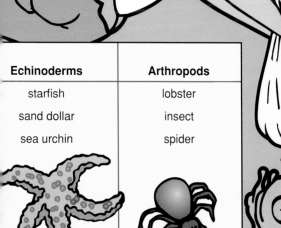

Echinoderms	Arthropods
starfish	lobster
sand dollar	insect
sea urchin	spider

For a catalog including invertebrates and other scientific supplies, contact:
Carolina Biological Supply Company
2700 York Road
Burlington, NC 27215
1-800-334-5551

(current as of April 2006)

Movin' and Groovin'

How do some invertebrates move and eat? Find out with these three "inverte-great" activities!

- **How a Sponge Eats:** Show students a natural sponge. Explain that this is really the sponge's skeleton that's been cleaned and dried. A live sponge has holes, or *pores,* through which water is squeezed to filter food. Let each student use a hand lens to examine the pores in a synthetic sponge. Then divide students into groups to complete the following experiment:

  Materials: 1 cup of water, 1 clear empty glass, 1 tablespoon of glitter, 1 large-holed synthetic sponge (large enough to cover the top of the glass), 1 plastic spoon, paper and pencil

  Steps:
  1. Use the spoon to stir the glitter (food) into the cup of water.
  2. Place the sponge over the empty glass.
  3. Predict what you think will happen to the food when it is poured on the sponge. Write your prediction.
  4. Slowly pour the food (glitter mixture) on the sponge.
  5. Carefully fold the ends of the sponge together; then squeeze the sponge so that the water from it goes into the empty glass.
  6. Record what happens to the food. *(The sponge filters the glitter from the water, trapping most of it in the sponge.)*

- **How a Squid Moves:** Explain that a squid travels by jet propulsion—taking water in and pushing it out—which moves it *backwards!* To demonstrate this unusual method of movement, squeeze the bulb end of a turkey baster. Put the tube end into a clear plastic tub of water. Release the bulb so that it fills with water. Tell students that this action mimics a squid taking in water under its mantle. Next squeeze the bulb, forcing the water out of the tube. Explain that this mimics the action of a squid as it pushes water out through a funnel under its head, making it move backwards.

- **Moving Into Research:** Follow up these two activities by assigning each student a different invertebrate to research (see the list on page 43). Have the student find out how his invertebrate eats, and also how it moves to catch prey and evade predators. Challenge him to share his findings in a presentation that includes a demonstration of how his animal moves.

Internet Invertebrates

Visit this interesting site for more information on invertebrates *(valid as of March 2006):*

- **http://www.mnh.si.edu** (Click on "Invertebrate Zoology" for current on-line exhibitions at The Smithsonian's National Museum Of Natural History.)

Investigating Incredible Invertebrates!

Invertebrates are animals without backbones. Pretend that a group of aliens has come to investigate the different *phyla* (groups) of invertebrates found on Earth, and that *you* are on the committee to answer their questions!

To get ready to answer their questions, complete ___ activities by _____. Use the list of invertebrates below and your science text, library books, encyclopedias, or the Internet for help. Color one of the invertebrates on this sheet each time you complete an activity.

1. Choose one of these invertebrate phyla: Sponges, Coelenterates, Flatworms, Roundworms, Segmented Worms, Mollusks, Echinoderms, Arthropods. Write a paragraph describing the phylum's basic characteristics for the aliens. Include the names of several animals that belong to this group.
2. Make a model of any invertebrate to show the aliens. Be sure to label the invertebrate's parts.
3. Choose an invertebrate from the box below. Write a friendly letter from the invertebrate to the aliens. In the letter, have the invertebrate tell what it eats, how it gets its food, and where it lives.
4. Pretend a classmate is one of the aliens. Teach him the spelling and the definition of each of the eight largest phyla of invertebrates (Hint: they're listed in #1).
5. Make a detailed drawing of an invertebrate listed below in its environment as a souvenir for the aliens. Remember to label the invertebrate's parts.
6. Pretend you are an alien. Write an e-mail message to the chairman of the committee that is investigating invertebrates. In the e-mail, list five questions about invertebrates that you want answered during your stay on Earth.
7. Choose a partner. Work together to create a fun game that will teach the aliens ten interesting facts about one of the invertebrate groups listed in #1. Test your game with two other classmates.
8. Make a shape book about an invertebrate to give to an alien as a memento. Share the book with a younger student (before giving it to the alien, of course!).

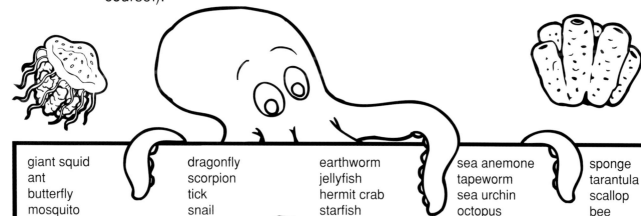

giant squid	dragonfly	earthworm	sea anemone	sponge
ant	scorpion	jellyfish	tapeworm	tarantula
butterfly	tick	hermit crab	sea urchin	scallop
mosquito	snail	starfish	octopus	bee
black-widow spider	slug	coral	lobster	sea cucumber

Note To The Teacher: Use with "Eight Fabulous Phyla" on page 40. Before duplicating, fill in the blanks with the number of activities to complete and the due date. Make one copy for each student. Use also with "Moving Into Research" on page 42.

Candy-Worm Dissection

How is a worm like a map? Believe it or not, they *are* alike! The 100–180 rings on an earthworm's body are like the lines on a map's grid. They help scientists locate the earthworm's organs. Scientists have learned this information through careful observation and a procedure called *dissection*. Dissection is the process of cutting into a dead animal to find out what its body is like inside. Follow the steps below to do a little dissecting of your own!

Materials: 1 Gummy Worm®, 1 plastic knife, 1 paper towel, 1 pencil

Steps:

1. Place the Gummy Worm® on the paper towel. Carefully count the number of rings on your worm. Record the number: _____.

2. Draw your candy worm in the space below. Show its exact number of rings.

3. Label the worm's rings in your drawing:
   Ring 3: Brain
   Rings 7–11: Five pairs of hearts
   Rings 17–18: Gizzard (stomach)
   (Note: Your candy worm won't have as many rings as real earthworms do! Add more rings to your drawing if you'd like.)

4. Carefully use the knife to cut the sections of the candy worm apart.

5. Look carefully at the outer surface of the candy worm. Also notice what the cut surface is like. Touch both surfaces. On the back of this sheet, describe the look and feel of these surfaces.

6. Use the information in Step 3 to label the drawing below with the names of the worm's organs.

7. Now eat your candy worm—it will taste much better than the real thing!

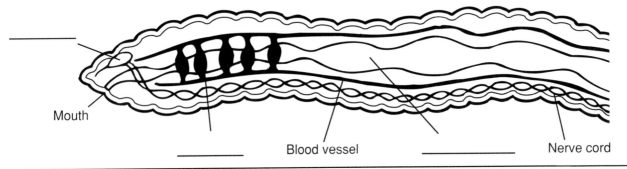

Mouth   _____   Blood vessel   _____   Nerve cord

Bonus Box: Pretend you are an earthworm that's just been caught by a child. The child plans to use you as fishing bait! On another sheet of paper, write a story telling how you persuade the child to let you go.

Home Sweet Invertebrate Home

Did you know that invertebrates prefer certain living conditions over others, just like people do? To learn more about the places that some invertebrates like to call home, follow the directions below with a partner.

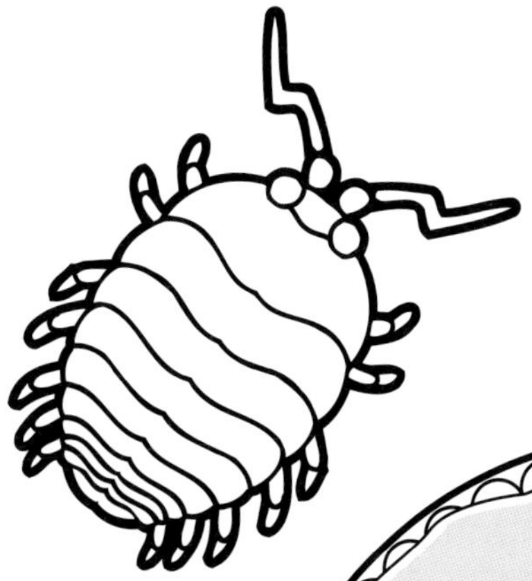

Materials:

1 roly-poly bug (also known as a pill bug)
1 large, round white Styrofoam® plate
one 9" x 12" sheet of white construction paper
one 9" x 12" sheet of black construction paper
pencil
scissors
water
plastic wrap (enough to cover plate securely)
tape
1 toothpick

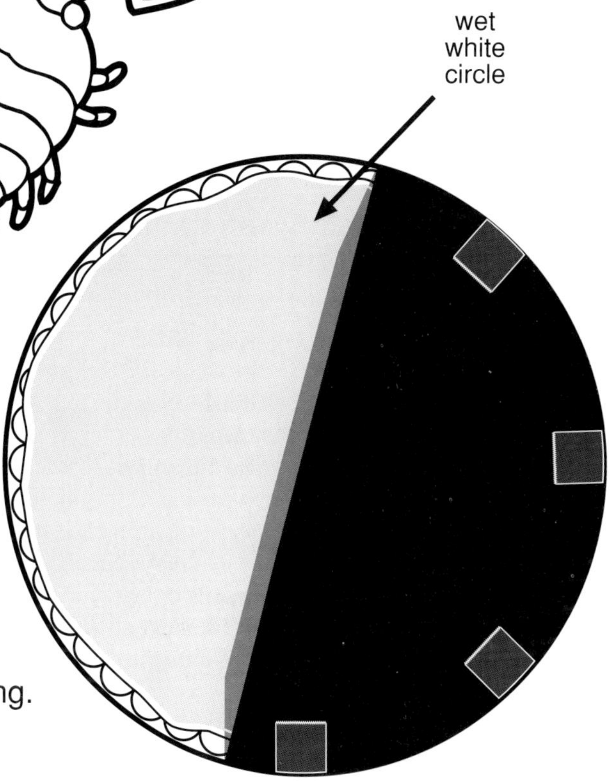

wet white circle

Steps:

1. Trace the plate on both the white paper and the black paper; then cut out the tracings.
2. Wet the white circle with water so that it has no dry spots; then press it to the bottom of the plate.
3. Fold the black circle in half; then tape this semicircle to the plate at the edges as shown.
4. Put the roly-poly onto the uncovered part of the plate; then cover the plate completely with plastic wrap. If necessary, tape the plastic wrap to the plate's edges to prevent the roly-poly from escaping.
5. Use the toothpick to make several tiny airholes in the plastic wrap.
6. Put the plate in a place where it will be undisturbed for at least 30 minutes.
7. Decide which section—the light (uncovered) part or the dark (covered) part—you think the roly-poly will prefer. Record your prediction below.
8. After at least 30 minutes are up, uncover the plate and find the roly-poly. Was your prediction correct? Record your observations below.

My Prediction:

I think the roly-poly will like the _____ section.

My Observations:

I found the roly-poly in the _____ section. I think it chose this section because

_____

_____.

Bonus Box: Roly-polies prefer damp environments. Pretend you are a roly-poly. On the back of this sheet, write a conversation between you and a bee about why you prefer a damp home.

Note To The Teacher: Use after "Spineless Math" on page 41. Roly-polies are found in damp places, such as under rocks and pieces of wood. Earthworms can also be used for this investigation. Duplicate this page for each pair of students. If desired, combine all the data and have students graph the results and draw conclusions.

Exploring Ecosystems

Eager to explore ecosystems? This collection of hands-on activities is the perfect vehicle for an exciting learning excursion!

by Dr. Barbara B. Leonard, Winston-Salem, NC

Who's Who on the Food Chain Gang?

Concept: Food chains

Time to teach about food chains? Then put this simple activity on the menu! A *food chain* is a group of living things that form a chain in which the first living thing is eaten by the second, the second is eaten by the third, and so on. A food chain always begins with plant life and ends with an animal. After explaining this information to students, discuss the definitions shown of *producers, consumers,* and *decomposers.* Then write the following food chain on the board: "seed → mouse → weasel → owl." Ask students what might happen if owls were removed. *(The weasels may increase in population and possibly run out of food.)* Weasels? *(The mice may increase in population and possibly run out of food, and the owls may decrease in population because of a lack of food.)* Mice? *(The weasels may decrease in population due to a lack of food.)* If a severe drought occurred? *(The food chain may struggle to survive if plants were in short supply.)*

Next, have each student research a food chain that consists of a producer and primary, secondary, and tertiary consumers. Afterward, give each child a black marker and four 1" x 8" paper strips in the following colors: green for the producer, orange for the primary consumer, blue for the secondary consumer, and red for the tertiary consumer. Have the student label the strips with her chain's members. Then have her staple the strips in order to form a chain as shown. Hang the chains from a bulletin board labeled "Meet the Food Chain Gang!"

Biological Fans

Concept: Biological hierarchy of living things

Just what is an ecosystem? The answer can be found by comparing the characteristics of an ecosystem to other levels studied in ecology. To introduce this biological hierarchy to students, list the levels shown on the board. Discuss each level, beginning with the *individual* and ending with the *biosphere.* Then have students suggest illustrations that could be drawn to represent each level.

Next, give each child colored pencils or markers and one-fourth of a cardboard pizza circle. Have the student divide the cardboard wedge into six bands as shown. Then have him label and illustrate the six levels. Encourage students to keep these easy-to-read study aids handy so they can refer to them throughout the unit.

Individual—one plant or animal that belongs to a specific species
Population—a group of plants or animals that belong to the same species
Community—many plant and animal populations living together in the same general area and depending on each other
Ecosystem—a community and its nonliving environment (soil, climate, water, air, energy, and nutrients)
Biome—many different ecosystems sharing the same geographical area and climate
Biosphere—the thin, life-bearing, outer layer of the earth's surface that contains all the biomes

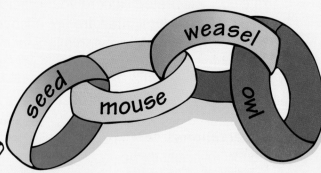

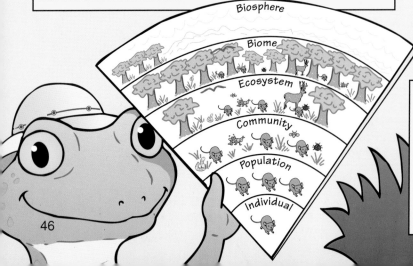

Producers—mainly green plants that use the sun's energy to produce food
Primary consumers—animals that eat plants (herbivores)
Secondary consumers—animals that eat other animals (carnivores) or both plants and animals (omnivores)
Tertiary consumers—animals that prey on secondary consumers
Decomposers—organisms such as fungi and bacteria that break down dead plant and animal material into nutrients

Making Mini Ecosystems

Concept: Creating and observing a miniature ecosystem

Want a close-up view of an ecosystem? Then make your own mini aquariums and terrariums with the simple-to-use plans listed below. Have each student make his own models, or have students help you make one of each for the class. After the models are made, instruct each child to record in a journal his observations about the animals' activities, physical changes in the bottles' environments, schedules for feeding, and schedules for changing the water in the aquarium. As you discuss students' observations, have them identify the following:

- biotic parts of each model *(the plants and animals)*
- abiotic parts of each model *(water, soil, rocks, air, sun, temperature)*
- food chain represented in each model *(aquarium—fish food → guppy, terrarium—lettuce or fruit → cricket)*
- plants' and animals' roles in the food chain *(plants—producers; animals—consumers)*
- factors to consider before more animals could be added to the models *(space, soil, air and oxygen supply, sunlight, temperature)*

After a few days of observation, release the cricket outside and send the guppy home with someone who keeps freshwater tropical fish.

Mini Aquarium

Materials: 20 oz. clear plastic bottle without cap, ruler, sand, water plant, guppy, small fish food pellets, gallon jug of water left standing for 24 hours, thermometer

Directions:
1. Cover the bottom of the bottle with a one-inch layer of sand.
2. Put the plant into the bottle.
3. Fill the bottle with water from the jug. Add the guppy and one or two fish pellets. Then insert the thermometer.
4. Each day, replace some of the water in the bottle with clean water from the jug. Keep the water temperature between 76°F and 86°F.
5. Add one or two fish pellets daily as needed.

Mini Terrarium

Materials: 2-liter plastic soda bottle with cap, scissors, ruler, soil from outside, small rocks, small plants (with roots), water, twig, cricket, lettuce leaf or slice of apple or orange

Directions:
1. Cut three inches from the bottom of the bottle. Then make six one-inch slits around the bottom edge of the top section as shown.
2. Fill the bottom of the bottle with rocks. Put one rock aside to use in Step 4.
3. Put the soil on top of the rocks. Then plant the plants in the soil.
4. Arrange the extra rock and the twig on the soil. Add a piece of lettuce or fruit.
5. Water the soil. Place the cricket inside and put the top back on the bottom.
6. Put the terrarium in a sunny spot (but not direct sunlight). Remove the top, as needed, to add food.

I Will Survive!

Concept: Flow of energy through a food chain

Make it easier for students to understand food chains with an outdoor simulation that's full of grasshoppers, birds, and a hawk—oh my! Just follow the directions shown. After Round 4, have students answer the questions below.

Materials:
copy of page 50
6 regular-sized (3.5 oz.) bags of popped microwave popcorn
13-gallon plastic garbage bag, labeled "Hawk"
3 gallon-sized resealable plastic bags, each labeled "Bird"
3 crepe-paper armbands, each labeled "Bird"
sandwich-sized resealable plastic bags, each labeled "Grasshopper"
  (enough for all but four students)
pinch clothespins (enough for all but four students)
class supply of index cards
class supply of small pencils
stopwatch
whistle
4 orange safety cones
yardstick
pencil

Round	Grasshoppers	Popcorn Pieces Collected by Grasshoppers	Birds	Grasshoppers Eaten by Birds	Popcorn Pieces Collected by Birds	Birds Eaten by Hawk	Popcorn Pieces Collected by Hawk
1							
2							
3							
4							

Getting ready: Place an index card and pencil inside each plastic "Grasshopper" bag. Use the safety cones to mark off a 50-foot-square area outside. Scatter the popcorn throughout the marked area. Then give one student the bag labeled "Hawk." Give three other students the "Bird" bags and armbands. Give each remaining student a clothespin and a "Grasshopper" bag. Explain that each plastic bag represents an animal's stomach.

Round 1: Send the grasshoppers into the area with instructions to pick up popcorn pieces with their clothespins and place the pieces in their bags. After 20 seconds, blow the whistle and call the grasshoppers to the sidelines. Have each grasshopper count the popcorn pieces in his bag, record the total on his card, and report the total to you. Calculate and record the total number of grasshoppers and popcorn pieces collected. Share the results with the students. If a grasshopper doesn't have any popcorn, pronounce him dead and send him to the sidelines permanently.

Round 2: Play as in Round 1, except send in the birds five seconds after the grasshoppers. Instruct the birds to tag the grasshoppers. Have each tagged grasshopper place his bag inside the larger bag of the bird that tagged him and then go to the sidelines permanently as an eaten grasshopper. Blow the whistle after 20 seconds. Then have the birds and surviving grasshoppers go to the sidelines to count, record, and report to you. Share the new totals with the students. If a bird never tags a grasshopper, pronounce him dead and send him to the sidelines permanently.

Round 3: Play as in Round 2, except send in the hawk five seconds after the birds. Have the hawk tag the birds. Have each tagged bird place his popcorn bag into the hawk's larger bag and then join the eaten grasshoppers on the sidelines as an eaten bird. Conclude the round as before and share the new totals with the students.

Round 4: Repeat Round 3.

Questions:
1. What represents the producers in the simulation? *(popcorn)*
2. What food chain is represented in this simulation? *(popcorn → grasshopper → bird → hawk)*
3. Which part of this food chain needs the most energy to live? *(hawk)*
4. Which consumer in the food chain starts with the largest population? *(grasshoppers)*
5. Do the consumers increase or decrease as you move up the food chain? *(decrease)*
6. What happens to the energy when a plant or animal dies? *(It eventually ends with decomposers, such as bacteria and fungi, that break down dead plant and animal material into nutrients that enrich the soil.)*

Can You Dig It?

Concept: How soil and water affect an ecosystem

Dig for answers about how soil and water can affect an ecosystem by having groups of students conduct this earthy experiment! Have each group follow the steps below. Afterward, have the experimenters graph the results. Then follow up with the questions below.

Materials for each group of students: six 8 oz. Styrofoam cups, sharpened pencil, paper towels, liquid measuring cup, 6 craft sticks, newspaper, trowel, 3 soil samples (1 from an area with no plants, 1 from a wooded area, 1 from a grassy area), water

Steps:

1. Make filter cups by punching holes in the bottoms of three cups with the pencil. Line the bottom of each filter cup with a small piece of a paper towel.
2. Place each soil sample on the newspaper. Observe the color and texture of each sample. Also note whether the sample contains plants whose roots are holding the soil together.
3. Fill each filter cup with a different soil sample, including any attached plants. Label the cup of soil containing no plants "A," the cup with soil from a wooded area "B," and the cup with soil from a grassy area "C."
4. Place two craft sticks slightly apart atop each remaining cup as shown. Stack a filter cup on each empty cup as shown.
5. Slowly pour eight ounces of water into cup A. When the dripping stops, remove the filter cup and craft sticks. Then measure and record the amount of water collected in the bottom cup.
6. Repeat Step 5 with cups B and C.
7. Record your conclusions about which soil retains the most water, which one allows water to pass through the fastest, and whether soils with plants hold more water than those without.

Questions:

1. Why are soil and water important to an ecosystem? *(For the most part, plants depend on soil and water to live and grow. Without plants, consumers could not live and grow.)*
2. How can soil differences affect an ecosystem? *(It is one factor that determines the type of plants and animals that can live there. Sandy soils, for example, drain faster than soils containing clay.)*
3. How does the amount of water in an area affect an ecosystem? *(All living things need water. If there is too much or too little water, plants and animals can die. Climate, topography, and soil type all affect the amount of water in an ecosystem.)*

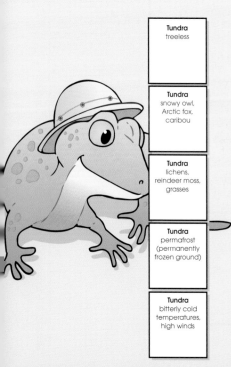

Tundra
treeless

Tundra
snowy owl, Arctic fox, caribou

Tundra
lichens, reindeer moss, grasses

Tundra
permafrost (permanently frozen ground)

Tundra
bitterly cold temperatures, high winds

The Build-a-Biome Game

Concept: Characteristics of biomes

Put on your hard hat—it's time to build a biome with this fun-to-play group game! Make a copy of the cards on page 51 for each group of four players. Glue each copy to a piece of tagboard. Then have the players cut out the cards and shuffle them. The object of the game is to be the first to collect all five cards for the same biome. Have students play according to these rules:

1. The dealer deals five cards to each player and places the remaining ten cards facedown in a stack.
2. The dealer draws the stack's top card and decides whether to keep it. If he doesn't want the card, he places it faceup next to the stack. If he wants the card, he takes it and discards a different card from his hand, placing it faceup next to the stack.
3. The next player to the right chooses the faceup card or draws a card from the pile and discards one from his hand.
4. Continue playing in this manner until one player has five matching cards.

To extend the activity, have students research characteristics of other biomes and make new cards to add to the game.

Round	Grasshoppers	Popcorn Pieces Collected by Grasshoppers	Birds	Grasshoppers Eaten by Birds	Popcorn Pieces Collected by Birds	Birds Eaten by Hawk	Popcorn Pieces Collected by Hawk
1							
2							
3							
4							

50

Note to the teacher: Use with "I Will Survive!" on page 48.

Game Cards

Use with "The Build-a-Biome Game" on page 49.

Tundra treeless	**Tundra** snowy owl, Arctic fox, caribou	**Tundra** lichens, reindeer moss, grasses	**Tundra** permafrost (permanently frozen ground)	**Tundra** bitterly cold temperatures, high winds
Temperate Deciduous Forest trees lose leaves in fall	**Temperate Deciduous Forest** deciduous trees: oak, hickory, maple, beech	**Temperate Deciduous Forest** deer, squirrels, foxes, birds, skunks	**Temperate Deciduous Forest** deep, rich soil	**Temperate Deciduous Forest** four seasons: spring, summer, fall, winter
Tropical Rain Forest warm and moist all year with average rainfall of about 200 cm	**Tropical Rain Forest** tree snakes, tree frogs, spider monkeys	**Tropical Rain Forest** located near the equator	**Tropical Rain Forest** dense canopy of vegetation, little light reaches the ground	**Tropical Rain Forest** orchids, bromeliads, large woody vines
Coral Reef found in warm, tropical waters	**Coral Reef** aquatic biome made of coral	**Coral Reef** sponges and algae grow on coral	**Coral Reef** very old, grows slowly	**Coral Reef** sea urchins, fishes, octopuses, snails, plankton
Savanna tropical or subtropical grassland	**Savanna** poor soil, few trees	**Savanna** termites, ants	**Savanna** animals in African savanna: elephants, zebras, giraffes, lions, rhinos, hyenas	**Savanna** three seasons: cool and dry, hot and dry, warm and wet
Desert *Most average less than 10 inches of rainfall per year*	***Desert*** *cacti, creosote bushes, mesquite plants*	***Desert*** *sidewinders, kangaroo rats, Gila monsters*	***Desert*** *extremes of high heat during the day and cooler temperatures at night in warm climates*	***Desert*** *dry air*

It's a Balancing Act!

Mother Nature knows all too well what a difficult job it is to keep the populations and communities in her ecosystems balanced. If even one little part of it gets out of whack, it can eventually affect the entire ecosystem.

Directions: Read each descriptor. Then decide whether nature is in balance or out of balance. Shade the correct seesaw seat to show your answer. If your answer is "OUT," write on the back of this page what you think must happen for there to be balance.

1. A coyote is stalking a jackrabbit that is munching on prairie plants. Suddenly they both stop, sniff the smoke in the air, and see the approaching wildfire.

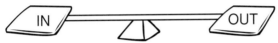

2. A herd of zebras is grazing on the savanna. The herd is being carefully watched by some lions.

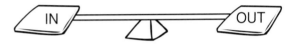

3. A chemical company is illegally dumping waste into a stream. The stream flows through a woodland and joins a river. Dead fish are being found along the river's banks.

4. Some mice are feeding on a swarm of grasshoppers eating alfalfa in a field. There aren't many mice because hunters in the area have stopped killing foxes.

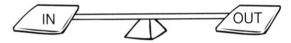

5. More and more souvenir hunters are gathering coral skeletons from reefs. Also, the number of crown-of-thorns starfish—animals that prey upon the coral that makes up the reefs—is increasing.

6. A marshland is being drained so that a new highway can be built. Plants are dying and the wildlife is scattering.

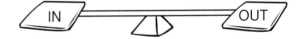

7. Many more squirrels than usual were born, survived, and reproduced last year. Since the foxes had lots of squirrels to eat, they stayed healthy and now their population is even larger.

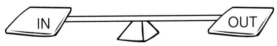

8. There has been a lot of rain on the prairie. Deer are grazing on a huge supply of grass. Farmers have been killing coyotes so that very few remain to feed on the deer.

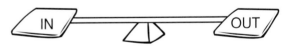

9. A school of fish that had been feeding on shrimp in the ocean has been attacked by seals. Now some of the seals are being eyed by a shark.

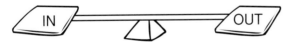

10. A disease has attacked the desert's mesquite trees. The disease has caused the population of kangaroo rats, who feed on the trees, to decrease. Now there are fewer Gila monsters.

Bonus Box: Based on the situations above, which do you think affects an ecosystem more: a natural event or a man-made event? Explain your answer on the back of this page.

©The Mailbox® • *Science* • TEC60859 • Key p.158

Earth Science

This Changing Earth

Hands-On Activities About Weathering and Erosion

Imagine Mother Earth getting face-lifts. She does, you know! How? From earth-changing processes such as weathering and erosion. Use the following hands-on activities to find out what causes the gradual and sometimes dramatic changes in Mother Earth's appearance!

by Dr. Barbara B. Leonard, Winston-Salem, NC

Earth-Changing Processes

Weathering occurs when rocks are broken up by ice, water, growing vegetation, chemicals, and temperature changes. *Erosion* is the removal and transportation of weathered material by agents such as water, glaciers, and wind.

Go With the Flow!

Topic: Movement of glaciers

One of the main agents of erosion are glaciers. Gravity pulls a mountain glacier downhill, bringing along rock and soil materials. Have students find out how a glacier moves with a simple simulation.

Materials for each group: paper cup, ⅓ c. cornstarch, ¼ c. water, measuring spoons, spoon, aluminum pie pan, plastic straw cut into three 1" pieces, cupcake liner, pencil

Steps:
1. Spoon the cornstarch into the cup. Then gradually add all but one teaspoon of the water. Stir until the mixture is smooth.
2. Place the cupcake liner in the pan as shown.
3. Pour the cornstarch mixture into the liner. Place the straw pieces on top of the mixture in three parallel lines as shown.
4. Prop up one end of the pan with a pencil. Quickly pull down the lower end of the liner to let the mixture flow. Observe how the straws move.

(The mixture represents a glacier that is flowing downhill. The liner represents valley walls. The middle straw moves faster than the outer ones, showing that the center of a glacier moves faster than the edges.)

Glacier Tracks

Topics: Ice erosion and deposition

What kinds of tracks and materials do glaciers leave behind as they flow downhill? Use the following demonstration to help students find out.

Materials: 5 oz. paper cup, water, dirt, 4 or 5 pieces of gravel, 12" square of heavy-duty aluminum foil, 2 pieces of sandpaper (1 coarse and 1 fine, each smaller than the foil), access to a freezer

Steps:
1. Place the dirt and the gravel in the cup. Add just enough water to cover the contents.
2. Cover the cup tightly with foil. Then place the cup upside down in the freezer overnight.
3. Take the cup from the freezer. Remove the foil and flatten it. Then place both pieces of sandpaper on the foil.
4. Peel away the cup's rim so that half of the frozen mixture is visible. Hold the bottom of the cup and rub the frozen mixture's flattened surface across the sandpaper until scratch marks can be seen. Explain that glaciers make similar marks as they move.
5. Turn the cup upside down on the sandpaper and foil. Then place the foil in the sun. After 15 minutes (30 minutes if the temperature is less than 60°F), lift the cup so students can observe the resulting puddle of water and loose dirt. Explain that when glaciers melt, similar rock deposits (called *till*) result.
6. Take the cup outside and rub it across the ground so students can observe the marks made on both the ground and the ice's surface.

Blowin' in the Wind!

Topic: Wind erosion

Show students how wind can carry sand from one location and deposit it in another with this group experiment. For a related activity, see the ready-to-use reproducible on page 57.

Materials for each group: egg carton, scissors, 5" x 7" piece of black construction paper, tbsp. each of salt and rock salt, tbsp. each of fine and coarse sand, small bowl, flexible drinking straw, safety goggles, newspaper

Steps:

1. Cover a workspace with newspaper.
2. Cut the egg carton apart at the fold. Place the two parts end to end as shown. Then place the construction paper on the carton top so that it slightly overlaps the adjacent edge of the carton bottom.
3. Mix the salt and rock salt in the bowl. Then pile the mixture on the black paper near the carton bottom as shown.
4. Bend the straw and place its short end next to the mixture's midpoint. Predict where the salt particles will land when you blow on them through the straw.
5. Put on the safety goggles. Then blow into the long end of the straw. Observe what happens. *(The heavier particles of the rock salt land in carton sections that are closer to the pile. The regular salt's lighter-weight particles land in sections that are farther from the pile.)*
6. Repeat Steps 3–5 with a mixture of fine and coarse sand. *(The coarser sand particles land in the closer sections. The finer particles land in the sections that are farther away.)*

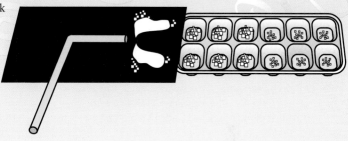

As the River Flows

Topic: Water erosion and deposition

What happens when water flows over land? Head outdoors and find out with this cool demonstration!

Materials: plastic splash block (available at home improvement stores), mixture of sand and dirt (enough to fill splash block), brick, small funnel, ½ gal. water, spoon

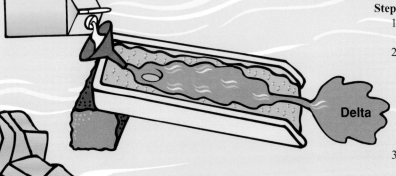

Delta

Steps:

1. Fill the splash block with the sand and dirt. Then place the brick under the enclosed end of the splash block to prop it up.
2. Hold the funnel at the raised end of the splash block as shown. Pour water into the funnel in a continuous stream. Have students note the path the water makes and what happens to the soil in its path. *(Gravity makes the water flow downhill. As the water flows over the soil, it carries soil particles and deposits them in a fan shape, creating a delta.)*
3. Repeat Step 2, this time placing the funnel at a different point on the splash block. See if the water takes a different path.
4. Smooth the soil in the splash block. Then make an S-shaped path in the soil with the spoon. Have students predict what will happen to the soil when water flows along this new path. Then pour water into the funnel and observe. *(The water should follow the path and remove soil from the outer part of each curve where the flow is fastest and deposit material on the inner part of the curve where the flow is slowest.)*

Excellent Books About Earth's Changes

Children of the Dust Bowl: The True Story of the School at Weedpatch Camp by Jerry Stanley
The Dust Bowl by David Booth
Earthsteps: A Rock's Journey Through Time by Diane Nelson Spickert
Out of the Dust by Karen Hesse
Shaping the Earth by Dorothy Hinshaw Patent

Wave Bye-Bye!

Topic: Water erosion

Raid the nearest Monopoly game to demonstrate how moving water can erode the land's surface along coastlines and the banks of streams and rivers.

Materials: rectangular aluminum roasting pan at least 3" deep; shoebox filled with mixture of sand, soil, and gravel; water; 3 plastic buildings from a Monopoly game (2 houses, 1 hotel); ruler

Steps:

1. Build a three-inch-wide bank of the sand-soil-gravel mixture along one long side of the pan as shown.
2. Place the buildings along the bank, putting the hotel closer to the edge than the houses.
3. Slowly fill the empty part of the pan with water to a depth of one-fourth inch.
4. Carefully slide the pan back and forth six times, making waves that wash against the bank. Have students observe what happens. *(The wave motion causes some soil to wash away with the water. Most of the sediment collects near the bank's edge.)*
5. Slide the pan back and forth six more times. Discuss any changes. *(The water's movement causes more erosion, washing soil away from the bottom of the bank first and making the water very muddy. Depending on the waves' angle of impact, the coastline may develop an irregular shape.)*
6. Slide the pan back and forth 12 more times. Discuss any changes. *(The houses and hotel begin to slide down the bank. This effect, known as* mass wasting *or a* landslide, *is due to gravity's downward pull on soil. The coastline may look uneven.)*
7. Conclude by asking students whether this kind of erosion should be slowed down and, if so, how. *(Answers will vary. Students might suggest planting vegetation or using sandbags.)*

Before

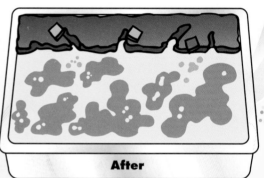

After

Before

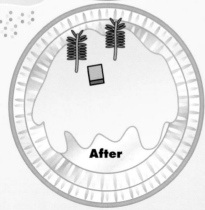

After

Where'd My Beach House Go?

Topic: Beach erosion

What are the hazards of having an oceanfront home? Challenge groups of students to find out by building and testing their own artificial beachfronts! For more information about beach erosion, including why the Cape Hatteras Lighthouse had to be moved, check out **whyfiles.org/091beach/** and its links *(current as of March 2006)*.

Materials for each group: aluminum pie pan, cup of wet sand, sprigs of pine needles, plastic house from a Monopoly game, water, ruler

Steps:

1. Pile the wet sand on one side of the pan.
2. Place the house on the sand. Push the pine needles deeply into the sand to represent trees.
3. Slowly fill the empty side of the pan with water to a depth of one-fourth inch.
4. Slowly move the pan back and forth six times to make waves that wash against the sand. Observe what happens. *(Some sand is washed back into the water.)*
5. Move the pan back and forth six more times. Observe what happens. *(The water eventually reaches the house and begins to erode the sand around it.)*
6. Continue moving the pan back and forth until the house moves. *(Sand eroding around a real beach house can take years. Bad storms can speed up the process. Trees remain in place because their roots anchor them, but they will eventually uproot if the underlying soil is not stable.)*

The Dust Bowl

In the 1930s, the southern Great Plains—Colorado, Kansas, Oklahoma, New Mexico, and Texas—suffered a seven-year drought. Because of poor farming practices and the loss of good soil, land which had once grown lots of crops became dry and dusty. Wind blew the dust for miles and darkened the sky for days. The area became known as the Dust Bowl. Because they could not grow crops, thousands of farm families fled the area.

Directions: Watch your teacher demonstrate how conditions such as those in the Dust Bowl can be simulated. Then answer the questions on the lines provided.

Creating a Dust Bowl

Materials: aluminum pie pan filled with a thin layer of damp dirt and potting soil, handheld electric hair dryer, newspaper

Steps:
1. Place the pan on the newspaper.
2. Hold the hair dryer at an angle about six inches away from the pan.
3. Turn the dryer on high. Blow hot air on the soil for about five minutes.
4. Turn off the dryer and observe.
5. Turn the dryer on high again, this time continuing until the soil is dry and loose (about ten to 15 minutes).

Questions:

1. Based on this demonstration, what conditions caused the Dust Bowl?

   _____

   _____

   _____

   _____

2. How might the first five minutes of the demonstration represent the first few years of the Dust Bowl? _____

   _____

3. What would your bedroom look like after several years of fine dust being blown around in the air? _____

   _____

4. If a drought developed where you live and lasted for ten years, what might the area look like? How would this lack of rain affect life in your town or city? _____

   _____

   _____

   _____

Bonus Box: Think of another natural disaster, such as a flood. How could that event change the land and lives of those living in your area?

Note to the teacher: Use with "Blowin' in the Wind!" on page 55. Demonstrate the Dust Bowl model for students. Then have each child answer the questions.

57

Shake, Rattle, 'n' Roll!

How are rocks broken down into smaller pieces of gravel, sand, and soil? Find out whether tumbling and crumbling have anything to do with it by conducting an experiment that really shakes, rattles, and rolls!

Materials for each group of four students: two 1" pieces of chalk, 2 sugar cubes, two 1" cinnamon sticks, 3 baby food jars with lids, clock with a second hand, 4 paper towels

Steps:

1. Study the chalk, sugar cubes, and cinnamon sticks. Then record your observations in the table at the right.
2. Place the chalk pieces in one jar. Place the cinnamon sticks in a second jar. Place the sugar cubes in a third jar. Tighten the lid on each jar.
3. Shake each jar for 30 seconds (three students can each shake a jar while the other student keeps the time).
4. Empty the jars' contents on separate paper towels. Record your observations in the table.
5. Place one piece of chalk, one cinnamon stick, and one sugar cube in a jar. Study the jar's contents and record your observations in the table. Then tighten the lid and shake the jar for 30 seconds.
6. Empty the jar's contents on the remaining paper towel. Record your observations in the table.

Material	Appearance Before Shaking	Appearance After Shaking
chalk		
sugar cubes		
cinnamon sticks		
all three items together		

Questions:

1. Which item lost the most material during the shaking? _____

_____

2. Which item represents softer rocks that weather more quickly? Explain. _____

_____

3. Which item represents harder rocks that weather more slowly? Explain. _____

_____

_____

Bonus Box: What would happen if soft rocks, such as gypsum, were shaken in a jar with harder rocks, such as calcite?

Note to the teacher: Divide the class into four groups to complete this experiment. After the experiment, explain that the friction created by items hitting each other in the shaken jars simulates the weathering of rocks by agents such as ice, water, growing vegetation, chemicals, and temperature changes.

Looks Like Stormy Weather!

Hands-on Activities for Studying Storms

Your students may not be able to chase a tornado or fly an airplane inside a hurricane. But they can learn to track clues that will help them predict that a storm's on the way! Complement your studies of weather with the following creative activities, teacher demonstrations, and reproducibles on severe storms.　by Gail Peckumn, Jefferson, IA

A Close-Up Look at How a Storm Develops

1 —Hot Air's on the Rise

How exactly does a hurricane develop? Three ingredients must be present.

- Warm water: During the summer and fall months, the sun continually warms tropical ocean waters.
- Moist air: Warm, moist air rises above the water and drifts up into the sky.
- Converging winds: Cooler air moves in to take the place of the rising warm air. As warm air continues to rise, the air pressure drops, making stronger winds.

Help students understand that warm air rises with the following demonstration:

1. Tape the bottom of one paper lunch bag to each end of a meterstick.
2. Balance the meterstick on your index finger. Hold it so that the opening of one bag is directly over a heat source (a lamp without its shade), but not touching it.
3. Ask students to observe what happens.

The air inside the bag will heat up, so the air expands and some of it escapes. This reduces the weight of the air inside the bag. The heavier, cooler air around the bag will exert a force on the lighter, warm air, causing the bag to rise. Remind students that they see warm, moist air rise when steam rises above boiling water. The same thing happens over warm ocean waters. The more heated water in the atmosphere, the more likely that a storm will occur.

2 —A Cold Front's Moving In

Cold air forces warm air upward, creating an area of low pressure. As warm, moist air rises, it can produce towering storm clouds. Show your students how this movement of cold air happens with the following demonstration. Remind students that since both air and water are considered fluids, water represents air in the demonstration.

1. Punch two holes in the bottom of a paper cup.
2. Secure the cup to the corner of a large, clear container (a plastic storage box or an empty aquarium) with duct tape. The bottom of the cup should be about two centimeters from the bottom of the container.
3. Fill another cup with ice-cold water and add a few drops of blue food coloring.
4. Fill the large container with hot water to about one centimeter from the top of the cup.
5. Quickly pour all of the cold, blue water into the cup. Have students view the bottom of the container to see what happens.
6. Have students touch the water in the paper cup that's inside the large container.

The cold, blue water will sink to the bottom of the container as it pushes up the hot water. The water in the cup will be warm because all of the cold water sank to the bottom of the container.

tape

cup with holes

plastic container

59

3 —Moisture's Building

Hot air can hold a lot of moisture. This moisture, in vapor form, rises in the atmosphere. Air temperatures become cooler with increased elevation, so all the moisture in the hot air starts to condense into clouds. The more moisture, the bigger the clouds. Demonstrate how hot air holds more moisture than cold air with the following activity:

1. Fill two glasses—one with hot water and the other with cold water and ice.
2. Let them sit for several minutes as students observe what happens.

Moisture will form on the outside of the cold water glass. Why? Because the cold water has cooled the air around the glass, and since cooler air cannot hold as much moisture as warmer air, the moisture in the air begins to condense into droplets on the glass.

Extend this demonstration by showing how clouds form.

1. Fill a small cake pan with ice.
2. Fill a large, widemouthed glass jar about ¼ full of hot water.
3. Light a match and hold it down inside the jar for a few seconds; then drop it in. (This forms dust particles around which water vapor can condense.)
4. Place the pan of ice over the top of the jar.
5. Have students observe what happens.

Warm air will rise off the water in the jar, then cool and condense when it hits the pan of ice. The result will be the formation of a cloud near the top of the jar. Whenever there is a large amount of heated, moist air, it can cool and condense into huge cumulonimbus storm clouds, producing thunder, lightning, and rain.

> A tornado in Broken Bow, Oklahoma, carried a motel sign 30 miles and dropped it in Arkansas!

> In early times, people thought that lightning and thunder were signs of the gods' anger.

4 —Pressure's Dropping

When stormy weather hits, high winds follow! Differences in air pressure cause winds. Demonstrate this concept with the following activity:

1. Blow a little bit of air into a balloon and hold the end so the air stays inside.
2. Ask your students where the air has greater pressure—inside or outside the balloon. (Inside.) Ask what will happen if you loosen your grip on the opening of the balloon. (The air will come sputtering out.)
3. Have a volunteer hold his hand in front of the balloon opening as you let the air out. Ask the class why the air left the balloon instead of staying inside it. (Air moves from an area of high pressure to an area of low pressure.)
4. Next fully inflate the balloon and hold its end. Ask students if the balloon has more air pressure inside than when you first blew it up. (Yes.)
5. Let out the air, as the same volunteer feels it escape. Ask the volunteer which time there was a stronger flow of air. (The second time.)

Share with your students that this is what makes the wind in a storm blow—but on a much larger scale! Like the air that rushed out of the fully inflated balloon, surface air is always on the move between high- and low-pressure areas, trying to even them out. The bigger the difference in pressure between the two areas, the harder the wind will blow.

Low Pressure

High Pressure

5 —Lightning's Flashing

What exactly is lightning? Demonstrate for your students how lightning is formed on a smaller—and safer—scale.

1. Blow up two large balloons and tie off the end of each one.
2. Tie a one-meter length of thread to each balloon.
3. Suspend the balloons from the top of a door frame so that they are about ten inches apart.
4. Label two sticky notes—one A and the other B—and attach a note to each balloon.
5. Have a student rub balloon A against her hair about a dozen times, then gently release the balloon.

The balloons will move toward each other and stay together. Why? Electrons are rubbed off the hair and collected on balloon A, giving it a negative electrical charge. Since like charges *repel* (push away) each other, the negative charges on balloon A repel the negatively charged electrons of balloon B. This causes the surface of balloon B to become more positively charged. Since the balloons now have opposite charges, they are attracted to each other.

Explain to your students that most scientists think this is what happens in a thundercloud. Light, rising water droplets and tiny pieces of ice collide with hail and other heavier, falling particles, creating electric charges. The heavier particles gain a negative charge; the lighter ones, a positive charge. The negatively charged particles fall to the bottom of the cloud and most of the positively charged particles rise to the top. Lightning occurs when these separated charges flow toward each other (or toward opposite charges on Earth), creating an electric spark.

Hurricane comes from a Carib Indian word for "big wind."

When a snowstorm's winds reach 39 mph, it's called a *blizzard*.

6 —Thunder's Rumbling

Is that thunder rumbling in the distance? The bright light that we see in a flash of lightning is called a *return stroke*. Return strokes heat the air in their paths, causing it to expand very quickly. It then cools and contracts. This rapid expansion and contraction causes air molecules to move, which produces the sound waves that we hear as thunder. To help students "experience" thunder, provide each small group with a 1" x 8" plastic strip (cut from a transparency), a small lump of modeling clay, a large paper clip, a ruler, and a piece of wool (any item made of 100% wool). Then direct each group to follow these steps:

1. Use the clay to stand the paper clip upright.
2. Wrap the wool around the plastic strip.
3. Quickly pull the strip through the cloth at least three times.
4. Immediately hold the plastic near the top of the paper clip. What happens? Each group should hear a snapping sound. Why?

Electrons are rubbed off the wool and onto the plastic. The electrons cluster together until their energy is great enough to move them across the air between the plastic and the metal clip. The movement of the electrons through air produces sound waves, resulting in a snapping sound.

Other Stormy Weather Activities

How Do Meteorologists Know a Storm Is Coming?

With modern technology, meteorologists can now gather more information than ever before, using such weather instruments as *barometers, thermometers, anemometers, radar, weather balloons, computers,* and *satellites.* Help students better understand two of these methods with the following activities:

Infrared Radiation

1. Have students place sheets of different-colored paper in a sunny area outside. Place a thermometer in the middle of each sheet.
2. After 15 minutes, have students record the temperature reading for each color of paper.
3. Return to the classroom and discuss why the temperatures were different. *(Each color of paper absorbs and gives off different amounts of heat.)*

Explain to students that this is an example of infrared radiation. Just as some objects give off more heat than others, so do different areas of the earth and atmosphere. Weather satellites measure the heat given off by the earth and the atmosphere. These infrared images provide clues that help in weather and storm prediction.

Doppler Radar

1. Take your students outdoors.
2. Give one student a bell and direct him to go to a point about 50 yards away from the rest of the class.
3. Instruct that student to run toward the class while continuously ringing the bell, then continue running about 50 yards past you while still ringing the bell.
4. Ask your students what they noticed about the sound of the bell.

Students should notice that the sound began soft and low in pitch, but increased in loudness and became higher in pitch as the runner got closer to the class. Then it became softer and lower in pitch again as the runner ran past the class. Doppler radar works in the same way. It detects whether particles in the atmosphere are moving toward or away from a radar signal that has been sent out from an antenna on the ground. This radar is used to detect precipitation and wind circulation within clouds, so it's especially helpful in predicting tornado formation.

Looking for great resources on storms? Check out:
Storms by Seymour Simon
Tornado by Stephen Kramer
Lightning by Seymour Simon
Hurricanes by Seymour Simon
The Magic School Bus Inside A Hurricane by Joanna Cole

Now That's Incredible!

Did you know that in one day, a hurricane can release enough energy to power the United States for six months? Below are some more amazing facts about storms. Read each fact; then simplify the boldfaced math terms by

- adding, subtracting, multiplying, or dividing
- changing a word form to a numeral form
- reducing a fraction

Write your answers in the blanks. The first one has been done for you.

1. There are about **40,000 + 5,000** thunderstorms in the world each day.   _45,000_

2. The temperature of the surface of the sun is about 10,800 degrees Fahrenheit. The air around a flash of lightning rises to about **5 x 10,800** degrees, or five times hotter than the sun!   _____

3. Lightning strikes the earth about **ten million** times a day.   _____

4. Lightning travels at a speed of up to **sixty thousand** miles per second.   _____

5. Ocean temperatures have to reach **536 – 457** degrees for a hurricane to form.   _____

6. In order to be classified as a hurricane, wind speeds have to be **37 x 2** miles per hour or more.   _____

7. Winds in a tornado can reach up to **30 x 10** miles per hour.   _____

8. Water droplets in clouds are so small that **100 x 100** could fit on the head of a pin.   _____

9. In 1967 Hurricane Beulah caused **7,100 – 6,959** tornadoes in Texas.   _____

10. In 1969 Hurricane Camille dumped **243 ÷ 9** inches of rain in eight hours in parts of Virginia.   _____

11. On March 18, 1925, tornadoes ripped through Missouri, Illinois, and Indiana, killing **394 + 295** people.   _____

12. In 1989 destruction from Hurricane Hugo totaled about **seven billion** dollars.   _____

Bonus Box: Look up *storms* in an almanac or in *Guinness Book of World Records*. Make up a math problem that includes a storm fact. Give your problem to a friend to solve.

Relief for the Disaster Relief Agency

Tornado Safety

①

Hurricane Safety

You have just been hired to take I. C. Hale's place at the Disaster Relief Agency. (He quit to become a storm chaser!) Mr. Hale had great ideas for information to be printed on some new safety brochures, but his desk looks like *it* was hit by a tornado!

Try to figure out which tips should be included on each brochure. Write the number of the tip on its matching brochure. The first one has been done for you. Hint: Some tips will be used on more than one brochure.

You'd better get a move on…storm season is fast approaching!

① Get out of an automobile.

② Stay away from windows.

③ If a *warning* is issued, this means that it looks like the storm will strike within 24 hours or less.

④ Go to a basement.

⑤ If you don't have a basement, go to an inside room or hallway on the lowest floor.

⑥ If you live on an island or near the coast or a river, you're likely to be evacuated.

⑦ If you're outside, lie flat in a nearby ditch.

⑧ Find shelter when a *warning* is issued for your area.

⑨ Get out of boats and away from water.

⑩ If caught in the storm, stay in your vehicle until rescue workers arrive.

⑪ Stay away from downed power lines.

Blizzard Safety

⑫ Listen to a local radio or TV station.

⑬ Do not take a bath or shower.

⑭ If you're outdoors, find a low spot away from trees, fences, or poles.

⑮ Always try to preserve body heat, and keep warm and dry.

⑯ Never try to outdrive the storm.

⑰ Don't talk on the telephone, except in an emergency.

⑱ If you live in a mobile home, seek other shelter.

⑲ Put lawn furniture and bikes in a safe place.

⑳ Do not try to drive through flooded streets.

Thunderstorm Safety

Bonus Brochure

Choose a brochure. On the back of this sheet, design and color its front panel.

RED

©The Mailbox® • *Science* • TEC60859 • Key p. 159

Stormy Effects

Storms are known for their terrible effects—on both people and property. See if you can complete the following cause-and-effect statements about storms. Read each cause; then choose a matching effect from the box and write it on the blank. Use encyclopedias, almanacs, your science textbook, and other resources to help you. The first one has been done for you.

Causes

1. Since the new hurricane was the fourth of the season, _____ *it was named David.*

2. The cloud was tall, dark, and anvil-shaped, _____

3. Because we had a blizzard warning, _____

4. Since the storm was called a *typhoon,* _____

5. Storm surges were predicted when the hurricane hit the coast, _____

6. Because thunderstorms pump lots of hot air from the earth's surface high into the air, _____

7. Since we have no basement, _____

8. Because Hugo was such a terrible hurricane, _____

9. Whenever I hear thunder, _____

10. We spotted a tornado while driving in a car, _____

11. Since the tornado was classified as an F-5, _____

12. There were 15 seconds between when I saw lightning and then heard thunder, _____

Effects

- we made sure we had blankets and food in the car before driving to town.
- they are called earth's "air-conditioning system."
- I know there has been lightning.
- so I knew the storm was three miles away.
- it was named *David.*
- so we evacuated the island.
- that name will never be used again.
- we knew houses and cars had been blown away.
- so we knew it was a cumulonimbus cloud.
- my family gathers in the bathroom in the center of our house during a tornado warning.
- so we stopped and took cover in a deep ditch.
- I knew that it wasn't located in the United States.

Bonus Box: When was the last time you were in a storm? On the back of this sheet, write three cause-and-effect statements about your experiences.

Water, Water, Everywhere!

Whether it trickles, freezes, or evaporates, water moves and constantly changes form. Invite students to splash around in the following activities, games, and investigations to learn more about this wonderfully unique substance!

by Daniel Kriesberg, Bayville, NY

Gotta Have Water!
Concept: Importance of water

Begin your study with a relay race that helps students realize the importance of water. Label two containers—one "Yes," one "No"—for each team of students. Also, make and cut apart one copy of the cards on page 69 for each team. Arrange each team's cards on a desk next to a masking-tape starting line; then place the team's containers an equal distance away from the starting line. Finally, position each team behind its line.

On your signal, Player 1 on each team takes a card, runs with it to his team's containers, and drops it in the container that indicates whether the item needs water. Then he runs back, tags Player 2, and goes to the back of his line. Continue play until each team has played all of its cards. Announce that the team that finished first and has the most correct answers wins. Then explain that *every* card should have been dropped into a "Yes" container. Pull a card from a "No" container and discuss how it can be linked to water. (For example, the people and factories that make a stapler need water.) Continue discussing the "No" cards. Then declare the team with the most cards in its "Yes" container the winner.

Dirty Water
Concept: Water pollution

Is water pollution a problem that can be improved over time? Pose this question to students; then treat them to the following simulation. Place a large, clear plastic cup that's three-fourths full of water on a table. Begin reading aloud *A River Ran Wild: An Environmental History* by Lynne Cherry. As you read, represent the changes that transformed a clean Nashua River into a polluted one by adding the following items to the cup:

- Add several fire-scorched twigs after reading about how the Indians set fires to clear brush from the forest floor.
- Add a handful of soil after reading about how the settlers cleared the forest.
- Add a handful of sawdust and several drops of red food coloring after reading about how paper mills dumped leftover pulp and dye into the river.

After reading about laws that were passed to stop the pollution, filter the "contaminated" water into an empty cup by pouring it through a funnel that's lined with two coffee filters. Have students compare the filtered water (the river after cleanup efforts) to a clear cup of water (the river before pollution). Help them note that the water's cleanliness improved but that some "pollutants" were difficult to remove.

H₂O's Unique Qualities
Concept: Properties of water

All you need to demonstrate water's many properties is a glass of lemonade and the simple investigations on this page! After the experiments, let students sip lemonade as you share *A Drop Around the World* by Barbara Shaw McKinney.

Materials for the class: large container of pink-lemonade-flavored powdered drink mix, tablespoon, water, 2 clear plastic cups, ruler
For each group of four students: 4 paper clips, 1 small plastic cup of water
For each student: clear plastic cup of water, plastic spoon, paper towel, ice cube

It dissolved!

• **Water can dissolve more substances than any other liquid.** Have each student stir one tablespoon of drink mix into his cup of water and observe how it dissolves. Explain that water can dissolve more substances than any other liquid. It can even dissolve oxygen, a gas. The small amount of oxygen dissolved in water is what aquatic plants and animals breathe.

• **Water in its solid form is less dense than its liquid form.** Have each child put an ice cube in her lemonade and watch it float. Explain that if ice were heavier than water and did not float, lakes, rivers, and oceans would freeze from the bottom up and kill most aquatic life-forms.

Frozen

Evaporated

• **Water is the only substance existing naturally in three states.** Fill two cups with one tablespoon of lemonade each. Measure and record the height of the liquid in each cup. Place one cup in a sunny place and the other in a freezer. Have students measure and record the heights of the lemonade daily for several days. Students will observe that the freezer's lemonade freezes and increases in height while the lemonade in the sun evaporates and leaves behind lemonade crystals. Explain that if water did not exist in all three states (solid, liquid, gas), there could be no water cycle.

• **Water is sticky and has capillary action.** Direct students to spill a little lemonade on their desktops; then have them soak it up with paper towels and observe how the liquid *adheres* to, or sticks to, the paper. Explain that water is easy to clean up because it can stick to other substances. Also explain that water can climb up a surface against gravity's pull. This property helps a column of water rise from a tree's roots hundreds of feet in the air to its stems.

• **Water has surface tension.** Have one student at a time in each group carefully float a paper clip in a cup of water. Explain that the water's top layer is *cohesive* (or sticky), making it strong enough to support objects heavier than itself.

Water Cycle Circles
Concept: The water cycle

Show students that if they can toss a ball, they can understand the water cycle! Gather a tennis ball for each group of five students. Also number and label five index cards for each group as follows: 1—Sun, 2—Evaporation, 3—Clouds, 4—Precipitation, and 5—Land, Groundwater, or Body of Water. (If you have more than 25 students, make an additional set of cards.)

Next, draw a simple diagram of the water cycle on the board such as the one shown. Review the diagram. Then give each child one labeled card. Have students circulate around the room and form teams comprising a complete set of numbered cards. Direct each team to put down their cards and form a circle (with students standing in numerical order according to their cards); then give a tennis ball to each child who held a Sun card. Explain that the ball represents a water molecule. At your signal, team members pass the ball around the circle as quickly as possible. As a student passes a ball, she announces her role in the water cycle. Periodically call out "Stop" and a number from one to five. Have the student who held that card explain her step in the water cycle to her teammates. Conclude by asking, "How long has your team's water molecule been circulating?" Then point out to students that the same amount of water circulating in the water cycle today has been doing so since the world was formed. Amazing!

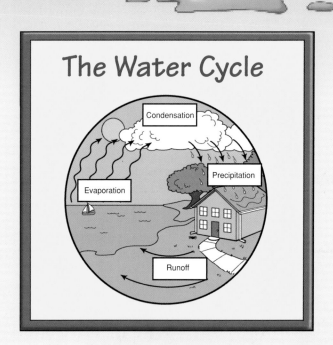

The Water Cycle

Condensation

Evaporation

Precipitation

Runoff

That's all there is?

Itty-Bitty Bits of Freshwater
Concept: Water conservation

Use this simple demonstration to convince students of the need to conserve freshwater. Display a clear glass filled with water. Announce that the water in the glass represents all the water in the world. Pour out 97 percent of the water, explaining that it represents the salt water in the world's oceans. Announce that the remaining 3 percent represents the world's freshwater. Pour out 2 percent more, explaining that this water is unavailable because it is frozen in ice caps and other glaciers. Tell students that half of the remaining 1 percent is groundwater (found beneath the earth's surface). Only about one-fiftieth of 1 percent of the earth's water fills rivers and lakes.

Have students consider how precious this small amount of water is and how pollution can affect it. Then write these questions on the board: How can freshwater be protected from pollution? How might the water in ice caps be used without upsetting the ecological balance? How might salt be removed from ocean water? Challenge each student to research one of the questions and write a plan suggesting a solution to the drinking-water dilemma. Set aside time for students to present their plans to the class.

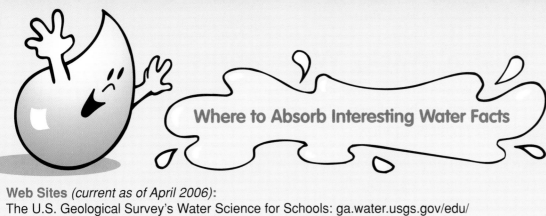

Where to Absorb Interesting Water Facts

Web Sites *(current as of April 2006)*:
The U.S. Geological Survey's Water Science for Schools: ga.water.usgs.gov/edu/
The Environmental Protection Agency's Office of Water: epa.gov/ow

Books:
Drip! Drop! How Water Gets to Your Tap by Barbara Seuling
A Drop of Water: A Book of Science and Wonder by Walter Wick
Water Dance by Thomas Locker

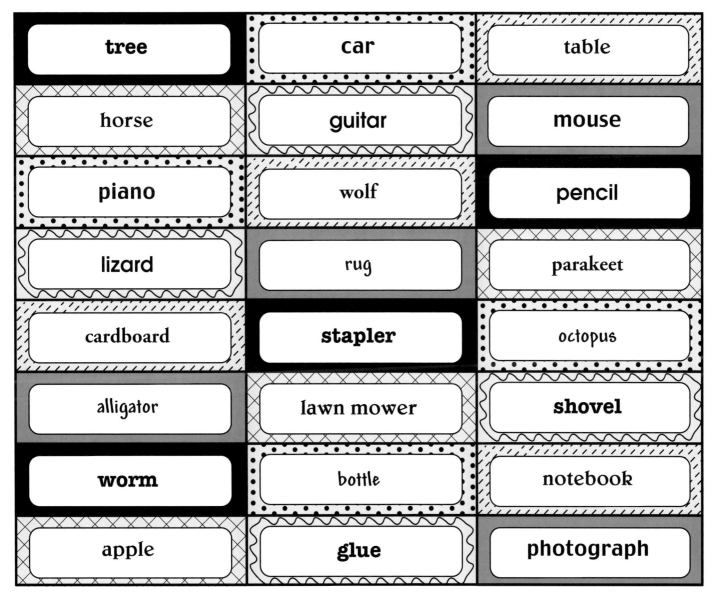

tree	car	table
horse	guitar	**mouse**
piano	wolf	pencil
lizard	rug	parakeet
cardboard	**stapler**	octopus
alligator	lawn mower	**shovel**
worm	bottle	notebook
apple	**glue**	photograph

Name _____

Wild 'n' Wacky Waterworks

Walter and Wilma work at the Workman Waterworks Company. They connect pairs of pipes along water lines. Help them do their job by following the directions below. If you match the pipes correctly, you'll learn some amazing facts about water!

Directions: Match the words written on one pipe with those written on another to form a complete sentence. There are ten different sentences altogether. Write them on the back of this page or on another sheet of paper.

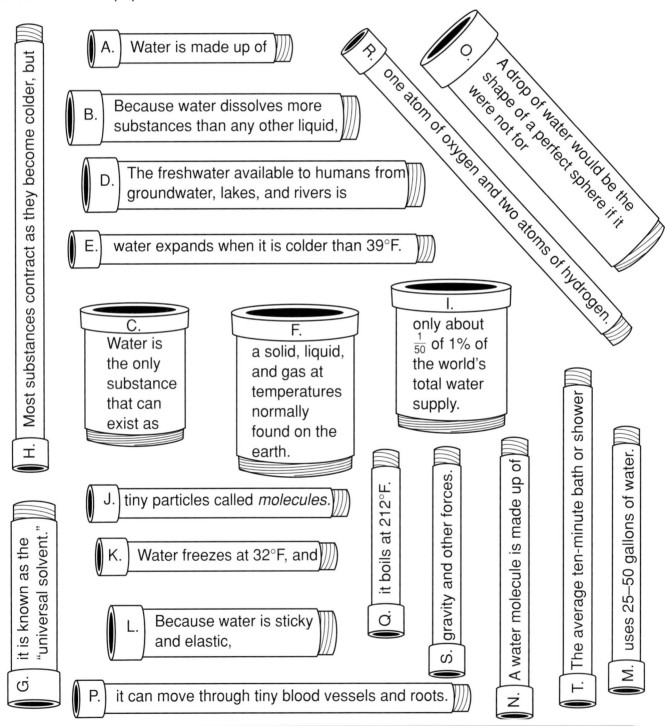

A. Water is made up of

B. Because water dissolves more substances than any other liquid,

D. The freshwater available to humans from groundwater, lakes, and rivers is

E. water expands when it is colder than 39°F.

H. Most substances contract as they become colder, but

R. one atom of oxygen and two atoms of hydrogen.

O. A drop of water would be the shape of a perfect sphere if it were not for

C. Water is the only substance that can exist as

F. a solid, liquid, and gas at temperatures normally found on the earth.

I. only about $\frac{1}{50}$ of 1% of the world's total water supply.

G. it is known as the "universal solvent."

J. tiny particles called *molecules*.

K. Water freezes at 32°F, and

L. Because water is sticky and elastic,

P. it can move through tiny blood vessels and roots.

Q. it boils at 212°F.

S. gravity and other forces.

N. A water molecule is made up of

T. The average ten-minute bath or shower

M. uses 25–50 gallons of water.

BONUS BOX: A tomato is about 95 percent water, an elephant about 70 percent, a human about 65 percent, and a potato about 80 percent. List these percentages on the back of this paper in greatest to least order.

Whole Lot of Quakin' Goin' On!

A Hands-on Project for Studying Earthquakes

Rock and roll—you may not mind hearing it on the radio, but it's definitely not something you want the ground under you to do! Yet that's exactly what happens during a powerful earthquake. Examine this fascinating force of nature with a hands-on project that challenges students to build earthquake-safe skyscrapers.

ideas by Diane Coffman, Deland, FL

What Is This Project?

For a science project that builds listening, thinking, reading, and cooperative skills, this easy-to-do activity is a real shaker and mover! After studying about earthquakes and their causes, teams of students work together to build quake-safe skyscrapers using a few inexpensive materials. Then they test their skyscrapers during a simulated earthquake. It's a project that results in sky-high learning and student interest!

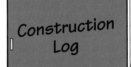

Preparing Materials

1. Make a class supply of the reproducibles on pages 74–76.
2. Divide the class into teams of five to six students. Label a separate large manila envelope for each team. Place copies of page 74 (one per team member) in each envelope. Also include a Construction Log made by stapling five sheets of notebook paper inside a folded sheet of construction paper.
3. Out of students' sight, put each of the following sets of items in a separate brown paper grocery bag:
   - Bag 1: one roll of masking tape, 50 plastic straws, pair of scissors
   - Bag 2: one roll of masking tape, 50 chopsticks or bamboo skewers
   - Bag 3: one brick of modeling clay, 50 plastic straws, pair of scissors
   - Bag 4: one brick of modeling clay, 50 craft sticks
   - Bag 5: one brick of modeling clay, 50 chopsticks or bamboo skewers
4. Decide on a space in which to store each group's skyscraper-in-progress and materials so they won't be disturbed.
5. Gather these materials to have ready for Day 5's skyscraper testing:
   - table or desk that can be shaken to simulate an earthquake
   - stopwatch or watch with a second hand
   - masking tape or modeling clay for fastening each skyscraper to the table prior to testing (optional)

Preparing Students

1. Ask students to share what they know or have even experienced about earthquakes. Discuss why some buildings might remain standing in an earthquake while others topple.
2. Give each student a copy of page 75. As a class, in teams, or individually, have students read the page, underlining important facts as they read. Then discuss the page together.
3. Give each student a copy of "Piecing It Together" on page 76. Read and discuss the page as in Step 2.
4. Explain that each student will be part of a team that will try to construct an earthquake-safe skyscraper. Each skyscraper will be tested to see how it holds up during a mock earthquake.

Introducing the Project

1. Divide the class into predetermined teams. Distribute the team envelopes.
2. Give each student a copy of "Quite Quake-Safe!" on page 76. Read and discuss the sheet together as a class.
3. Have each student take a copy of page 74 from his team's envelope. Read page 74 as a class. Then have each group decide on job roles.
4. Go over these guidelines for the project:
   - You may not trade building materials or bring more from home.
   - The skyscraper must be at least 20 inches tall. Remember: your goal isn't to build the tallest skyscraper but an earthquake-safe one.
   - The blueprint must be completed before starting to build.
   - Only the team in charge of a skyscraper may touch or move it.
   - At the end of each day, the Log Keeper (with the help of teammates) must fill in the Construction Log telling what the team accomplished that day.
5. Ask each Materials Manager to choose a bag of construction materials (without looking inside the bags). Label each bag with the team's name or number.

Constructing and Testing the Skyscrapers: A Five-Day Plan

Day 1:

- Have teams experiment with their materials and share ideas based on what they discover and on the information from "Quite Quake-Safe!" (page 76).
- When a group gets an idea, have its Architect begin drawing a blueprint. The blueprint should illustrate a side view of the building, showing it "open" so that beams and/or joints are visible. Remind each group to keep a careful count of how many beams and joints its building will have.
- Have the Materials Manager make sure that the team has enough materials for its building based on the blueprint.
- Direct the Log Keeper to write the Construction Log entry for the day. *(Continued on page 73.)*

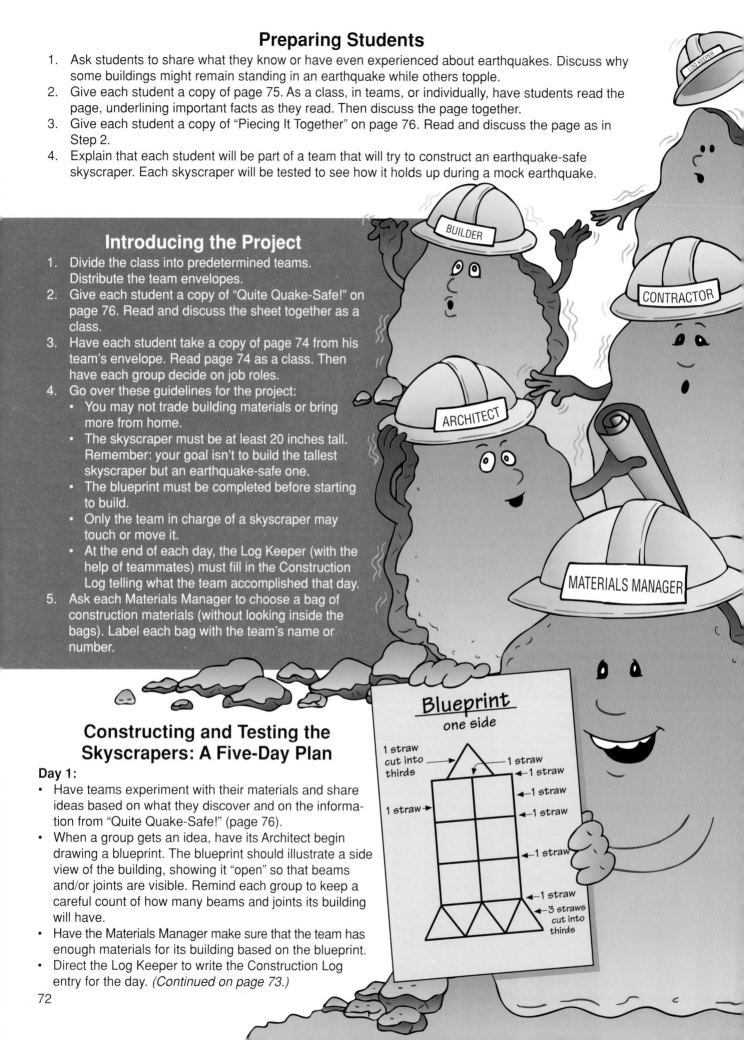

Blueprint
one side

1 straw cut into thirds
1 straw
1 straw
1 straw
1 straw
1 straw
1 straw
3 straws cut into thirds

Day 2:

- Have each team complete and turn in its blueprint. While the team waits for the blueprint to be approved by you, have team members choose a name for their construction company and make a sign to label the skyscraper.
- Instruct each Materials Manager to estimate how much of her team's building materials will be used and write that figure in the Construction Log.
- If time permits, let teams begin building their skyscrapers.
- Remind each Log Keeper to fill in the Construction Log entry for the day.

Day 3:

- Provide time for teams to work on constructing their skyscrapers.
- Remind each Log Keeper to write the log entry for the day.

Day 4:

- Have each team finish its skyscraper and test it to see if any modifications are needed. (See Day 5 for guidelines on how to test the building.)
- Check each skyscraper to make sure it's at least 20 inches tall. If not, have the team modify the structure.
- Direct each Materials Manager to count her team's leftover materials and write that figure in the Construction Log.
- Remind Log Keepers to update their logs.

Day 5: Test Day

- Ask the class to gather around the table that will represent the earth. Go over these guidelines for testing:
  - Only the group whose skyscraper is being tested is allowed to move the table for the test.
  - The earthquake will last 20 seconds. The teacher will be the timekeeper.
- In turn, have each group practice starting and stopping on your command by simulating the earthquake *without* the skyscraper on the table. Direct students to move the table or desk horizontally rather than vertically. After the practice, have the team test its skyscraper.

After the Tests

After each skyscraper has been tested, meet together as a class to discuss the following questions:

- Which designs worked? Which didn't?
- What materials worked best?
- What could have been done differently to make each skyscraper successful?
- Which groups worked well together and why?

Finally ask each team to write final recommendations for its building materials and design ideas. Have the team place the recommendations, the Construction Log, and the blueprint in its manila envelope to turn in. Evaluate the projects on these criteria:

- Blueprint completed
- Blueprint closely resembles skyscraper
- Construction Log completed daily
- Final recommendations completed

Sky-High Construction Project

Shake, rattle, and roll! It's time to put on your hard hat and take part in the Sky-High Construction Project. As part of a special construction company, you will help design and build a model skyscraper. Then your company will test the skyscraper under earthquake conditions. Use this sheet to help plan and complete this rockin' and rollin' project.

Company Name: _____

Jobs: Write each team member's name beside his or her job.

_____ *Log Keeper:* With help from team members, keeps Construction Log telling what group accomplished each day.

_____ *Architect:* Draws blueprint using ideas provided by team members.

_____ *Materials Manager:* Receives supplies. Responsible for daily mainte-nance of supplies. Counts number of materials used in skyscraper construction. Counts all mate-rials at beginning and end of project.

_____ *Contractor:* Makes sure skyscraper is built according to blueprint.

_____ *Builder* (may be two people): Does most of actual building of skyscraper under direction of Contractor.

Work Checklist

Day 1:
___ Read this page of information.
___ Experiment with team's building materials.
___ Begin drawing blueprint.
___ Take inventory of supplies.
___ Begin Construction Log.

Day 2:
___ Finish blueprint and turn it in to teacher for approval.
___ Choose name for construction company and make a sign to label skyscraper.
___ Estimate how much of building materials will be used; write estimate in log.
___ Begin building.
___ Update log.

Day 3:
___ Build skyscraper.
___ Update log.

Day 4:
___ Finish skyscraper and test it.
___ Count leftover materials and write figure in log.
___ Update log.

Day 5:
___ Test skyscraper.
___ Write final recommendations.
___ Turn in blueprint, Construction Log, final recommendations.

Note to the teacher: Use with "Preparing Materials" on page 72 and "Introducing the Project" on page 72.

We're on Shaky Ground!

What happens when you feel the earth move under your feet? Read to find out!

The *crust* is the top layer of the earth. It is made of rocks that form the land and ocean floor. Picture a cracked hard-boiled egg. Pieces of eggshell cling to the egg. That is similar to how the earth's crust looks, with all the pieces fitting together like a puzzle. Each piece, or *plate,* is really a large slab of rock. Because these plates are moving very slowly in different directions, there are breaks, or *faults,* in the earth's crust. Most earthquakes happen at faults. A famous fault in the United States is the San Andreas fault in California. There have been several major earthquakes along this fault.

As the rocks on one side of a fault push and grind against the rocks on the other side, energy builds up. When the energy builds up too much, sometimes the rocks suddenly snap past each other. Then an earthquake happens. The place where this happens is called the *focus.* The energy from the earthquake quickly spreads out from the focus in all directions. For a big earthquake, the shocks may last for several minutes.

Scientists who study earthquakes are known as *seismologists.* They measure the *magnitude,* or strength, of earthquakes with the Richter scale. Each earthquake is given a number that represents its strength at the focus. Seismologists get this number using a *seismograph.* It is an instrument that records and measures the time, size, and direction of an earthquake. Each Richter scale number means the earthquake is ten times stronger than the number before it. For example, an earthquake that measures 6 is ten times stronger than one that measures 5.

Scientists also use the Mercalli scale to measure earthquakes. It uses observations to rate an earthquake on a scale of 1 to 12. For example, an earthquake that is rated 2 is felt by only a few people. One that is rated 12 destroys whole towns.

Earthquakes can sometimes be predicted by foreshocks. A *foreshock* is a small earthquake that happens before a larger one in the same area. Sometimes animals behave strangely before an earthquake. They may try to leave an area or act scared. After an earthquake, a place can have *aftershocks.* These are small earthquakes that happen days or even weeks after a larger earthquake.

There are almost half a million earthquakes every year. In fact, one happens somewhere about every 30 seconds! But only about 1,000 of these quakes cause damage. The worst earthquake in the United States hit Alaska in 1964. It measured 9.2 on the Richter scale.

Note to the teacher: Use with "Preparing Materials" on page 71 and "Preparing Students" on page 72. For a reading comprehension activity, have each student number the paragraphs. On the back of this page or another sheet of paper, have the student write a title or main idea for each paragraph.

Piecing It Together

Scientists think that the earth's crust is made of about 10 big plates and about 20 smaller ones. The plates move slowly on a thick layer of hot rock in the *mantle*. As they move, the plates bump each other, move apart, and slide past one another.

All that moving around strains rocks that are near the edges of the plates. This produces areas where the rock has lots of breaks, or *faults*. Rock sometimes gets locked in place along these faults. Because the rock isn't able to slide, pressure builds up on both sides of the fault. Eventually the rock may snap and move, creating an earthquake.

If an earthquake happens on land, buildings can topple, roads can break apart, and people can be hurt. Earthquakes that happen in the ocean can produce giant waves called *tsunamis*. These huge waves can travel as fast as 500 miles per hour! Tsunamis cause lots of damage if they flow over an island or a city on the coast.

Look at a world map. The continents look a little like puzzle pieces. In fact, you may notice that they look like they could fit together to make one big piece of land. Could they have once been one huge *supercontinent* that later broke apart? A man named Alfred Wegener thought so. He called this supercontinent *Pangaea*. He believed that Pangaea began to break into smaller continents about 200 million years ago. These smaller continents slowly drifted to where they are today.

Africa

South America

©The Mailbox® • *Science* • TEC60859

Note to the teacher: Use with "Preparing Materials" on page 71 and "Preparing Students" on page 72. As an extension, give each student a duplicated world map. Have the student cut the continents apart. Then have him try to put the pieces together to make one large supercontinent. If desired, let the student glue the arrangement of pieces onto a sheet of construction paper.

Quite Quake-Safe!

If buildings don't stand up well during an earthquake, people can be hurt or even killed. So architects and builders use special methods to make their buildings more earthquake-safe.

One method is to build structures without odd shapes that can snap off in a quake. Another idea is to make sure the building is heavy on the bottom, not the top. For example, if a floor is heavier than the one below it, it will collapse during a quake. Quake-safe buildings also have regular shapes (like squares) from top to bottom. This spreads out the weight evenly over the entire building instead of loading it up on just one spot.

Some quake-safe buildings have flexible beams. Instead of breaking, the beams bend like a bendable straw during a quake. A method called *crossbracing* also makes a building more quake-safe. If you cut out the bottom of a box and push on the sides, the box bends out of shape easily. But tape an X diagonally across the bottom and the box holds its shape better. Cross-bracing can be seen on many bridges.

Some buildings have rubber and steel pads under them. The pads absorb some of the earthquake's force so it won't go up the building. Other structures have a large concrete block at the top sitting on a slippery container of oil. The block is attached by springs to the sides of the building. During an earthquake, when the building sways, the springs push and pull the building back to the center.

Buildings constructed on hard ground, packed sand, or gravel are more quake-safe. Soft soil often moves during an earthquake. Buildings on soft soil aren't as stable during quakes.

©The Mailbox® • *Science* • TEC60859

Note to the teacher: Use with "Preparing Materials" on page 71 and "Introducing the Project" on page 72. Explain that the building shown is the Transamerica Pyramid in San Francisco. It is designed to be twice as strong as building codes require for this area.

Our Mysterious Ocean

Drop anchor right here to pull in a netful of activities that clear up everyone's notions about oceans!

with contributions by Kathleen Scavone, Middletown, CA

A Wealth of Water
Topic: Area of the world's oceans

For this seaworthy activity, gather a supply of gallon-size plastic bags (one for every four students). Cut each bag along the seams, as shown, to make two sheets. Next, have students estimate how much of the world is covered by water. Then give each pair of students the materials listed and guide them through the steps below. Conclude by having students share their findings. Compare their quotients to 0.75, or three-fourths, the approximate area of the earth that is covered by water.

Materials for each pair of students: sheet cut from plastic bag, sheet of 1 cm grid paper, copy of a world map, 4 paper clips, 3 markers (1 black, 1 brown, 1 blue), scissors, calculator, ruler (optional)

Steps:
1. Clip the plastic sheet atop the centimeter grid. Trace the grid on the plastic sheet with the black marker.
2. Clip the plastic grid atop the map, trimming the plastic to fit the map, if necessary. Extend the grid, if needed.
3. With the plastic grid clipped to the map, color the land brown and the water blue.
4. Count and record the whole brown squares. Then count and record the partial brown squares. Divide the number of partial squares by two. Add the quotient to the number of whole squares to find the total brown squares.
5. Repeat Step 4 with the blue squares.
6. Find the number of colored squares by adding the total number of brown squares to the total number of blue squares.
7. Divide the total number of blue squares by the total number of squares to calculate how much of the earth is covered by water.

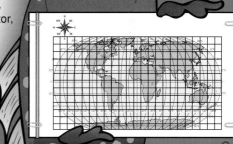

Wow! Since water covers about 75% of the earth's surface, we have lots of room to swim!

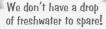

We don't have a drop of freshwater to spare!

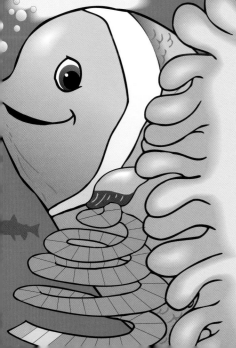

A Whole Lot of Salty
Topic: Amount of saltwater versus freshwater

Part of what makes our planet unique is its abundance of water. But precious little of it is usable freshwater. Convince students of the need to conserve freshwater with an easy model-making activity. Begin by having students discuss the questions below. Then give each child three crayons (green, yellow, and blue), scissors, and a copy of page 80 to complete as directed. Suggest that students take the resulting water spirals home as reminders not to carelessly let freshwater whirl down the drain!

Questions:
1. What percent of the earth's water do you think is salty? *(about 97 percent)*
2. Other than oceans, what are other sources of water? *(ice caps and other glaciers, lakes, rivers, groundwater)*
3. What percent of the earth's water do you think is frozen in ice caps and other glaciers? *(about two percent)*
4. What percent of the earth's water do you think is in rivers, lakes, and underground? *(about one percent)*
5. What are some ways that water could be conserved? *(Answers will vary. Possible answers: take shorter showers, fix leaky pipes, wash dishes by hand rather than by a dishwasher)*

Fishing the Ocean's Zones
Topic: Ocean zones and animal adaptations

Use this fishy game to help your students understand how marine organisms can be classified according to where they live. In advance, write the name of each sea organism and clue on the right (not the italicized items) on half of an index card. Attach a small magnetic strip to the back of each card. Then, on the board, draw and label the diagram below.

Next, use the diagram to explain that the ocean can be divided into layers according to the amount of sunlight each receives: *the sunlight zone, the twilight zone,* and *the midnight zone.* Point out the role sunlight plays in the temperature and the types and number of organisms living in each zone. Then divide students into two teams. Give Player 1 on Team A a card. Have him read the card's clue and then stick the card in the correct zone. If correct, award his team a point. Then have Player 1 on Team B take a turn. But if incorrect, give the card to Player 1 on Team B. If his answer is incorrect, place the card in its correct zone and discuss the reason with the class. Then continue play with Player 2 on Team A. After every student has had a turn, declare the team with more points the winner. For a related activity, see the reproducible on page 81.

sperm whale—70°F *(sunlight zone)*
sea cucumber—15,000 feet *(midnight zone)*
viperfish—50°F *(twilight zone)*
plankton—70°F *(sunlight zone)*
tuna—500 feet *(sunlight zone)*
squid—2,000 feet *(twilight zone)*
shark—500 feet *(sunlight zone)*
tripod fish—34°F *(midnight zone)*
hatchetfish—49°F *(twilight zone)*
dolphin—300 feet *(sunlight zone)*
anglerfish—9,000 feet *(midnight zone)*
octopus—1,000 feet *(twilight zone)*
blue marlin—55°F *(sunlight zone)*
snipe eel—41°F *(midnight zone)*
rattail fish—2,500 feet *(twilight zone)*
seal—200 feet *(sunlight zone)*
Portuguese man-of-war—0 feet *(sunlight zone)*
humpback whale—68°F *(sunlight zone)*
jellyfish—2 feet *(sunlight zone)*
lantern fish—38°F *(midnight zone)*
gulper eel—7,000 feet *(midnight zone)*
krill—65°F *(sunlight zone)*
anchovies—7 feet *(sunlight zone)*
hammerhead shark—1,000 feet *(twilight zone)*
coelacanth—35°F *(midnight zone)*

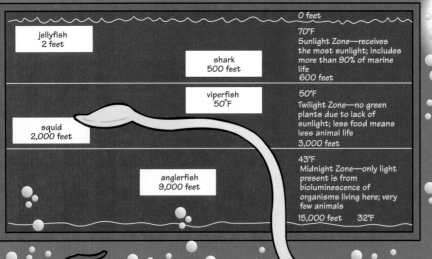

	0 feet
jellyfish 2 feet	70°F Sunlight Zone—receives the most sunlight; includes more than 90% of marine life
shark 500 feet	600 feet
viperfish 50°F	50°F Twilight Zone—no green plants due to lack of sunlight; less food means less animal life
squid 2,000 feet	3,000 feet
	43°F Midnight Zone—only light present is from bioluminescence of organisms living here; very few animals
anglerfish 9,000 feet	15,000 feet 32°F

Skittish About Pollution
Topic: Effects of pollution on the ocean

Garbage and other wastes have been dumped into the ocean throughout history. When fewer people were polluting, the ocean was big enough to absorb it. Today, however, the world's population is so large that if pollution doesn't stop, the ocean environment will suffer irreparable damage. Already, many ocean species have become endangered.

Challenge students to consider the impact that pollution has on marine organisms with this two-part activity. Pair students and have each pair research an ocean animal (see the list in "Fishing the Ocean's Zones" above). Then have the twosome write a short skit in which the researched animal complains to another of its species about how their ocean habitat is being affected by increasing pollution. If desired, challenge the pair to include a *soliloquy* in which one animal mutters to itself about the situation. Then have each twosome present its skit to the class.

This oil is yucky. Why can't those hu[man]s spill stuff in their backyards?

Coastal Weather vs. Inland Weather

Topic: Ocean's effect on climate and weather

Does ocean weather have its own special characteristics? Have pairs of students find out with this "weather-ific" investigation! Ask each twosome to pick either an east-coast or a west-coast state. Next, have the pair select two cities within that state, one inland and one coastal. Instruct the partners to use encyclopedias, weather-related Web sites, and other resources to compare the average yearly precipitation of their cities. Have each duo share its data with the class. As students share, tally on the board the times that yearly precipitation for a coastal city exceeds that of an inland city. Afterward, ask students if their data supports the generalization that coastal areas are wetter than inland areas. Then share that because water from the ocean evaporates, winds blowing from the ocean are moister than those coming from inland areas. Follow up by having each twosome compare its cities' average winter and summer temperatures. Then ask students if they can make a generalization about the ocean's effect on temperature *(in general, coastal cities have warmer winters and cooler summers than their inland counterparts)*.

Friend or Foe?

Topic: Consequences of human action on the ocean

Examine the interaction between man and ocean with an activity that results in a terrific deep-sea display. List on the board the examples of human-ocean interaction shown. Instruct each student to copy one example and the headings shown below on the unlined side of an index card. Then have her add an advantage and a disadvantage of that interaction in each corresponding column. After each student shares her card, give her a sheet of paper, scissors, glue, and crayons, markers, or colored pencils. Have the student draw, color, and cut out an outline of an ocean animal. Then have her glue the labeled index card to the cutout. Display the completed cutouts on a bulletin board that has been covered with blue paper. Add the title "Man and Ocean...Friends or Foes?"

Human-Ocean Interaction

Oil tankers cross the ocean between countries.

People use boats to observe whales and fish.

Many industries are located near the coast.

Offshore drilling collects oil and gas from the ocean floor.

Seawalls stand between the ocean and some cities.

Many of the world's largest cities are on the coast.

Tourists visit the oceans and coasts.

Boats called *trawlers* use nets to fish in the ocean.

Pros	Human–Ocean Interaction	Cons
Seawalls protect the shore from erosion.	Seawalls stand between the ocean and some cities.	Seawalls may damage the natural environment.

Water Whirl

About how much of the earth's water is salty? Fresh? Make a swirling model that will help you remember!

The whole strip represents 100% of the earth's water. So each section represents 1%!

Directions:

1. Color sections 1–97 of the strip green.
2. Color sections 98 and 99 yellow.
3. Color section 100 blue.
4. Cut out the strip along the bold line. Then cut it on the dotted lines.

Key

green—saltwater (about 97%)
yellow—freshwater that is frozen in ice caps and other glaciers (about 2%)
blue—freshwater that is beneath the earth's surface and in rivers and lakes; the only form usable to humans (about 1%)

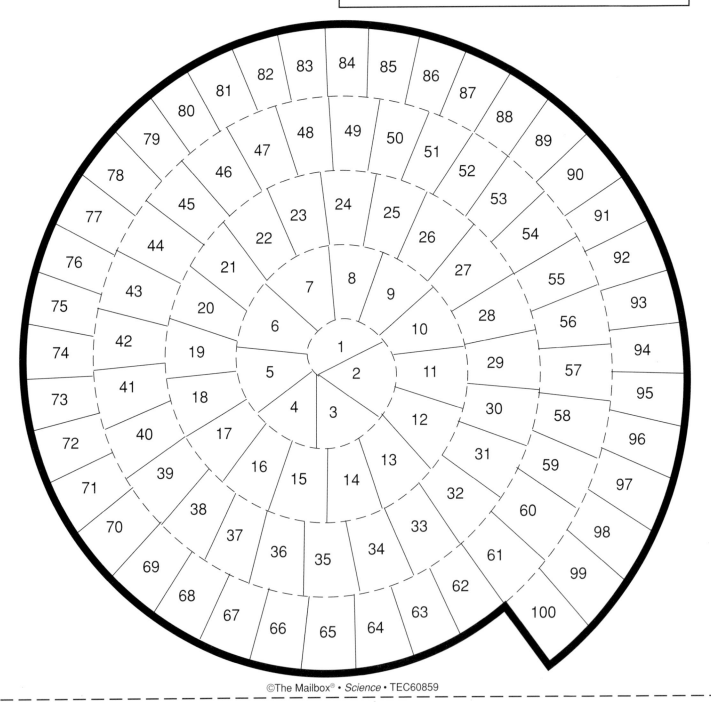

©The Mailbox® • *Science* • TEC60859

Note to the teacher: Use with "A Whole Lot of Salty" on page 77.

Creeps of the Deep

Dr. Ichabod Fish is a world-famous marine biologist working at Ocean Adaptation Station #7. He knows it's no accident that many ocean animals have special shapes, body parts, and behaviors to help them survive in their ocean environment! Follow the directions to help Dr. Fish match each picture to its description.

Directions: Research each "creepy" ocean animal pictured below. Then cut out each picture and glue it inside the box that matches its description.

1. has one or two sharp, poisonous spines on the middle of its tail	2. can hide its pancake-shaped body in the sand or mud	3. has organs along its head and body that help it create light
4. has poisonous dorsal spines	5. has a spiny head and wartlike skin that is the color of some rocks	6. has organs in its body that produce electricity
7. is covered with spines and can puff up like a balloon	8. has a flat body that makes it hard to see when viewed head-on	9. has a large mouth and sharp teeth; uses a "fishing lure" to catch its prey

Bonus Box: Based on the descriptions above and your research notes, write five true-or-false questions for a classmate to answer. Then discuss the answers together.

©The Mailbox® • *Science* • TEC60859 • Key p. 159

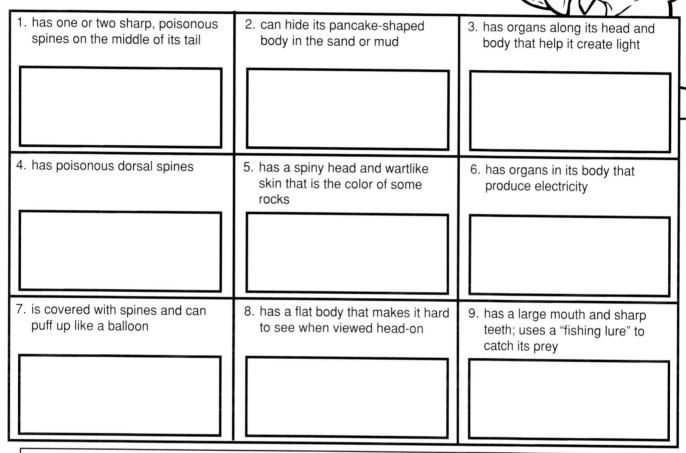

porcupine fish | skate | electric eel

lionfish | stonefish | lantern fish

stingray | angelfish | anglerfish

Note to the teacher: Students will need scissors, glue, and access to encyclopedias or other resources to complete this page.

IT'S A JUNGLE OUT THERE!
Studying Tropical Rain Forests

From the mossy floor to the lush canopy above, the rain forest is a remarkable environment that simply invites investigation. Lead your students on an exotic expedition through the rain forest with the following activities, literature suggestions, and reproducibles.

with ideas by Simone Lepine

*Look for helpful background information on rain forests in the yellow boxes.

Layer Upon Layer

The year-round growing season in the rain forest gives plants ample opportunity to grow... and grow...and grow! Four layers divide the rain forest into distinct areas:

- **Emergent Layer:** Towering over the rest of the canopy are the tallest of rain forest trees, a few reaching over 200 feet in height. Blown about by the wind, this layer is hotter and drier than the canopy beneath it.
- **Canopy:** Most animals of the rain forest live in this green and leafy layer, 80–150 feet above the ground. Large broad leaves catch and block both rain and sunlight.
- **Understory:** This layer extends about 40–50 feet from near the ground. It is made up of tall shrubs, mosses, algae, and fungi. Also found here are young trees whose growth has been stunted by the lack of sunlight.
- **Forest Floor:** In the dark, humid world of the forest floor live decomposers, such as termites and fungi, which quickly process the five tons of litter the other layers produce in a year. Animals such as jaguars, tapirs, and ocelots roam the floor hunting their prey.

The Invisible Tree

A tree that's 230 feet tall is hard to imagine—but not after doing this activity! Have each student cut a five-foot length of string. Then head outdoors or to the gym, taking along a tape measure and two orange cones or other markers. Once outside, follow these steps:

1. Have students lay their strings end-to-end in a line. Place a cone at both ends of the line. Ask, "How many feet of string do we have?" *(5 x the number of students)*
2. Tell students that a tree in the emergent layer can be as tall as 230 feet. Then ask, "How many more strings do we need to add to our line to equal 230 feet?" *(Forty-six five-foot lengths equal 230 feet.)* Have that number of students remove their strings from the line and lay them end-to-end behind one cone; then move the cone to the new endpoint.
3. After students have studied their invisible tree, explain that the canopy is about 150 feet above the ground. Challenge each child (except two helpers) to estimate where the canopy would fall on the tree and stand at that point beside the string. Have your helpers use a tape measure to discover the closest estimate.
4. Have students estimate where the understory (at 33 feet from the ground) would fall. Choose new helpers to measure and find the closest estimate.

As a fun extension, divide the class into pairs. Have each pair estimate the number of steps needed to walk the length of the tree; then have students test their guesses.

High-Rise Dioramas

Looking for a top-notch rain forest project? Look no further! Several weeks before the project, ask each student to bring in a shoebox and a paper-towel tube. Divide students into three large teams: Emergent Layer, Canopy, and Understory-Floor. Provide each team with reference books (see the suggested list on pages 86 and 87) so students can research their assigned rain forest section. After the research is completed, regroup students into smaller teams of three, each with one person from each large group. Then have the teams follow the steps below:

Steps for the team:

1. Paint three paper-towel tubes brown to resemble a tree trunk. Let them dry.
2. Stack three shoeboxes atop each other. Decide as a group where to position the tree trunk (see the illustration). Then cut holes in the boxes and insert the tubes as shown. Use tape to secure the tubes to the boxes if necessary.
3. Give each group member the box for the layer he researched.

Steps for each team member:

4. Using art materials, create a scene in your box that includes at least four different animals and three plants that live in your rain forest layer.

When the three boxes are finished:

5. Stack the boxes in the correct order; then tape them together with masking or packing tape.
6. From green paper, cut out a treetop and other leaves to tape to the trunk and box as shown.

A Rain Forest of Words

Do your students speak "rain forest-ese"? If not, help them learn with this vocabulary activity! Give each student a file folder and two to three copies of page 91. Post a list of rain forest words (see the sample list below). Then have the student complete each copy of page 91 as directed, storing the finished pages in her folder. When all copies have been completed, have the student cut out the pages along the bold lines and staple them inside her folder. Then let her decorate the front of the resulting book to complete her "pic-tionary" of rain forest words.

Possible words: bromeliad, buttress, camouflage, canopy, carnivore, cloud forest, consumer, crown, decomposer, deforestation, emergent tree, epiphyte, forager, fungi, herbivore, indigenous people, jungle, liana, niche, parasite, understory

Rain Forest Pocket Book

Fit a whole rain forest into a pocket? It's possible with this nifty research project! Duplicate page 88 on white construction paper for each student. Then guide the class through the following steps:

1. Fold the paper into three sections as shown so that the picture is on top.
2. Color the picture with crayons or colored pencils (no markers).
3. Cut the front page along the three dotted lines that divide the drawing; stop at the dots. Do **not** cut the back page.
4. Seal the bottom of each section with clear tape to make four small pockets. Then staple the left side of the book as shown.
5. Research the four layers of the rain forest. Write your notes on the inside pages of the book. As you come across other cool facts, write each one on a small piece of paper. Fold the paper and place it inside the appropriate pocket.

When the unit is completed, pair students; then have each child share her pocket book with her partner.

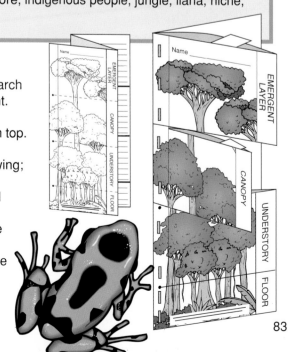

Animal Mystery Boxes

Turn report writing into a project that's more fun than a barrel of rain forest monkeys! Give each student a copy of page 90. Have him research a rain forest animal from the list on page 90 and complete the page. Then have him follow these steps to make an Animal Mystery Box about his critter.

Steps:

1. Cover an empty cereal box with white paper.
2. Cut one shape from construction paper. Label the cutout "Rain Forest Mystery Animal" and add your name. Then glue the cutout to the front of your box.
3. Cut out additional shapes. Label each with a fact about your animal from page 90. Do **not** mention your animal's name in any fact.
4. Glue the cutouts on all sides of your box. Add other decorations such as vines and leaves.
5. Cut a 5" x 12" piece of white poster board. At the top, write "Pull up. Who am I?" as shown. At the bottom, write the name of your animal. In the middle, draw and color a picture of your animal.
6. Cut a five-inch slit in the top of the box. Insert the card so only "Pull up" shows.

When all the boxes are done, have students place them on their desks. Tell students that they will be going on a jungle safari in the classroom; then invite students to wander around the room to examine the different boxes. Don't step on the anaconda!

Less Is...More!

So why all the fuss about protecting the rain forest anyway? Help answer that question with this eye-opening activity. Divide students into several groups. Give each group four rolls of pennies (one roll = 50 pennies). Direct each group to open two rolls and neatly lay the 100 pennies end-to-end on a flat surface. Explain that only about 6 percent of the earth's surface is covered by rain forests. Ask students how many of the lined-up pennies this figure represents *(six)*. Ask each group to move six pennies slightly away from the others in the line. Then ask how the rain forest area compares in size to the rest of the earth *(a very small area)*.

Next tell students that 50 percent of all species of animals and plants live in tropical rain forests. Instruct each group to open its two remaining penny rolls; then have the group's members stack 50 percent, or 50 pennies, atop the six pennies that represent the rain forest area. Have them stack the other 50 pennies atop the remaining 94 until they run out. Ask students, "How does the rain forest compare to the rest of the earth now?" Discuss why this ecological environment is so important. Follow up this discussion by having each student complete the reproducible on page 89.

WANTED:

Rain Forest Scientists

It's a bird! It's a plane! No, it's a botanist hanging from the rain forest canopy! Expose students to the types of scientists who study the rain forest—and sharpen their writing skills—with this activity. Divide the class into five groups: botanists, entomologists, ecologists, zoologists, and anthropologists. Have each group research its scientist to find out what he/she studies and how to become an expert in that field. Then have the group write a classified ad, searching for a scientist in its field to work at a tropical rain forest lab. Direct each group to copy and illustrate its ad on a poster to display in the classroom. After groups have shared their posters, have each student choose one type of scientist and write a letter of application to the lab explaining why he would like to work there.

A Tropical Medicine Chest

The tropical rain forest is like a big medicine cabinet that we've just begun to clean out! About 25 percent of all medicines used today start from somewhere in the rain forest. That figure is amazing because man has studied only 2 percent of the 250,000 species of plants in these forests for this purpose. Some of the medicinal plants that have been discovered in the rain forest and the problems they help treat include the following:

- *Ouabain plant:* heart problems, rheumatoid arthritis
- *Indian yam:* rheumatoid arthritis, rheumatic fever
- *Chaulmoogra:* leprosy, skin infections
- *Calabar bean:* glaucoma, high blood pressure
- *Quinine (bark of red cinchona tree)*: malaria
- *Curare*: multiple sclerosis (also used as a muscle relaxer during surgery)
- *Rosy periwinkle:* Hodgkin's disease, childhood leukemia
- *Moreton Bay chestnut:* HIV

A Pharmacy in the Forest

Help students understand the medical treasures hidden in the rain forest with this activity. Cut out 25 green paper leaves. Write "10,000" on each leaf; then give one to each of 25 students. Tell students that each leaf represents 10,000 different species of plants and that altogether the leaves represent the 250,000 plant species found in the rain forest.

Next display four empty pill bottles. Holding up one bottle, announce that about 25 percent, or one-fourth, of all medicines originate in the rain forest. Share the uses listed in the box above. Then explain that only about 2 percent of rain forest plants (about 5,000) have been studied. To represent this number, ask a student to tear her leaf in half and drop one piece into a pill container. Ask everyone to hold up their leaves to demonstrate how many species still hold potential for medical uses. Finally explain that 50,000 plant species in the rain forest become extinct each year. Ask how many leaves that number represents (five); then have five students throw their leaves in the trash. Discuss with students the implications rain forest destruction has for future medical research.

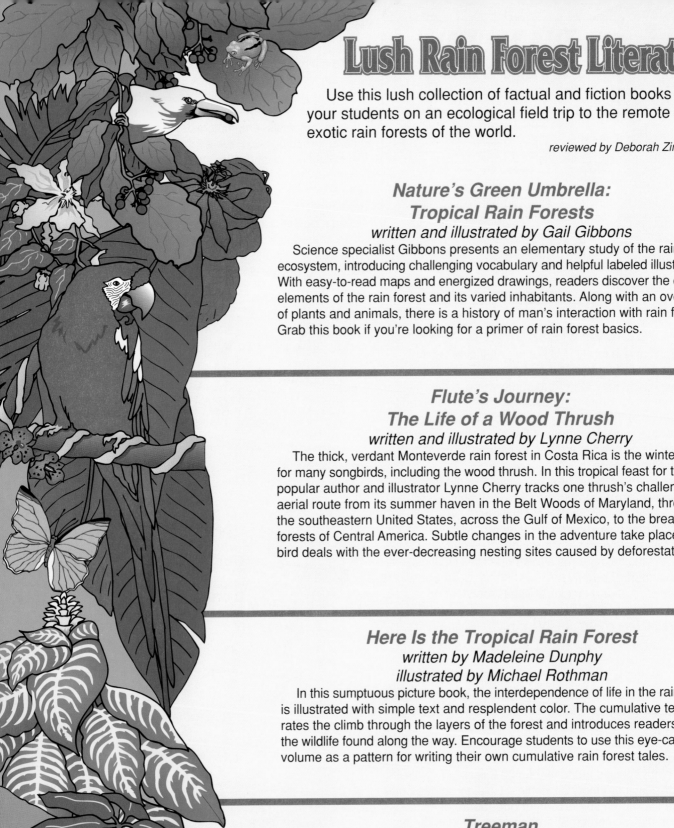

Lush Rain Forest Literature

Use this lush collection of factual and fiction books to take your students on an ecological field trip to the remote and exotic rain forests of the world.

reviewed by Deborah Zink Roffino

Nature's Green Umbrella: Tropical Rain Forests
written and illustrated by Gail Gibbons

Science specialist Gibbons presents an elementary study of the rain forest ecosystem, introducing challenging vocabulary and helpful labeled illustrations. With easy-to-read maps and energized drawings, readers discover the essential elements of the rain forest and its varied inhabitants. Along with an overview of plants and animals, there is a history of man's interaction with rain forests. Grab this book if you're looking for a primer of rain forest basics.

Flute's Journey: The Life of a Wood Thrush
written and illustrated by Lynne Cherry

The thick, verdant Monteverde rain forest in Costa Rica is the winter home for many songbirds, including the wood thrush. In this tropical feast for the eyes, popular author and illustrator Lynne Cherry tracks one thrush's challenging aerial route from its summer haven in the Belt Woods of Maryland, through the southeastern United States, across the Gulf of Mexico, to the breathtaking forests of Central America. Subtle changes in the adventure take place as the bird deals with the ever-decreasing nesting sites caused by deforestation.

Here Is the Tropical Rain Forest
written by Madeleine Dunphy
illustrated by Michael Rothman

In this sumptuous picture book, the interdependence of life in the rain forest is illustrated with simple text and resplendent color. The cumulative text narrates the climb through the layers of the forest and introduces readers to the wildlife found along the way. Encourage students to use this eye-catching volume as a pattern for writing their own cumulative rain forest tales.

Treeman
written by Carmen Agra Deedy
illustrated by Douglas J. Ponte

Celebrated Cuban storyteller Deedy weaves a whimsical tale of three Amazon rain forest creatures that discover a sack of holiday mail that has dropped from a passing airplane. The forest dwellers—who have never even heard of Christmas or Santa—decide that St. Nick must be the Treeman, who leaves a tree in exchange for presents. While celebrating their new tree, the three amiable amigos gaze at the smoke from a burning rain forest and decide that one tree at a time *can* make a difference. The narrative rolls naturally and comfortably with delightful drawings.

Amazon Basin:
The Vanishing Cultures Series
written and photographed by Jan Reynolds

Traveling deep into the Amazon rain forest, photographer and author Jan Reynolds focuses on the Yanomama people to capture their native attire, housing, food, gatherings, and rituals. The engaging narration follows one family through the routines of the day while the close-up photos show off the lush tropical setting of their village. Don't skip the thought-provoking author notes at the back of the book, which remind the reader that deforestation has social as well as ecological ramifications.

Jungle
written by Theresa Greenaway
photographed by Geoff Dann

Part of the popular Eyewitness Series, this fact- and photo-packed book will be eagerly ogled by even the most reluctant reader. Two-page chapters and well-captioned pictures make for a resource that covers an array of rain forest topics. A must-have reference book for any rain forest exploration.

At Home in the Rain Forest
written by Diane Willow
illustrated by Laura Jacques

Towering kapok trees shade howler monkeys and toucans while passionflower butterflies flit softly through the shadows. Meet the creatures that inhabit the dark, dewy realm of the rain forest in Diane Willow's well-written book. Brilliant paintings illustrate the colors and camouflage in this exciting introduction to the large and small animals of the Amazon rain forest.

Other Recommended Books

Rain Forests: Habitats of the World Series
written and illustrated by Sheri Amsel
Clear text engages all senses in an informative description of the rain forest.

Rain Forest
written by Joy Palmer
Part of a series on world habitats and conservation, this easy reader includes a handy glossary of rain forest terms and a list of addresses for finding more information.

Animals and Plants: _____

Animals and Plants: _____

Animals and Plants: _____

Animals and Plants: _____

Emergent Layer

Description: _____

Canopy

Description: _____

Understory

Description: _____

Floor Description: _____

| EMERGENT LAYER | CANOPY | UNDERSTORY | FLOOR |

Name _____

©The Mailbox® • Science • TEC60859

Note to the Teacher: Use with "Rain Forest Pocket Book" on page 83.

It's a Numerical Jungle out There!

The rain forest isn't just filled with all types of plants and animals. It's also loaded with numbers, as you'll see from reading these math miniprojects. Choose _____ projects; then complete them by this date: _____.

A   Only 6% of the earth is covered by rain forests, yet more than 50% of the world's species of plants and animals live there! Use a metric ruler or meter stick to measure two lengths of string: one to represent 6% and one to represent 50%. *(Hint: Use a scale of 1% = 1 cm.)* Cut the two strings. Then tape the strings to the back of this paper. Next to your strings write a brief statement telling why this statistic is so amazing.

B   If you travel in Central and South America, you'll find 57% of the world's rain forests. About 25% are in Southeast Asia. The rest are in Africa. In the circle, draw a pie chart that illustrates these figures. Don't forget to label each piece of the pie.

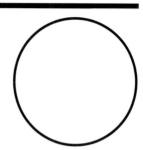

C   What makes a tropical rain forest a tropical rain forest? First of all, there must be lots of, well, rain! Rain forests average 80 or more inches of rain a year. Another factor is temperature. The average yearly temperature in the tropical rain forest is about 80 degrees Fahrenheit. How do these figures compare with where you live? Use a local newspaper and other reference materials to help you fill in this chart.

	Tropical rain forest	**My area**
Yearly precipitation	80" and up	
Average temperature	80°F	
Humidity	80%	Today:

D   The rain forest is home to many species of plants and animals. For example, in just 2.5 acres of rain forest in the country of Peru, you could find nearly 300 species of trees! In that same amount of land in the state of Ohio, you would only find about 10 species. Use the key to fill in each box so that it shows the number of species of trees.

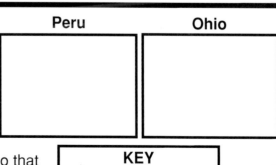

Peru   Ohio

KEY

▲ = 10 species

©The Mailbox® • *Science* • TEC60859 • Key p. 159

Note to the Teacher: Use with "Less Is...More!" on page 84. Before duplicating, fill in the number of projects and due date. Provide students with the following materials: string, scissors, tape, metric rulers or meter sticks, and a local newspaper and other reference materials (such as an almanac or encyclopedia).

Critter Twitter

What's everyone twittering about? The mysterious
animals that live in the tropical rain forest, that's what!
Choose one animal from the box below. Then research
this critter and fill in the blanks.

1. Lives in a rain forest on this/these continent(s): _____

2. Invertebrate or vertebrate: _____

3. Level of the rain forest where animal lives *(check one):* ____forest floor ____understory

   ____canopy ____emergent layer

4. Size of animal when fully grown: _____

   _____

5. Eating habits: _____

   _____

   _____

6. Adaptations that help animal survive in the rain forest: _____

   _____

   _____

   _____

7. Description of animal's appearance: _____

   _____

   _____

   _____

8. Other interesting facts: _____

   _____

   _____

anaconda	cobra	kinkajou	sloth
anteater	flying lemur	macaw	spider monkey
armadillo	galago	marmoset	swallowbill butterfly
army ant	gibbon	ocelot	tapir
boa constrictor	harpy eagle	okapi	tarantula
bushmaster snake	howler monkey	paca	tarsier
chimpanzee	hummingbird	peccary	toucan
coati	jaguar	poison dart frog	tree frog

©The Mailbox® • *Science* • TEC60859

A Lush Lexicon

What's a *lexicon?* It's a dictionary—and now it's your turn to write your very own! Write each rain forest word on a leaf below. In the box next to the leaf, draw a picture to illustrate or represent the word. Then cut along the two dotted lines and fold back the flap. Write the definition of the word on the back of the flap.

Note to the Teacher: Use with "A Rain Forest of Words" on page 83.

Somewhere Out There

Lost in space? Return to Earth by packing the following intergalactic activities into your next space unit!

by Hellen Harvey

Planet Poetry

Schedule a rendezvous between the nine planets and poetry with this fun writing activity! Divide students into nine groups, one for each planet. Have each group research to find five to ten facts about its planet. After the groups have gathered their facts, change orbits by forming five new groups: (1) Mercury and Venus, (2) Earth and Mars, (3) Jupiter and Saturn, (4) Uranus and Neptune, (5) Pluto. Direct each new group to write a *couplet*—two lines that rhyme—using a fact about the first planet for Line 1 and a fact about the other planet for Line 2. (Instruct the Pluto group to use two facts about Pluto for its couplet.) Encourage groups to write more than one couplet and choose the one they like best. When students have finished their couplets, compile the rhymes into a class poem as shown at the right.

Neighbors in Space

Mercury is the planet closest to the Sun;
Venus, called the morning star, is the brightest one.

Earth, our planet, is 4.5 billion years old;
Life probably never existed on Mars, we're told.

Jupiter is the biggest planet with the largest mass;
Saturn has an atmosphere that's mostly just one gas.

Uranus spins on its side as it orbits the sun.
Named for the Roman god of the sea? Neptune's the one!

Pluto is the most distant planet of the nine,
To revolve around the sun, it sure takes its time!

Is Anybody out There?

Send students on a creative mission that just might convince aliens to pay our piece of real estate a visit! In the 1970s, unmanned space probes—the *Pioneer 10* and *11* and *Voyager 1* and *2*—attempted to communicate with other intelligent life-forms via engraved plaques and recorded messages. Have students design their own space probe plaques by following these steps:

1. Trace the bottom of an aluminum pie pan on white tracing paper. Cut out the resulting circle.
2. With a pencil, draw an object, a diagram, or a symbol that depicts the current decade in the circle. Include the object's name.
3. Tape the circle inside the bottom of the pie pan, drawing side down. Use a pushpin to punch holes through the paper and pan along the drawing's lines and the object's name.
4. Turn the pan over. Glue magazine pictures depicting life on Earth to the outside rim as shown.

Display the plaques on a bulletin board as a shining reminder of what's important to inhabitants of the third rock from the sun!

Don't Mess With Gravity!

Astronauts must adapt to very different gravitational forces in space. Simulate this challenge by moving a chair to the front of the room. Place a glass of water on the floor next to the chair. Ask a student to lie across the chair with his stomach on the chair's seat and his head bent down toward the glass of water. Instruct the student to grasp the glass with his hands and take a drink. *(This will be difficult to do because gravity is pulling the water to Earth's center.)* Next place a straw in the glass and ask the student to drink the water using the straw. *(Earth's gravitational pull still makes this difficult to do, even though more force—the sucking action—is pulling the water toward the student's mouth.)* Follow up by having each student describe in his journal how difficult it must be for astronauts to perform ordinary tasks in space. Then challenge them to research the ways astronauts complete those tasks.

Are We There Yet?

The distance from Earth to the sun is absolutely astronomical! Actually, it's *1 AU*—one astronomical unit—which is a term scientists use to measure distances in space. One AU is equal to 93 million miles. About how long would it take to travel this distance in a car, a plane, or a space shuttle? Use a calculator, your division skills, and the steps in the box below to find out!

Follow these steps. Round all answers to the nearest whole number. Write your answers in the chart below.

1. To find the hours traveled:
   - For a car, divide 93,000,000 miles by 60 mph
   - For a plane, divide 93,000,000 by 550 mph
   - For a space shuttle, divide 93,000,000 by 25,000 mph
2. To find the days traveled, divide the hours traveled by 24 (the hours in one day).
3. To find the months traveled, divide the days traveled by 30 (the average days in one month).
4. To find the years traveled, divide the months traveled by 12 (the months in one year).

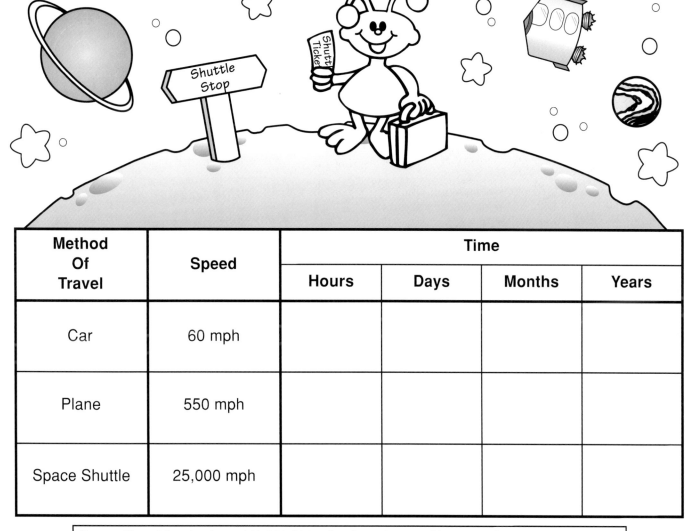

Method Of Travel	Speed	Time			
		Hours	**Days**	**Months**	**Years**
Car	60 mph				
Plane	550 mph				
Space Shuttle	25,000 mph				

Bonus Box: Mars is about 141,600,000 miles from the sun. How many hours would it take to travel by car from Mars to the sun? Days? Months? Years? (Use paper and pencil.)

Shuttling Through

3, 2, 1...liftoff! Launch your amateur astronauts on a tour of the solar system using these out-of-this-world activities!

Dr. Barbara B. Leonard, Winston-Salem, NC

Earth's Nearest Star

The sun is a yellow star. Its innermost region is the *core,* where nuclear reactions occur. As hydrogen changes into helium, the energy produced moves outward through the remaining layers and leaves the sun. The largest layer is the *radiative layer.* Above the radiative layer is the *convection layer.* Then comes the *photosphere,* or surface, where sunspots are visible. The photosphere is the innermost layer of the sun's atmosphere. The middle region of the sun's atmosphere is the *chromosphere.* It is made of hot gas that moves violently. Above the chromosphere is the *corona.* The gases of the corona are constantly expanding outward into space. A *solar prominence,* a cloud or sheet of gas, can rise up above the chromosphere and extend into the corona.

Schedule shuttle stops at these great Web sites! *(current as of March 2006)*

- Genesis mission Web site, part of NASA's program to study the sun: www.genesismission.org
- StarChild Web site sponsored by NASA's Goddard Space Flight Center (click on Level 2 links): starchild.gsfc.nasa.gov/docs/StarChild/StarChild.html

A Sun of Your Own

Concept: The sun's structure

Send students on a "sun-sational" tour of everyone's favorite star with this model-making activity. Share the facts above about the sun's structure. Also, invite shuttlers interested in learning more about the sun and the solar system to browse the suggested Web sites above. Then distribute the materials and guide students through the steps that follow.

Materials: 9" x 12" sheet of yellow (or orange) construction paper, 12" square of waxed paper, scissors, ruler, black fine-tipped marker, 2 paper clips, glue, pattern on page 96

Steps:

1. Cut a 3" x 9" strip from the construction paper to make a nine-inch square. Set the strip aside.
2. Fold the nine-inch square in half and in half again to make a $4\frac{1}{2}$-inch square.
3. Cut out the pattern on page 96 and clip it to the $4\frac{1}{2}$-inch paper square. Cut along the dashed lines. Remove the clips and pattern and unfold the circle.
4. Fold the waxed paper square in half twice. Trim the paper's outer edge into a curve similar to that on the pattern. Fringe the edge of the folded waxed paper. Then unfold the circle.

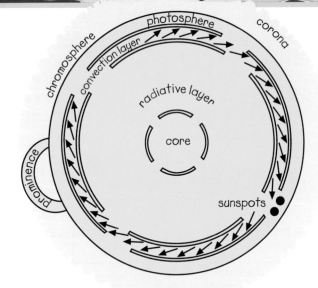

5. Glue the yellow circle to the middle of the waxed paper circle.
6. Label the sun's layers as shown. Add curved arrows to the convection layer to represent the movement of energy to the photosphere. Draw two to three dots on the photosphere to represent sunspots.
7. Cut a prominence from the 3" x 9" paper strip. Glue it to the edge of the chromosphere so that it extends into the corona.

the Solar System

Swinging Into Orbit

Concept: A planet's orbit around the sun

Take a closer look at how planets orbit the sun with this hands-on investigation. Review with students that an *orbit* is the path a planet travels to make one trip around the sun. Then give each student a ten-centimeter length of plastic straw, one meter of string, a ruler, and two small washers. Direct the student to thread the string through the straw and tie a washer to each end of the string.

Next, have the student hold the straw (representing the sun) upright in her right hand with about 15 centimeters of string dangling from the top. Have her hold the bottom of the string in her left hand. Direct the student to stand a safe distance from her classmates and whirl the top washer counterclockwise (the direction planets would revolve if viewed from above the sun's north pole). Have her gradually release more string as she whirls it until she has demonstrated a range of orbits with different diameters. Conclude by asking students to estimate and then measure the string's length when it was orbiting the fastest *(about 15 cm)* and slowest *(about 80 cm)*. Then have them predict which planet orbits the sun the fastest *(Mercury)* and slowest *(Pluto or Neptune)*. For a "space-tacular" follow-up activity, see "Oh, What a Trip!" below.

Oh, What a Trip!

Concept: The elliptical orbit of planets

Help students visualize the oval-shaped path of a planet's orbit with this eye-opening investigation.

Materials: 2 pushpins, 9" x 12" sheet of cardboard, 8½" x 11" sheet of white paper, metric ruler, 22 cm length of string, colored pencils (red, blue, and black), tape

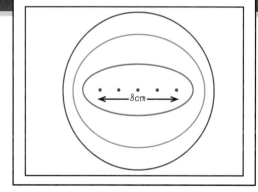

Steps:
1. Tape the white paper atop the cardboard.
2. Insert the pins into the center of the paper so they are eight centimeters apart (see the illustration). One pin is a *focus,* or fixed point, and represents the sun.
3. Tie both ends of the string together to form a loop. Wrap the loop around the pins as shown.
4. Place the red pencil inside the loop, extending it until the string is tight. Keeping the string taut, carefully move the pencil around the paper to make a complete revolution. The resulting oval shape is called an *ellipse.* The path of a planet as it revolves around the sun is an ellipse.

5. Move the pins so they are four centimeters apart. Repeat Step 4 using the blue pencil. Explain how the blue path differs from the red *(bigger and more like a circle).*
6. Move one pin two centimeters closer to the other. Remove the other pin. Repeat Step 4 using the black pencil. Explain how the black path differs from the others *(forms a circle).*

At the end of the activity, point out to students that the orbits of the planets are elliptical, with the sun always at one of the foci (Kepler's first law of planetary motion).

Relatively Speaking...
Concept: Relative size and distance of planets

Help students grasp the size of the planets and how far apart they are with this hands-on activity. Divide students into teams of four: pilot (team leader), mission specialist I (recorder), mission specialist II (materials manager), and copilot (encourager). Distribute a copy of page 97 and the materials listed to each team. Remind students that *scale* is the ratio between measurements on a map or model and the actual measurements (as in a scale of one inch equals one kilometer). Discuss page 97 with students, calculating the first answer on each chart together, if necessary. Then have the teams complete the page as directed.

When students have completed all three assignments, tape each planet model (see the materials list on page 97) to a different index card and label it. Head outside with the class, taking along the models, a 50-meter measuring tape, and a basketball to represent the sun. Use the basketball to anchor the front end of the measuring tape on the ground. Select one student to stand at the 40-meter mark; then have nine other students position the planet models on the tape using the scale of one meter equals one astronomical unit. Mission accomplished!

Meteorites Away!
Concept: How craters are formed

Invite your amateur astronauts to create a meteor shower of sorts with this data-collecting activity. Gather the materials listed on page 98 and divide students into groups of four or five. Then give each group the materials and a copy of page 98 to complete as directed. Afterward, have students compare the craters created by the marble and grape or the Ping-Pong ball and golf ball. Then have students discuss whether meteorites of similar size but different mass create similar craters (*those with greater mass create deeper craters*).

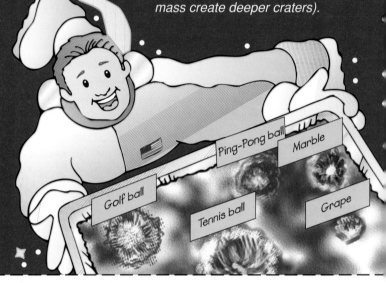

Pattern
Use with "A Sun of Your Own" on page 94.

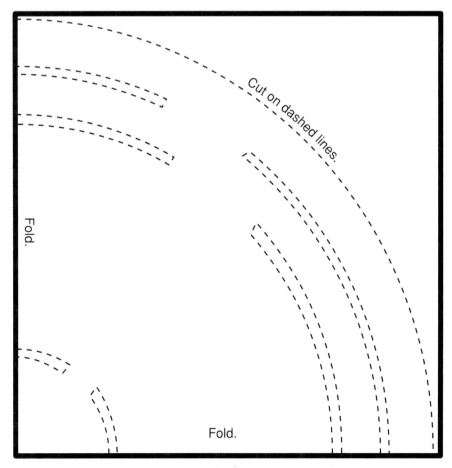

Cut on dashed lines.

Fold.

Fold.

Mission Prep 101

Welcome, junior astronauts! You've been recruited to conduct a special study of the solar system aboard the next shuttle. To prepare for this mission, your team must complete three important assignments. Good luck!

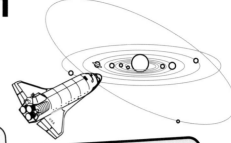

Materials for each team: calculator, metric ruler, 40 cm strip of paper or adding machine tape, 9 planet models (3 poppy seeds, 1 medium grape, 2 mustard seeds, 2 peppercorns, 1 piece of M&M's or Skittles candy)

Assignment I: Notice that the distances in the chart below are in millions of kilometers. Simplify these numbers by converting them to *astronomical units* (AU). One AU is equal to the average distance between the earth and the sun (149.6 million km). To calculate astronomical units, use a calculator to divide each planet's distance from the sun by the earth's distance from the sun. Round each answer to the nearest tenth and record it in the chart.

	Mercury	Venus	Earth	Mars	Jupiter	Saturn	Uranus	Neptune	Pluto
Distance from sun (millions of kilometers)	57.9	108.2	149.6	227.9	778.3	1,427	2,871	4,497	5,914
AU			1						

Assignment II: Draw a line segment 40 cm long on the strip of paper. Mark each centimeter. Label the beginning point "Sun." Using the scale one centimeter equals one AU, plot and label points along the line segment to show each planet's relative distance from the sun. Use the millimeter marks on your ruler to plot tenths of units.

Assignment III: Study the chart below. Notice that the scale of each planet's diameter has been changed from kilometers to millimeters. Measure the diameter of each of the planet model items in millimeters. Select the model that best represents the diameter of each planet and record it in the chart. Then place each model on its corresponding point on the distance line created in Assignment II.

Diameter	Mercury	Venus	Earth	Mars	Jupiter	Saturn	Uranus	Neptune	Pluto
Actual (km)	4,880	12,100	12,756	6,794	143,200	120,000	51,800	49,528	~2,330
Scaled (mm)	0.49	1.21	1.28	0.68	14.32	12.0	5.18	4.95	0.23
Model									

Note to the teacher: Use with "Relatively Speaking…" on page 96.

Names _____

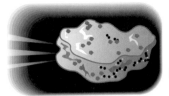

Meteorites Away!

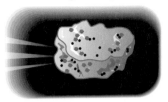

Create a shower of meteorites and see the kinds of crater creators they become!

Materials for each group: 5 lb. bag of flour, 9¼" x 11¾" aluminum pan, brown tempera paint, meterstick, ruler, newspaper, balance scale, tweezers, toothpicks, pencil, paper strips, objects to represent meteorites: grape, marble, Ping-Pong ball, golf ball, tennis ball

Steps:

1. Place the pan on the newspaper. Fill the pan with flour to a depth of three inches. Sprinkle tempera paint over the flour's surface.

2. Record the name of each meteorite object in the chart at the right.

3. Weigh each meteorite object and record its mass in the chart.

4. Select a meteorite object and hold it above the pan at a height of 20 centimeters. Drop the object. Then carefully remove it from the resulting *impact crater,* or bowl-shaped hollow. Use tweezers to remove the smaller objects. Label the crater with a paper strip.

Meteorite Object	Mass	Crater	20 cm	60 cm	1 m	2 m
		Width				
		Depth				
		Width				
		Depth				
		Width				
		Depth				
		Width				
		Depth				
		Width				
		Depth				

(Header note: the four rightmost columns are grouped under "Height of Drop")

5. Measure the crater's width and depth and record the measurements in the chart. To measure small craters, mark the measurements on a toothpick with a pencil. Then use a ruler to measure from the tip of the toothpick to each mark.

6. Repeat Steps 4–5 with each remaining meteorite object.

7. Repeat Steps 4–6, dropping each meteorite object from a height of 60 centimeters, then 1 meter, and finally 2 meters.

8. Label the following parts on the crater drawing on the left: floor, wall, rim, *ejecta* (material thrown out of the crater), *rays* (the streaks extending outward from the rim).

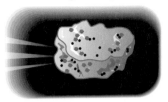

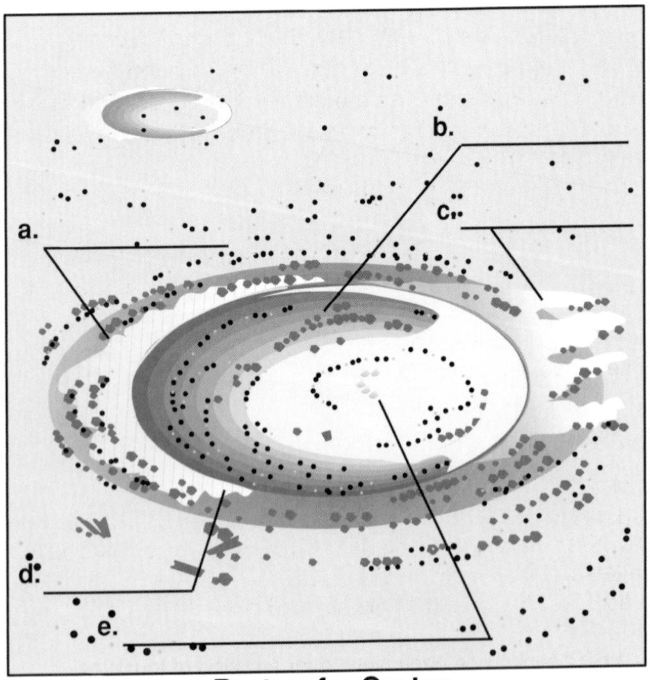

Parts of a Crater

a.
b.
c.
d.
e.

Bonus Box: Predict the crater depth of each meteorite object above if it were dropped from a height of 80 meters. Write your predictions on the back of this page.

Note to the teacher: Use with "Meteorites Away!" on page 96.

Ready, Set, Recycle!

Introduce your students to the benefits of recycling—the perfect way to celebrate Earth Day—with four environment-friendly, hands-on projects.

ideas by Deborah Mayo, Jena, LA

Project 1: Can-Collection Contest

Skill: Collecting and graphing data

Motivate students to reduce waste by involving them in a little recycling rivalry. Invite other classes in your grade level (or schoolwide) to join in a recycling contest. First, provide each participating class with a large collection box to hold its cans. Announce a place to store the overflow of cans. Also, demonstrate for each class how to use a magnet to tell whether a can is made of aluminum or another metal *(a magnet will not attract aluminum)*. Then set a date for the collecting to begin. On a bulletin board in a main hallway, display a pictograph that tracks the cans each class collects. After several weeks, sell the cans to a recycling center and treat the winning class to a pizza party. Donate any remaining money to a local environmental project, or use it to purchase new equipment for your school or classroom.

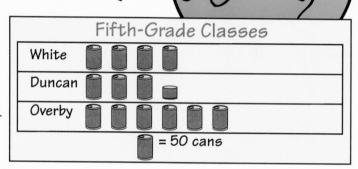

Fifth-Grade Classes	
White	🥫🥫🥫🥫
Duncan	🥫🥫🥫🥫
Overby	🥫🥫🥫🥫🥫🥫🥫

🥫 = 50 cans

Project 2: Landfill Logistics

Skill: Distinguishing between biodegradable and nonbiodegradable materials

Let students discover which trash items decay faster than others by conducting a landfill-simulation project. Use the directions below to help each student construct his own mini landfill, or make a single one the whole class can study. To avoid mold-sensitivity problems, store the project(s) in an area other than the classroom. At the end of the project, have students discuss the predictions and answers on their recording sheets (page 101).

Hummpf! The food and paper scraps are decaying, but this aluminum can hasn't changed a bit!

Materials:
large clear plastic box with a lid
wooden craft sticks
enough soil (not commercial) to fill the box
5 trash items (aluminum can, baby food jar, plastic bottle cap, eggshells, potato peelings, piece of newspaper, piece of Styrofoam, fabric scrap, piece of fruit, etc.)

2 to 3 cups of water
copy of page 101 for each student
ruler

Directions:
1. Fill the box with about two inches of soil.
2. Use a craft stick to draw lines in the soil to divide it into five equal sections. Select five items to bury. Bury one item at a time in a different section of the soil. Cover some items completely with soil. Leave others partly uncovered. Record each item on the recording sheet.
3. Add enough water to moisten the soil. Then put the lid on the box and place it in a sunny area.
4. Stir and examine the mixture with a craft stick twice each week over a period of four weeks. Record on the sheet any changes that are observed (odors, organisms, amount of decay).

Project 3: Earth-Friendly Fact Finders

Skill: Researching a topic

Want to fill your room with facts about recycling and pollution? Then try this Earth-friendly project! Pair students; then have each twosome research two facts about recycling or pollution. Next, give each pair of students two medium-sized circles cut from blue poster board. Have the partners draw and color the continents of the Western Hemisphere on one circle and the continents of the Eastern Hemisphere on the other. Direct the twosome to staple the blank sides of its circles together at the edges, leaving an opening at the top. Using a black marker, have the pair write one fact on one circle and the remaining fact on the other. Then have each pair stuff its project with paper, staple the opening closed, and hang it from the ceiling using a length of yarn.

Every person in the United States creates about four pounds of trash each day.

An aluminum can takes about 500 years to biodegrade in a landfill.

Project 4: Rags-to-Riches Soil

Skills: Observing, drawing conclusions

Challenge students to transform plain dirt into fertile compost in just a matter of weeks with this "get-rich-quick" soil project. Use the directions below to help each student make his own container of compost. Or make a single one the whole class can study. To avoid mold-sensitivity problems, store the project(s) in an area other than the classroom. Have students discuss the answers written on their recording sheets (page 102) together.

Materials:
plastic gallon milk jug with top
ruler
craft sticks
pair of panty hose
soil (not commercial)
water
scissors
tape
9" square aluminum (or metal) pan

small pebbles
5 nonmeat food items
   (potato or onion peelings,
    carrot pieces, tea bags,
     coffee grounds, etc.)
leaves
grass clippings
copy of page 102 for each
   student

Directions:
1. Cover the bottom of the pan with pebbles and set it aside.
2. Using scissors, poke 20 to 30 holes in the bottom of the milk jug. About an inch below the handle, cut the jug into two sections.
3. In the top section, cut out five to six small windows. Tape a small piece of panty hose material over each opening.
4. Fill the bottom section with about two inches of soil. Place the food items, leaves, and grass clippings atop this layer. Cover the materials with another layer of soil.
5. Add just enough water to dampen the soil.
6. Push the top section of the jug down into its bottom section so that the edges of one overlap the other. Put the jug in the pan atop the pebbles.
7. Each day, remove the jug's top section and stir the mixture in the bottom with a craft stick. As needed, add water to keep the soil *damp*, not wet.
8. Twice each week—once at the beginning and again at the end—measure the depth of water in the pan and observe the landfill. Record the measurement and observations on the chart.

Landfill Logistics

Find out which landfill items decay faster than others with this cool investigation.

Directions: In the chart below, write the five items you buried in the soil. On the lines, predict whether items will decompose fast or slow. Then use the chart to record your observations twice each week—once at the beginning and again at the end. To complete the project, answer the questions below the chart on another sheet of paper. Use encyclopedias or other reference materials for help.

Predictions

Fast Decomposers: _____   Slow Decomposers: _____

Date	Odor(s)	Presence of insects, molds, etc.	Item — Amount of decay	Item — Amount of decay	Item — Amount of decay	Item — Amount of decay	Item — Amount of decay

1. How is the model like a real landfill?

2. Are landfills a good thing? Why or why not?

3. How does recycling affect landfills?

4. Why do some objects decay faster than others?

5. What could happen if *leachate,* the substance formed when liquid from rotting garbage mixes with rainwater, seeps from a landfill?

Bonus Box: Will there be landfills 100 years from now? Explain your answer.

©The Mailbox® • *Science* • TEC60859 • Key p. 159

Note to the teacher: Use with "Project 2: Landfill Logistics" on page 99. Allow students to use encyclopedias and other reference materials to answer the questions.

101

Rags-to-Riches Soil

Recycle food scraps and other trash items to create fertile soil with this "get-rich-quick" activity!

Directions: In the chart below, write the name of each item you buried in the soil. Use the chart to record your observations twice each week, once at the beginning and again at the end. After making your last entry in the chart, write a paragraph on the lines summarizing what happened to the soil.

Date	Odor(s)	Depth of water in pan	Item	Item	Item	Item	Item
			Amount of decay	Amount of decay	Amount of decay	Amount of decay	Amount of decay

Write your rags-to-riches paragraph here.

_____

_____

_____

_____

_____

_____

_____

_____

_____

©The Mailbox® • *Science* • TEC60859

The Second Time Around

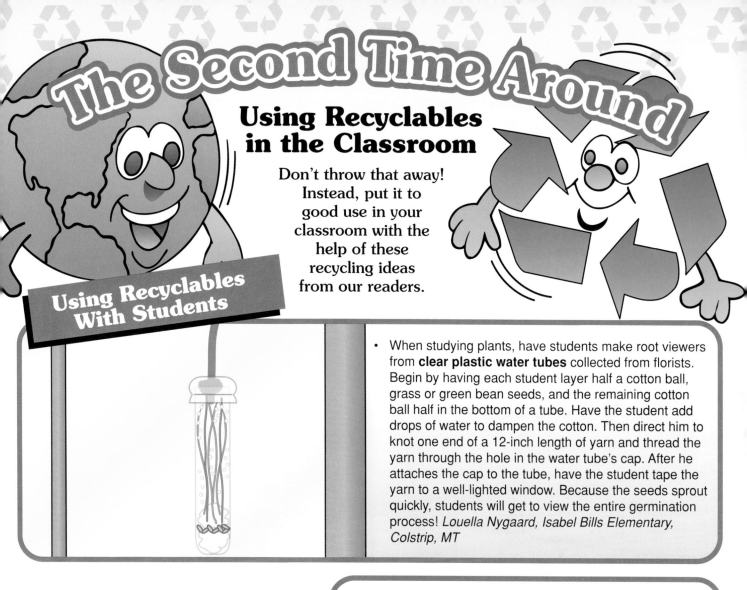

Using Recyclables in the Classroom

Don't throw that away! Instead, put it to good use in your classroom with the help of these recycling ideas from our readers.

Using Recyclables With Students

- When studying plants, have students make root viewers from **clear plastic water tubes** collected from florists. Begin by having each student layer half a cotton ball, grass or green bean seeds, and the remaining cotton ball half in the bottom of a tube. Have the student add drops of water to dampen the cotton. Then direct him to knot one end of a 12-inch length of yarn and thread the yarn through the hole in the water tube's cap. After he attaches the cap to the tube, have the student tape the yarn to a well-lighted window. Because the seeds sprout quickly, students will get to view the entire germination process! *Louella Nygaard, Isabel Bills Elementary, Colstrip, MT*

- Culminate the study of any biome by having students create terrarium-like models from **two- and three-liter plastic soda bottles.** First, cut a hand-size hole in the side of each bottle and fill its bottom with sand. Have each student fill her terrarium with various natural and hand-made materials to represent the chosen biome. Then have her attach a paragraph describing the biome's location, terrain, and plant and animal life. *Rebecca McCright and Melissa Nuñez, Washington Elementary, Midland, TX*

- Make it easy for students to draw perfect circles by saving unsolicited **CD-ROMs** that come in the mail. Collect enough for a class set. When teaching geometry or circle graphs, the disks are easy to trace anytime a circle is needed. They also make great tracers on overhead projectors, chalkboards, or whiteboards. *Lisa Hoegerman, Vista Campana Middle School, Apple Valley, CA*

- Teach propaganda techniques with the help of **empty product containers,** such as oatmeal boxes, spice shakers, and hair spray bottles. Divide students into groups and give each group several containers. After a group studies the advertising on its containers, have group members use art materials to turn one container into an original must-have product. Then have the group use various propaganda techniques to write television or radio ads to sell its product. *Rebecca McCright*

You'll never have a hair out of place if you use our Heavenly Hair hair spray!

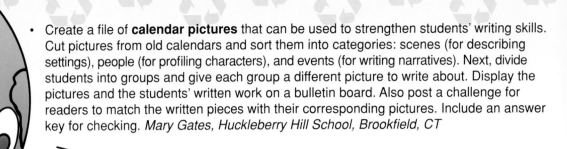

- Create a file of **calendar pictures** that can be used to strengthen students' writing skills. Cut pictures from old calendars and sort them into categories: scenes (for describing settings), people (for profiling characters), and events (for writing narratives). Next, divide students into groups and give each group a different picture to write about. Display the pictures and the students' written work on a bulletin board. Also post a challenge for readers to match the written pieces with their corresponding pictures. Include an answer key for checking. *Mary Gates, Huckleberry Hill School, Brookfield, CT*

- Brew endless ideas for writing prompts by clipping the unique artwork pictured on **tea bag boxes,** such as that on boxes of Celestial Seasonings tea bags. Store the clippings in a file box at a writing center. Have each student choose a clipping and write about what might have been going on before, during, and after the pictured scene. Or have her write a character sketch about a person or animal depicted in the artwork. *Kelly Cook, Dana Elementary, Dana, NC*

Using Recyclables to Organize Your Classroom

- Save the **tops of dried-up markers** to use as game pieces. Or use them to form cooperative groups. Just place the exact number and color of tops needed in a container. Then have each student draw out a top. *Toni O'Neil, Ramsey Robertson Elementary, Harbor Beach, MI*

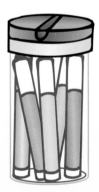

- Put empty plastic **Parmesan cheese containers** to use as marker holders. Use each container to hold a set of large or small markers. To remove a marker, simply lift or remove the hinged lid. *Sheila Wigger, Clara Barton School, Alton, IL*

- Cover **Crystal Light drink mix containers and Pringles potato chip cans** with Con-Tact covering and use them to hold pencils or paintbrushes. Use **plastic trays from frozen dinners** to sort small items, such as beads or noodles, for projects. Also retrieve items that are examples of cylinders, cubes, and rectangular prisms from recycling bins to help students identify geometric solids. *Amie L. Tedeschi, Triangle Day School, Durham, NC*

- Create sturdy magazine holders from 92-ounce **laundry detergent boxes.** Cut away each box top and the top two inches of each side. Make a wide cut (as shown) on one narrow end of each box. Then cover the inside and outside of the box with Con-Tact covering. *Karen Miller, Happy Valley Elementary, Johnson City, TN*

- Don't throw away those leftover pieces of **bulletin board border** after trimming a display. Instead, give them to students to use as colorful bookmarks! *Jamie Drewry, Wilson Elementary, Lawton, OK*

- Use **Lunchables lunch combinations trays** to help you organize paper clips, thumbtacks, and other small desk supplies. Also decorate small six-ounce **Pringles potato chip cans.** They're great for holding rulers! *Colleen Dabney, Toano Middle School, Williamsburg, VA*

- Don't put those precious **pieces of laminating film** in the garbage! Larger pieces can become desk mats when students paint or glasslike covers for framed pieces of artwork. Students can decorate medium-sized pieces with permanent markers to create stained-glass suncatchers for your windows. Smaller pieces can even hold small amounts of glue for art projects. *Doreen Placko, St. Patrick School, Wadsworth, IL*

- Collect plastic **film containers** to use whenever a student loses a tooth at school. They're just right for carrying the tooth safely home for the tooth fairy's visit. *Peggy Dickerson, Mattituck-Cutchogue School East, Cutchogue, NY*

- Hold on to empty **plastic-wrap and aluminum-foil rolls and boxes.** They're perfect for storing posters up to 18 inches wide. Just remove the metal tear strip, roll the poster around the empty tube, and place it in the box. Then tape the box closed, add a label, and it's ready to stack and store anywhere! *Julia Alarie, Essex Middle School, Essex, VT*

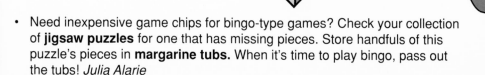

- Need inexpensive game chips for bingo-type games? Check your collection of **jigsaw puzzles** for one that has missing pieces. Store handfuls of this puzzle's pieces in **margarine tubs.** When it's time to play bingo, pass out the tubs! *Julia Alarie*

CLOSE ENCOUNTER WITH ENERGY ALTERNATIVES
INVESTIGATING RENEWABLE SOURCES OF ENERGY

More than any other generation, today's kids need to be aware of the need to become less dependent on nonrenewable sources of energy, such as oil and other fossil fuels. Give your students a close encounter with the world of renewable energy sources through the following out-of-this-world activities.

with ideas by Cynthia Wurmnest

SAVING SUNSHINE: SOLAR ENERGY

Searching for a renewable source of energy? Look up! Large amounts of energy from the sun hit our world every day. This energy can be used to produce electricity if properly collected, concentrated, and stored. Help students investigate the storage of solar energy with this activity, which compares the heat-retaining ability of four substances. First divide the class into teams; then give each team a copy of page 109 and the following materials:

- 4 dark plastic trash bags
- 4 same-sized, clear plastic cups
- 4 different colored pencils
- equal amounts of dried pinto beans, shredded white paper, soil, and water
- watch or clock
- 4 twist-ties
- 4 thermometers*
- spoon

When all groups have completed the experiment as directed on page 109, meet together to discuss results and determine the most efficient heat-retaining material. (*If desired, perform the experiment as a class, holding each of four teams responsible for measuring the temperature of only one cup. Have teams share their data; then have each student complete his graph on page 104 and answer the questions.)

To make nifty folders to hold student work during this close encounter with energy alternatives, see page 112!

These Earth creatures are most friendly. See how they wave at us...

WORKING WITH THE WIND: WIND ENERGY

Throughout history, people have used wind energy to do many jobs, including produce electricity. To illustrate the wind's ability to generate an electrical current, obtain a galvanometer (check a local high school's science department) or a current detector (available at a hardware store). Position two large electric fans about six inches apart facing each other. Plug in one fan and turn it on high. When the blades of the *unplugged* fan start to turn, touch the current detector to the metal ends of its plug. Surprise! The detector registers an electrical current.

Next display a picture of a windmill. Explain that windmills in history have provided power to pump water, grind grain, or generate electricity. Today's windmills, called *wind turbines,* are used to produce electricity. Ask, "What might be the advantages of wind energy?" *(It is free and produces little pollution; it doesn't have to be mined or pumped from the earth.)* Explain that wind speed must be greater than 7.5 miles per hour to produce electricity. Ask, "What might be wind energy's disadvantages?" *(Winds are too weak or infrequent in many places. Wind turbines are noisy and can be hazardous to birds. They can also interfere with TV and radio signals.)*

That's Hot Stuff!: Geothermal Energy

Heat energy from deep inside the earth—such as that evidenced by geysers like Old Faithful—is called *geothermal energy*. Simulate the nature of a geothermal energy source with this simple demonstration. Position a table or desk at least five feet from where students are sitting. Turn a metal kitchen funnel upside down in a pan that has been filled halfway with water. Heat the pan on a hot plate or another safe heat source. As the water heats, it will come out of the top of the funnel. (Be sure to wear oven mitts and stand back from the table.) Turn off the hot plate; then explain to students that in many places around the world, hot water and steam like this come out from cracks in the earth's surface. Hot melted rocks underground heat the water to high temperatures and sometimes the water boils to produce steam. The steam can then be used directly or be harnessed to produce electricity. Ask students the following questions to further explore geothermal energy:

- How could geothermal energy be used to heat homes safely? *(Homes can be directly heated with the steam through radiators. Or the steam can be used to drive turbines in a power plant to make electricity.)*
- Why do you think this energy source is relatively inexpensive? *(The only cost to geothermal energy is the equipment to use it. The fuel is free.)*
- What might be drawbacks to geothermal energy? *(You have to be located near a geothermal source to take advantage of it. There aren't many geothermal sources near big cities where the need is greatest. Also, hot water and steam can't be transported over long distances without losing energy.)*

Workin' Waterwheels: Water Power

For centuries, people have used water to power machines. Today, water, or *hydroelectric,* power is used to generate electricity. Water power causes little pollution, plus the water used to generate electricity can meet other needs later. On the downside, few rivers have good locations for building power plants or dams. And locating power plants in wilderness areas can upset those environments forever.

Help students discover the power of water by having them construct and test their own simple waterwheels. Provide each pair of students with the half-page reproducible on page 110 and the materials listed on it. Help students follow the steps to make their own simple waterwheels. Then have them use their models to test three early types of waterwheels as described on page 110. At the end of the activity, discuss students' answers to the question at the bottom of the page. Point out that people improved on the primitive Greek mill waterwheel, resulting in the more powerful over-shot waterwheel. Then have each student write in her science journal about a modern machine she would like to improve and the improvements she would make.

YESTERDAY AND TODAY: ENERGY CONSERVATION

That old horse-drawn carriage of 100 years ago didn't move as fast as our four-wheel-drive vehicles, but it also didn't cost much in terms of energy. For a fun exercise that gets your class thinking about the energy costs of progress, give each child a copy of the half-page reproducible on page 110. Have students or pairs of students complete the page. Then provide a sharing time to discuss their answers. As an extension, challenge student groups to design posters illustrating the contrasts between today's convenient, energy-guzzling machines and yesterday's inefficient, energy-saving devices.

ON THE WEB

- *U.S. Department of Energy's Energy Efficiency and Renewable Energy Network:* This helpful site contains background information for students and more. Check it out at eere.energy.gov/kids/.
- *Watt Watchers of Texas:* This program makes elementary students aware of energy use and conservation both at home and at school. It also includes links to other sources of information on renewable energy. Find it at wattwatchers.org. *(Current as of March 2006)*

THERE'S A CRISIS IN TECHNO TOWN!: CULMINATING ACTIVITY

Wrap up this unit with a fun simulation that provides an unforgettable review of renewable energy. Divide students into five groups. Choose one group to serve as the Town Council of Techno Town. Assign a renewable energy source to each of the other four groups: solar, geothermal, hydroelectric, and wind. Then read the following news release:

> Today Techno Town officials called a news conference to announce a series of public hearings on a recent energy crisis. Power outages have bothered this community recently, causing outraged citizens to lose the use of computers, home entertainment systems, and jet-train transportation into the town's business district. Outages are blamed on the lack of fuel to run the Techno Town Power Plant, which generates all electricity for the community. Officials are expected to announce a competition among highly respected energy experts to choose a new alternative energy system for the town. Experts began arriving today. More details as they become available.

Announce that students will become the energy experts hired to propose a solution to Techno Town's problem. Each group must research its energy source, then prepare a presentation for the Town Council that includes an opening statement, a list of their system's advantages and disadvantages, a brief description of the equipment needed, and a closing statement.

On Presentation Day, give each student a copy of the note-taking form on page 111. Seat the Town Council together and instruct all students to take notes on each presentation. After the presentations, have the Town Council meet to discuss each energy source and make its decision. Require that the council write and issue a formal announcement giving reasons for its decision.

Saving Sunshine

WHEW!

Yikes! As the owners of Positively Plants Greenhouse, you and your team are spending a fortune heating the greenhouse on cold winter nights. It's time to save a little sunshine! One idea is to fill several big black barrels with something that will absorb solar heat during the day. Then you can use the heat to warm your greenhouse at night. But what substance will hold the most heat in the barrels?

To find out, perform the following experiment. (Your teacher will provide the materials.) After you complete Steps 1–8, answer the questions. Then enjoy your toasty warm greenhouse!

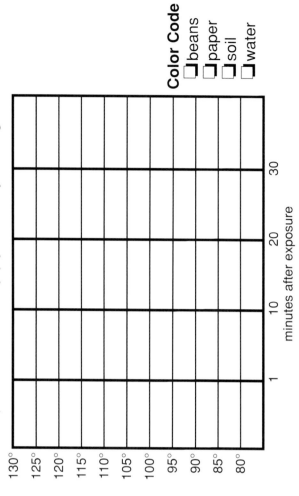

130°
125°
120°
115°
110°
105°
100°
95°
90°
85°
80°

1   10   20   30

minutes after exposure

Color Code

☐ beans
☐ paper
☐ soil
☐ water

Steps:

1. Use the colored pencils to color in the Color Code boxes. Be sure to use a different color for each box.

2. Use the spoon to fill each cup with a different substance. Be sure the amounts are as equal as possible.

3. Put each cup into a separate trash bag; then use a twist-tie to close each bag around its cup.

4. Place the four cups in the sun for one hour.

5. After the hour is up, move the cups to the shade. Unwrap each cup from its bag.

6. Place a thermometer in each cup. Leave it there for one minute.

7. Check the temperature of each cup after one minute is up. Use the colored pencils and Color Code to plot the temperature on the graph.

8. Repeat Step 7 after 10 minutes, 20 minutes, and 30 minutes.

Questions: Write your answers on the back of this sheet.

a. Did all the substances absorb the same amount of solar energy? Explain your answer.

b. Which substance would be best to use to fill the barrels? Why?

Bonus Box: What might be a disadvantage to using solar energy? Write your answer on the back of this page.

Note to the Teacher: Use with "Saving Sunshine: Solar Energy" on page 106.

Yesterday and Today

Name _____ Critical thinking

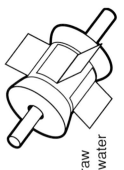

ENERGY EFFICIENT

A hundred years ago the old horse-drawn carriage didn't move as fast as today's four-wheel-drive vehicle. But it also didn't need gasoline to make it run. Nor did it hurt the environment the way today's vehicles do. Yes, that old horse-drawn carriage was slow, but it sure was an energy saver!

Can you match up an energy saver from yesterday with an energy user of today? Try to fill in each blank below. Complete blanks 10–12 with three pairs of your own. The first one is done for you.

Yesterday	Today
1. horse-drawn carriages	1. cars and trucks
2. _____	2. electric stove
3. horse-drawn plow	3. _____
4. _____	4. vacuum cleaner
5. washtub	5. _____
6. _____	6. clothes dryer
7. candles	7. _____
8. mixing spoon	8. _____
9. _____	9. calculator
10. _____	10. _____
11. _____	11. _____
12. _____	12. _____

Bonus Box: On the back of this sheet, list ten electrical devices that you can't imagine living without. Then write a paragraph describing how you would cope without these devices if you had to do without electricity for one week.

Note to the Teacher: Use with "Yesterday And Today: Energy Conservation" on page 108.

Which Waterwheel Works Wonderfully?

Names _____ Experiment

All through history, people have used waterwheels to help make power to run their machines. Investigate three early waterwheels with this wet and wild experiment!

Materials:
large, empty thread spool
4" x 6" index card
ruler
dishpan
scissors
masking tape
plastic drinking straw
squeeze bottle of water

Make your waterwheel:
a. Measure and draw four 1-inch squares on the index card. Cut out the squares.
b. Bend each square into an L-shape as shown above. Tape them to the spool to make your waterwheel's "fins."
c. Insert the straw into the spool's hole. Be sure the spool can spin loosely around the straw.

Test these types of waterwheels:
- *Greek mill:* Stand the waterwheel up in the dishpan as shown. Shoot a stream of water along the pan's bottom so that it touches the fins.
- *Undershot waterwheel:* Hold the straw horizontally over the pan. Shoot a stream of water under the wheel so that it touches the fins.
- *Overshot waterwheel:* Hold the straw as you did for the undershot waterwheel. Shoot a stream of water over the wheel so that it turns.

Which waterwheel would generate the most power? _____

Greekmill   undershot   overshot

Note to the Teacher: Use with "Workin' Waterwheels: Water Power" on page 107.

There's a Crisis in Techno Town!

No power to run computers or video games! No electricity to keep refrigerators or air conditioners going! What is Techno Town to do now that it is running out of fuel to keep its power plant in business?

Fill in this chart with the main points that your group has found out about your assigned energy source. Then take notes during the other teams' presentations. Finally, fill in the space at the bottom with your opinion about the best energy source for Techno Town. Be sure to give at least three reasons for your choice.

Renewable Energy Source	Advantages	Disadvantages
hydroelectric		
wind		
solar		
geothermal		

The best energy source for Techno Town is:

Note to the Teacher: Use with "There's a Crisis in Techno Town!: Culminating Activity" on page 108.

Unit Folder Cover Pattern

At the beginning of your unit, give each student a copy of this page, a blank file folder or manila envelope, markers or colored pencils, scissors, and glue. Have her cut out, color, and personalize the pattern, then glue it to the front of her folder. During the unit, have the student use the folder to store all notes, lab sheets, group work, and other handouts pertaining to renewable energy sources. Direct the student to write the name of each item she places in her folder on the contents list. If desired, award bonus points to each student who turns in an organized and complete folder at the end of the unit.

MY CLOSE ENCOUNTER WITH ENERGY ALTERNATIVES

WELCOME! TOURIST INFORMATION AVAILABLE!

This folder belongs to

Contents

Physical Science

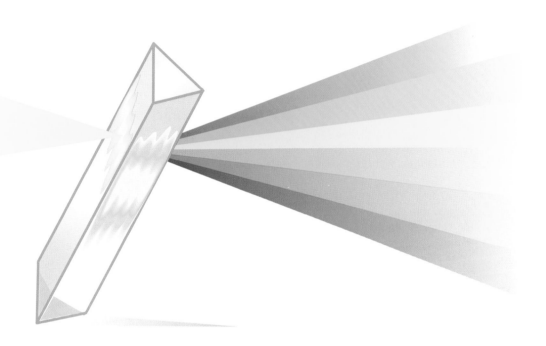

Physics for Kids

When you hear the word *physics,* do you instantly think, "I could never teach that!" Bet you can! All you need are the following easy-to-do-and-understand activities that teach kids important principles about matter and energy.

ideas by Terry Healy

What Is Physics, Anyway?

Physics is the study of matter and energy. Through performing experiments, physicists try to find laws that can describe the universe. The following activities teach some basic principles of physics. Most of the materials can be found in your classroom or home. Ask parents to help you collect any other items.

Resources on Physics

Learn more about teaching physics or find great physics-related activities in these books and Web sites *(current as of March 2006).*
- *Mechanics Fundamentals: Funtastic Science Activities for Kids* by Robert W. Wood
- *Magic Science: 50 Jaw-Dropping, Mind-Boggling, Head-Scratching Activities for Kids* by Jim Wiese
- *How Come?* by Kathy Wollard
- *365 Simple Science Experiments With Everyday Materials* by E. Richard Churchill, Louis V. Loeschnig, and Muriel Mandell
- Amusement Park Physics: http://www.learner.org/exhibits/parkphysics/
- Rader's Physics4Kids: http://www.kapili.com/physics4kids/index.html

Bernoulli's Ball
Materials: handheld blow-dryer, 3 Ping-Pong® balls

Explore an important law of physics with a demonstration that seems to defy gravity. Hold a blow-dryer so that the nozzle points up; then turn it on. Place a Ping-Pong® ball in the middle of the air stream and release it so that the ball remains suspended in midair. Ask students why they think the ball stays suspended. Then explain that this demonstrates a law of physics called *Bernoulli's principle.* This law states that when air flows very fast, its pressure is low; when air flows slowly, its pressure is high. Because air coming from the dryer is moving very fast, the area surrounding the ball has low pressure. The air outside this low-pressure area has a higher pressure, which keeps the ball in place. The force of the air from the dryer pushes the ball up while gravity pulls it down, keeping the ball suspended. Ask students how Bernoulli's principle might be used in real life. Then explain that engineers use this law to design the wings of airplanes. For fun, challenge a student to add a second and then a third ball. But watch out—the balls may take flight!

I'll Huff and I'll Puff...
Materials: plastic funnel, Ping-Pong® ball

Follow up the activity on page 114 with another easy-to-do activity that demonstrates Bernoulli's principle. Place a Ping-Pong® ball inside a plastic funnel. Ask students, "If I point this funnel up and blow into it as hard as I can, will I blow the ball out?" After tallying responses, tilt your head back and blow steadily into the funnel as shown. Surprise—you won't be able to blow the ball out! Ask students why; then explain that this demonstration illustrates Bernoulli's principle like the previous one using the blow-dryer. The flow of air rushing out of the funnel surrounds the ball and creates an area of low pressure on the ball's underside. The greater pressure of the atmosphere holds the ball in the funnel.

Next, ask students if blowing harder into the funnel will make the ball move. Then try it. Have students predict why the ball stays more firmly in place. *(The harder you blow, the more you lower the pressure on the ball's underside and the more the atmosphere's pressure will push the ball into the funnel.)*

A "Spudtacular" Straw
Materials: bowl of water, paper towel, large potato, paper drinking straw

Investigate the physics principle of *inertia* with this "spudtacular" demonstration! Follow these steps:

1. Soak the potato in the bowl of water for 30 minutes.
2. Pat the potato dry with a paper towel. Then place it on a table.
3. Ask students, "Do you think I can pierce the potato with this paper straw without damaging the straw?" Tally their responses on the board.
4. Hold the straw about two feet above the potato. Then thrust it straight down into the potato. The straw will penetrate the potato without bending.

Explain that this demonstration illustrates a law of physics called Newton's first law of motion, or the law of inertia. It was first stated by Sir Isaac Newton, an English scientist and mathematician in the 1600s. The law states that an object at rest tends to stay at rest unless acted on by an outside force. An object in motion will tend to continue moving in a straight line at a constant speed. In this demonstration, the potato is an object at rest that remains at rest. The straw is an object in motion that keeps moving in a straight line. Explain to students that hay straws growing in fields have been driven into wooden boards during extremely strong winds such as those experienced during a tornado.

The Balloon 500

Materials per group: drinking straw, 12' length of string, 2 chairs, small binder clip, balloon, measuring tape, tape

For a science lesson that your kids will talk about for days, make "vroom" for this experiment! Divide the class into groups. Then distribute the materials above, making sure to give each group the same size balloon. Guide students through these steps.

1. Run the string through the straw. Then tape one end of the string to the back of a chair as shown. Tape the other end of the string to another chair. Move the chairs apart so that the string is taut. (Make sure your chairs are aligned with those of the other groups.)
2. Put two four-inch strips of tape across the straw as shown.
3. Blow up the balloon and close it with a binder clip. Measure the balloon's circumference. Write your group's name and the circumference on the board. Then attach the balloon to the straw using the tape.
4. Gently pull the straw until the clipped end of the balloon almost touches the chair.
5. At your teacher's signal, release the binder clip. Observe which balloon wins the race.

binder clip

Give each group a new balloon and repeat the race. Then ask, "Is there a relationship between the circumference of the balloon and the race results?" Examine the circumferences listed on the board and discuss the question. Then explain that this race illustrates Newton's third law of motion, which states that "for every action, there is an equal and opposite reaction." When a rocket lifts from a launchpad, it expels gas out of its engine (the action, called *thrust*). The rocket then moves in the opposite direction (the reaction). In this experiment, the balloon (rocket) with the largest circumference will expel more air (gas), giving the balloon greater thrust.

Attention Race Fans!
The Balloon 500
Is
Today!!!

Picturing Physics

Materials per student: copy of page 118; crayons, markers, or colored pencils

Examples of Newton's third law of motion are all around us! For instance, when you hit a baseball with a bat, the bat exerts a force (action) on the ball. The ball exerts an equal and opposite force on the bat—proven by the tingly feeling in your hands! Explore this principle further with the reproducible on page 118. Give each student or student pair a copy of the page and the materials listed above. Have students complete the activity as directed. Then discuss their cartoons together. If desired, have students cut out their pictures and post them on a bulletin board titled "Picturing Newton's Third Law of Motion."

Roller Coaster Physics

Materials per group: 6' length of ¾" or 1" plastic tubing, 5 or 6 BBs, masking tape, ruler, copy of page 119, pencil, wall space

What kid isn't thrilled by a speeding roller coaster? Turn that fascination into a lesson on potential and kinetic energy with the reproducible activity on page 119. Before distributing the materials, divide the class into groups. Designate a wall space for each group to use in completing the experiment. Also provide time for each group to demonstrate its coaster design.

The Great Sipper Challenge

Materials per student: copy of the reproducible below and the materials listed on it

Quench your students' thirst for hands-on science with the "sip-sational" experiment below. Provide each student with the materials listed. Then have her complete the activity as directed. Discuss students' results and their answers to questions 1 and 2. Explain that when a person sucks on a straw, he creates lower pressure in his mouth. The atmosphere outside the straw exerts greater pressure—so much greater that it actually pushes the liquid up the straw. If you could reduce the pressure in your mouth and lungs to create a perfect vacuum (which you can't), you could sip water from a straw that was about 30 feet long! But since you can only lower the pressure in your mouth by a certain amount, the water can't rise more than about six feet. End the activity by having students answer and discuss question 3.

Name _____

Experiment: air pressure

The Great Sipper Challenge

Thirsty? Then pucker up for this experiment that investigates the physics behind a drinking straw!

Materials: cup of water, 8 plastic drinking straws, ruler, scissors, tape, pencil

Steps:
1. Answer question 1.
2. Cut two half-inch slits into one end of a straw as shown. Repeat with another straw.
3. Connect the two straws at the slits so that they overlap. Tape the joint.
4. Try to sip water through your long straw.
5. Repeat Steps 2 and 3 to connect another straw to your long one. Repeat Step 4.
6. Continue adding straws until you can't get a sip up the long straw.
7. Answer questions 2–3 on the back of this page.

½-inch slits

Answer these questions on the back of this sheet.
1. How many straws do you think you can connect and still sip water into your mouth?
2. How many straws did you successfully use to get a sip of water?
3. How does a drinking straw work?

Picturing Physics

If you've ever heard of Sir Isaac Newton, you can thank an apple. Newton was an English scientist and mathematician in the 1600s. According to a legend, the young Newton saw an apple fall from an apple tree. He thought about the accident and figured out an important scientific principle. It's known as Newton's third law of motion.

Look out below!

Directions: Read Newton's law and the examples below. In each photo, draw a cartoon that illustrates a real-life example of this principle. On the lines, explain how the picture illustrates Newton's law.

For every action, there is an equal and opposite reaction.

Examples:
- When you hit a baseball with a bat, the bat exerts a force (action) on the ball. The ball exerts an equal and opposite force on the bat—proven by the tingly feeling in your hands.
- You exert a force (action) on a trampoline when you jump on it. The trampoline exerts an equal and opposite force that causes you to bounce up.

Note to the teacher: Use with "Picturing Physics" on page 116. Have students complete this page independently or in pairs. Provide students with crayons, markers, or colored pencils. If desired, have students cut out their photos to display on a bulletin board titled "Picturing Newton's Third Law of Motion."

Roller Coaster Physics

You're riding on the world's largest roller coaster. As you race down the track, you're the perfect example of kinetic energy. *Kinetic energy* is the energy of moving objects. As you sit in your stopped car at the crest of the roller coaster's highest hill, you're an example of potential energy. *Potential energy* is stored energy that can be changed into kinetic energy.

Design your own roller coaster to experiment with potential and kinetic energy. Just follow the steps below.

Materials: 6' length of ¾" or 1" plastic tubing, 5 or 6 BBs, masking tape, ruler, pencil, large wall space

Steps:

1. On your group's wall space, tape the tubing to make a roller coaster that has hills, valleys, and loops. (See the example.) Remember that the only power the coaster (a BB) will have is gravity and kinetic energy.

2. Release one or more BBs in the starting end of the tubing. If the BBs don't make it up a hill or get all the way through your model, revise the design. To remove a BB, untape the tubing and lower one end until the BB falls out. **Do not suck on the tube.**

Sample Design

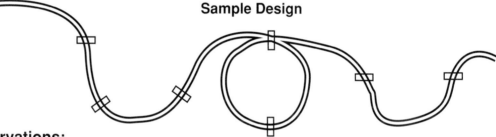

Observations:

1. What happened on your first trial? _____
   _____

2. Did you have to rework your model? _____ What did you learn as you reworked the model? _____
   _____

3. Measure the difference between the height of your first hill and the lowest point of your first valley. What is the difference? _____ What is the difference between the highest point of your design and the lowest point? _____
   _____

4. Draw a diagram of your roller coaster on the back of this page. Label the following:
   • the point of the greatest potential energy
   • the point where the greatest potential energy is converted to kinetic energy
   • the point where the BBs travel the fastest
   • the point where the BBs travel the slowest

Conclusion: On the back of this sheet or on another sheet of paper, explain why a roller coaster car doesn't need an engine to drive it. Use the terms *potential energy* and *kinetic energy* in your explanation.

Chemistry for Kids

Creative, Hands-on Activities for Teaching Chemistry

Why teach about chemistry? Because chemistry is all around us and is an important part of everyday life, from burning campfires to digesting food! So turn your students into a happy herd of budding chemists with the following hands-on activities.

by Cindy Mondello

Background Information

Anything that takes up space and has weight is *matter*. *Chemistry* is the study of matter and the changes that take place with that matter. Chemical changes take place when a substance breaks down or combines with another to produce one or more new substances that have different properties. Chemists study why a chemical change takes place and how it can be controlled. This knowledge has led to the development of many inventions, including synthetic fibers, drugs, and other useful substances.

Chemistry involves all of the senses: hearing, sight, smell, taste, and touch. It helps us understand and explain many of the events that we observe in daily life.

Safety in the Science Classroom

Make safety the first order of business when conducting any science experiment that involves chemicals by following these tips:

- Store equipment and materials properly.
- Always supervise students when they work with chemicals. Give clear, complete directions before students begin.
- Remind students not to taste or touch substances without your permission.
- Warn students not to touch their eyes, mouths, faces, or bodies when working with chemicals.
- Direct students to wash their hands thoroughly after completing an activity.
- To avoid waste, dispense chemicals in small containers.
- Insist that students measure amounts carefully. No dumping!
- Be especially careful with candle flames. Tie back long hair and roll up loose sleeves.
- Make sure students are aware of fire drill and other emergency procedures.

Materials List

Ask students and their parents to help you gather the following inexpensive, easy-to-find materials to use with the activities on pages 121–125.

- tall, slender glass jar
- 7-Up
- peanuts (do not request if you have students with peanut allergies)
- small foam cup
- bowl or pot
- deep glass measuring cup
- metal spoon
- hard-boiled egg (peeled)
- food coloring
- Ziploc bags
- 2 small pieces of cardboard
- small blocks of wood
- 12-oz. clear drinking glasses
- rulers
- paper
- paper towels
- bucket or bowl

- balloons
- 20-oz. soda bottle
- hot and cold water
- pennies
- saucers or small plates
- white vinegar
- salt
- sand
- baby food jars
- large glass jar
- light-colored cooking oil
- corn syrup
- craft sticks and plastic spoons
- stopwatch or watch with a second hand

A Chemistry Magic Show
Teacher Demonstrations:
Building an interest in chemistry

Mystify your kids and get them excited about chemistry right from the start by performing these magical "How'd *that* happen?" demonstrations.

- **Performing Peanuts:** Fill a tall, slender glass jar with 7-Up. Drop several peanuts into the jar. *They're up! Now they're down! The carbon dioxide gas from the soda collects on the peanuts, making them lighter than the soda. The peanuts then float to the surface. When the peanuts reach the surface, the carbon dioxide gas is released into the air, making the peanuts sink to the bottom again.* **Warning:** Do not conduct this demonstration if you have students with peanut allergies.

- **Disappearing Liquid:** Mix exactly one cup of rubbing alcohol and one cup of water together in a bowl or pot. Stir well. Allow a student volunteer to use a measuring cup to measure the mixture carefully and then pour it into another container. *Be ready for a surprise and exclamations of "It shrank!" When water molecules connect, small empty pockets are formed. These pockets are filled with the alcohol molecules, causing the combined volume to be less than two cups.*

- **Vanishing Cup:** Place a small foam cup in a deep glass measuring cup. Pour a small amount of acetone into the measuring cup. *Hey, where did the foam go? The acetone dissolves the Styrofoam cup and releases the trapped gases. All that remains is a very small amount of the solid material, explaining why foam is so lightweight.*

- **Egg in a Bottle:** Remove the shell from a hard-boiled egg. Light a small strip of paper with a match and drop it into a glass bottle. (A two-quart glass apple-juice bottle works well.) Place the egg, narrow end down, on top of the bottle. *Watch the egg closely—it will make its move in a flash! The burning paper heats up the air in the bottle, causing it to expand and force its way out of the bottle. The paper then stops burning when the egg is placed on top of the bottle. The air cools and contracts, forcing the egg to be sucked into the bottle.*

- **Rising Water:** Rinse out four empty 16-ounce glass bottles. Add food coloring to two of the bottles; then fill them to the top with hot water. Next add cold water to the remaining two bottles. Place a small piece of cardboard on top of one of the cold bottles and invert the bottle over a hot-water bottle. Repeat with the other two bottles, this time inverting the hot-water bottle over the cold one. Carefully remove both pieces of cardboard from the bottles. *In the first setup, the warm water in the bottom bottle is less dense than the cold water in the top bottle, so it rises into the bottle of cold water. The denser cold water flows down into the bottle of hot water. In the second setup, the cold water in the bottom bottle doesn't rise since it is denser than the warmer water above it.*

Chemical Connections on the Web

Want to kid around with chemistry while surfing the Internet? Check out the following Web sites (current as of March 2006) to learn more about the wonderful world of chemistry:
- http://www.chem4kids.com

The Truth of the Matter
Student Experiment: Forms of matter

Give meaning to matter with this simple classroom activity. Begin by explaining to students that matter comes in three physical states: solid, liquid, and gas. Then provide each student pair with three Ziploc® bags, a small block of wood, one cup of water, a ruler, and a copy of page 124. Have the pair follow the directions on the reproducible to learn more about three important states where no one lives!

That's 'un-baaaa-lievable'!

It's a Matter of Space
Student Experiments: Characteristics of matter

Show students that all matter—even matter you can't see—takes up space with the following experiments.

Problem: How can a piece of paper stay dry when submerged in water?

Materials for each group of students: 12-ounce clear drinking glass, piece of paper or paper towel, bucket or bowl (taller than the glass), water

Steps:
1. Fill the bucket half full with water.
2. Wad the paper into a ball; then push it into the bottom of the glass. The paper wad must remain against the bottom of the glass when the glass is turned upside down. If it falls out, make the paper ball a little larger.
3. Hold the glass vertically with its mouth pointing down.
4. Push the glass straight down into the bucket of water.
5. Without tilting it, lift the glass out of the water.
6. Remove the paper, smooth it out, and examine it. Record your observations.

The paper will be dry. Why? The glass is filled with paper and air. The air prevents the water from entering the glass, thus keeping the paper dry. This demonstrates that even though gases cannot always be seen, they do take up space.

Problem: Can a balloon be inflated inside a bottle?

Materials for each student: one 20-ounce soda bottle, balloon

Steps:
1. Blow up the balloon to test it for defects. Slowly release the air from the balloon.
2. Hold on to the mouth of the balloon and push the bottom inside the bottle.
3. Carefully stretch the mouth of the balloon over the mouth of the bottle.
4. Try to inflate the balloon by blowing into it. Record your observations.

The balloon (solid matter) only expands slightly. The bottle is filled with air (gaseous matter). Blowing into the balloon causes the air molecules inside the bottle to move slightly closer together. The air takes up space in the bottle, thus preventing the balloon from inflating. This demonstrates that matter cannot occupy the same space as other matter at the same time.

"Ch-Ch-Ch-Changes!"
Student Experiments: Chemical changes

Chemical changes happen every day. Where? For starters, right inside your body! The food you eat combines with oxygen and causes a chemical change. The result is a release of heat and energy. Every time you take a drive in your car, a chemical change takes place as gasoline is burned. Chemists also produce chemical changes that result in new products that help make our lives better and easier. Investigate some simple chemical changes with the experiments that follow.

Problem: How can a penny turn green?
Materials for each group: saucer or small plate, paper towel, white vinegar, 3–5 pennies
Steps:
1. Fold the paper towel twice to make a square; then place it on the saucer.
2. Carefully pour just enough vinegar into the saucer to moisten the paper towel.
3. Place the pennies on top of the wet towel.
4. Wait 24 hours; then remove the pennies.
5. Describe the pennies' appearance. Were there any changes?
6. Save the pennies for the next experiment.

The chemical name for vinegar is acetic acid. *The acetate in this acid combines with the copper on the pennies to form the green coating composed of* copper acetate.

Problem: How can the green pennies be cleaned?
Materials for each group: green-coated pennies from the experiment above, 1 tablespoon salt, 4 tablespoons white vinegar, baby food jar, spoon, water, paper towels
Steps:
1. Mix the salt and vinegar in the baby food jar.
2. Place several pennies in the jar.
3. Wait for a few minutes; then remove the pennies.
4. Rinse the pennies with water, and dry them on paper towels.
5. Describe the pennies' appearance. Is there any change?

The vinegar and salt combine to produce a new chemical called hydrochloric acid. *This acid has the ability to shine the copper pennies instantly.*

Red, White, and "Oooooo!"
Teacher Demonstration: Density of matter

One way a chemical can be identified is by its density. *Density* measures how tightly packed the particles of a substance are. The higher the density, the more tightly packed the particles. Help students learn that liquids have different densities with a demonstration that serves up a liquid sandwich!

Materials: 3 small jars or glasses, 1 large glass jar, rubbing alcohol, light-colored cooking oil, corn syrup, red food coloring, blue food coloring, 2 craft sticks
Steps:
1. Fill three small jars with equal amounts of the following liquids (one liquid per jar): cooking oil, corn syrup, and rubbing alcohol.
2. Add several drops of blue food coloring to the corn syrup and several drops of red food coloring to the alcohol. Stir each with a craft stick.
3. Pour the three liquids into a larger jar in the following order: corn syrup, oil, alcohol.
4. Ask students to describe what happens.

The corn syrup will sink to the bottom of the jar because it's the most dense of the three liquids. The alcohol, which is the least dense, will float on top of the oil. The oil will float in between the syrup and the alcohol.

124

As a Matter of Fact

Did you know that there are three important states where no one lives? Well, as a matter of fact, there are! Get the facts straight on these three states of matter by following the directions below with a partner.

Materials: 3 Ziploc® bags, small block of wood, cup of water, ruler

Steps:

1. Place the block of wood in one bag.
2. Carefully pour the cup of water into another bag; then seal it.
3. Blow air into the third bag and quickly seal it.
4. Use the information below to guide you in examining the three states of matter in your bags. Then answer the questions that follow.

SOLID MATTER: Wood

Can you easily see the wood? _____

Does the piece of wood take up space? _____

Gently squeeze the wood. Can you change its shape with a squeeze? _____

Poke the wood with the ruler. Does the ruler go through the wood? _____

What can you conclude about solids? _____

LIQUID MATTER: Water

Can you easily see the water? _____

Does the water take up space? _____

Lay down your bag and gently press your hand on the bag. Can you make the water fill the whole bag? _____

Gently squeeze the bag of water. Can you change the water's shape with a squeeze? _____

Open the bag and put the ruler through the water. Can you do this easily? _____

What can you conclude about liquids? _____

GASEOUS MATTER: Air

Can you easily see the air? _____

Does the air take up space? _____

Gently squeeze the bag of air. Can you change its shape with a squeeze? _____

Open the bag and put the ruler through the air. Can you do this easily? _____

What can you conclude about gases? _____

Bonus Box: List five examples of each state of matter on the back of this page. Try to think of examples that no one else will think of.

Note to the teacher: Use with "The Truth of the Matter" on page 122. After discussing the questions, have students share their Bonus Box answers as you list their responses on the board. Then divide the class into three groups, one per state of matter. Have each group create a poster about its state, using the list on the board, pictures cut from old magazines, and other art materials.

And the Race Is On!

Will food coloring dissolve faster in hot water or cold water? Rev up your engines and start the race to find out!

Materials: 2 baby food jars, 2 bottles of food coloring, hot water, cold water, stopwatch or watch with a second hand

Steps:

1. Fill one jar with very cold water.
2. Fill the other jar with an equal amount of hot water.
3. At exactly the same time, drop three drops of food coloring into each jar.
4. Use a stopwatch to time how long it takes for the food coloring to spread throughout each jar.

Observe: Compare the movement of the color in the two jars.
How long did it take for the color to spread through the hot water? _____
How long did it take for the color to spread through the cold water? _____
In which jar did the color spread more rapidly? _____
Why do you think this happened? _____
_____

A Mixture Mix-Up

Kendra the Chemistry Whiz Kid has experienced a mishap. Someone mixed up her mixtures! Help Kendra decide which mixture is the *solution* and which is the *suspension* by following the directions below.

> • **Solution:** a mixture of substances that are evenly mixed and do not easily separate
> • **Suspension:** a mixture of substances that do not dissolve and can be easily separated. A suspension must be constantly shaken for its substances to remain mixed.

Materials: 2 clear plastic cups, sand, salt, water, 2 spoons

Steps:

1. Fill one cup three-fourths full of water. Add one spoonful of sand and stir.
2. Fill a second cup three-fourths full of water. Add one spoonful of salt and stir.
3. Compare the two mixtures. Which is the solution, and which is the suspension? Record your conclusions on the lines below. Be sure to include reasons for your conclusions.

_____
_____
_____

Note to the teacher: Use "And the Race Is On!" to demonstrate the movement of molecules. Use "A Mixture Mix-Up" to demonstrate the differences between a solution and a suspension.

Investigating Invisible Forces

Electrifying Activities About Electricity and Magnetism

May the forces of electricity and magnetism be with your students as they investigate the following "electri-cool" activities and experiments!

by Dr. Barbara B. Leonard, Winston-Salem, NC

May the Magnetism Be With You!

Topic: Magnetism

Invite students to explore the force of magnetism with these "magnet-ificent" challenges!

Materials for each pair of students: three 1⅛" ring magnets, pencil, compass, craft stick, masking tape, transparency, iron filings

Steps:

1. Thread three magnets on a pencil so they repel one another. (Like poles must be facing each other.) Push the magnets together. Describe what you feel *(the repelling force between like poles).*

2. Stand a ring magnet on its side. Bring a compass near it. Determine the magnet's north and south poles. *(The painted tip of a compass's magnetic needle, the north end, swings away, or repels, when near the north pole. The tip is attracted to, or points toward, the magnet when near the south pole.)*

3. Use a loop of tape to affix a magnet to one end of a craft stick. Place another magnet on its side nearby. Slide the stick toward the second magnet until this second magnet moves away from the stick. (If the magnets attract instead of repel, flip the second magnet and try again.)

4. Cover a ring magnet with a transparency. Sprinkle iron filings on the transparency. Describe what you see. *(The alignment of the filings illustrates a magnetic field around the magnet. More filings will concentrate at the poles since the magnetic field is stronger in those areas.)*

A Simple Circular Path

Topic: Electrical energy's circular path

What path does electrical energy travel? To find out, give each pair of students a flashlight bulb, a D battery, and 15 cm of 22-gauge hookup wire (available from electronics stores such as RadioShack). Strip an inch of plastic from both ends of the wire. Then challenge students to use the materials to light the bulb. Have them also draw each arrangement they try. After discussing the drawings, guide students to conclude that the configurations that make the bulb light are circular (see the illustrations) and are called *circuits.* Explain that a lighted bulb represents a *closed circuit,* a path that is complete so electricity can flow freely. Ask students how to open a circuit and interrupt the flow of electrical energy to turn off the bulb. *(Remove a wire from the battery or from the bulb's base.)* Conclude by connecting this investigation to a classroom light switch. *(Turning the switch on completes the circuit, while turning it off breaks the circuit.)*

Create **personal battery testers** for students to use! Just cut strands of miniature holiday lights into single-bulb sections. Then strip an inch of plastic from each end of a section as shown. To complete a circuit, hold the wires on a battery as shown. If the bulb lights, the battery is good!

Electricity in Action

Topic: Open and closed circuits

Electrify your students by helping them build two devices that demonstrate open and closed circuits.

Buzzer Beater

Materials for each group: 50 cm thin, uninsulated copper wire; 9 cm x 20 cm piece of cardboard; 2 brads; D battery; 1.5–3.0 volt buzzer (available from an electronics store such as RadioShack); 30 cm hookup wire with ends stripped; 3 paper clips (2 large, 1 small); masking tape; pint-jar lid; pencil; ruler

Steps:

1. Tape the large paper clips to the battery's ends as shown. Place the battery in the lid.
2. Use the pencil to make a hole three centimeters from each short end of the cardboard. Fasten a brad through each hole.
3. Connect each end of the copper wire to a brad. Bend the wire in the shape of a roller coaster track.
4. Snap the small paper clip over the left brad. Connect the buzzer's black wire to the paper clip and its red wire to the paper clip at the battery's positive (raised) end.
5. Connect one end of the hookup wire to the paper clip at the battery's negative (flat) end. Bend a hook at the other end of the wire and hold it around one end of the copper track. Try to move the hook along the track without making the buzzer sound. *(If the hook touches the roller coaster track, you've created a closed circuit which will cause the buzzer to sound.)*

Step 3   Step 7

Do-It-Yourself Flashlight

Materials for each student: toilet paper tube cut in half vertically, 10 cm wire with ends stripped, 12 cm wire with ends stripped, 2 brads, 2 D batteries, flashlight bulb, 2 small paper clips, masking tape, 1" x 2½" strip of index card, pencil, 7 cm aluminum foil circle with 1 cm center hole

Steps:

1. Place the strip atop the outside center of a tube half. Use a pencil to make two holes about an inch apart through the strip and tube.
2. Insert a brad through each hole. Snap one end of a paper clip over a brad.
3. Inside the tube half, hook one end of the ten-centimeter wire to a brad and tape it in place as shown. Then tape the wire's other end to one battery's negative (flat) end. Bend the wire, if necessary.
4. Repeat Step 3 to attach the 12-centimeter wire to the remaining brad as shown.
5. Position the negative (flat) end of the second battery atop the positive (raised) end of the first battery. Tape the batteries together.
6. Open the remaining paper clip into an S shape and bend it to form a 90-degree angle as shown. Tape the paper clip's smaller hook outside the top of the tube.
7. Slide the flashlight bulb into the paper clip's larger hook. Wrap the wire from the tube's top tightly around the bulb's metal base. Adjust the paper clip so the bottom of the bulb touches the battery's positive end. Tape in place.
8. Tape the second tube half to the first one at the sides so the tubes fit tightly around the batteries. Tape across the tube's bottom to support the batteries.
9. Slip the foil circle over the bulb and tape it to the tube. Turn on the flashlight by swinging the paper clip to touch the other brad.

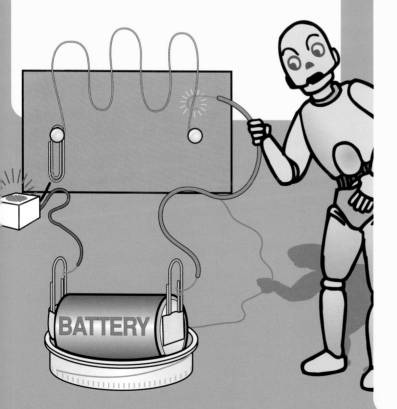

BATTERY

Sticky-Note Circuit Boards

Topic: Completing circuits on a circuit board

Construct simple circuit boards in a snap with these easy-to-follow directions!

Materials for each pair or group: two 3" x 3" sticky notes, three ¼" x 4" strips of aluminum foil, clear tape, personal battery tester from "A Simple Circular Path" on page 126, D battery, access to a hole puncher, scissors

Steps:

1. Place a sticky note on your desk with its gummed edge at the top. Punch three holes on each side and number the holes as shown. Then flip the note so the gummed edge is faceup.
2. Use a foil strip to cover a hole on the left side and on the right side of the note. (Trim the strip if needed.) Cover the strip with tape to hold it in place. Repeat with the other holes as shown.
3. Holding the second sticky note facedown and so its gummed edge is at the bottom, press it onto the first note so that the foil strips are sandwiched between the notes. Flip the resulting circuit board so its holes are faceup.
4. To determine which pairs of holes make a complete circuit, place the top (positive end) of the battery on one hole. Hold one end of the tester's wire to the battery's bottom (negative end). Touch the other wire to a hole on the opposite side of the note. If the circuit is complete, the bulb will light. Make a drawing to show which pairs of holes make complete circuits.

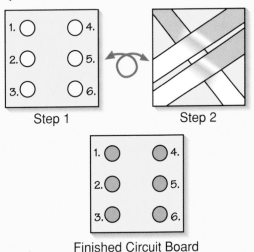

Step 1   Step 2

Finished Circuit Board

It's All in the Lineup!

Topic: Parallel and series circuits

Use the following investigation to help students understand the difference between parallel and series circuits.

Materials for each pair of students: 2 D batteries, 3 personal battery testers from "A Simple Circular Path" on page 126, 2 large paper clips, masking tape, half of a toilet paper tube

Steps:

1. Tape the batteries together, positive end to negative end. Then cradle them in the tube half as shown.
2. Tape a paper clip on the raised metal tip of the top battery. Tape a second clip to the bottom battery as shown.
3. Connect the battery testers as directed below.

Parallel circuit—Connect each end of each tester to a different paper clip. Observe the lighted bulbs. Pull one bulb from its socket. What happens? Remove a second bulb. What happens? *(When one bulb is removed, the other bulbs remain lighted because each light makes its own complete circuit.)*

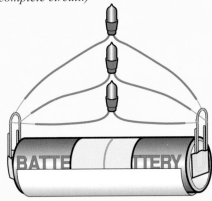

Series circuit—Twist the wires of all three testers together end to end. Connect the unused ends of the first and third testers to the paper clips as shown. Observe the lighted bulbs. Then pull one bulb from its socket. What happens? *(The lights go out because the energy is flowing in one path, and the circuit is broken.)* Replace the bulb. Then remove the middle tester from the strand. What happens? *(The circuit is broken and the bulbs will not be lighted.)* Now connect the loose ends of the remaining two testers. What happens? *(The bulbs are lighted because the circuit is complete again.)*

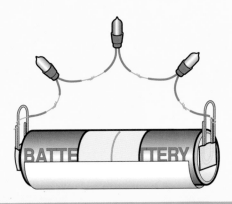

Team members_____

Making the Grade

Duke has just radioed your research team that he and his crew have very little copper wire on their spacecraft. Let him know which of the onboard materials he could use in an emergency to conduct electricity. Follow the steps below to see which materials make the grade.

Materials that allow electric current to flow through them easily are called conductors.

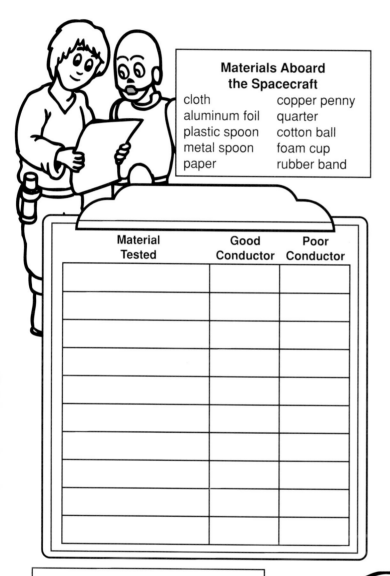

Materials Aboard the Spacecraft

cloth   copper penny
aluminum foil   quarter
plastic spoon   cotton ball
metal spoon   foam cup
paper   rubber band

Material Tested	Good Conductor	Poor Conductor

Materials: D battery, personal battery tester

Directions:

1. List the materials Duke has on board in the chart on the left.
2. To test each material, hold it on one end of the battery as shown. Touch the end of one tester wire to the material. Touch the end of the other tester wire to the other end of the battery as shown. If the bulb lights, the material is a good conductor. Make a ✓ mark in the chart to show your results.
3. Complete a message to Duke on the lines below.

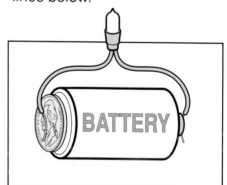

BATTERY

Duke,
    You can use the following materials if you run out of copper wire: _____
_____
_____
_____

Bonus Box: Poor conductors are sometimes called *insulators*. Look at the items you identified in the chart as poor conductors. Why do you think electricians wear or use items made of these materials?

A Temporary Picker-Upper

Uh-oh! Sam just spilled a box of paper clips on the spaceship's floor. If he had a magnet, he'd pick up the clips in a flash. But all he has are the materials listed below. He knows that electricity flowing in a coil can magnetize an iron bar and create an *electromagnet*. Help him pick up the clips by making an electromagnet according to the directions below.

Materials: 2 D batteries, 2 lengths (4" and 36") of hookup wire with ends stripped, masking tape, large steel nail, knife switch, small screwdriver, 10 to 20 paper clips

Directions:

1. Wrap the 36-inch wire around the nail ten times, leaving the ends free.
2. Tape one end of the wrapped wire to one end of a D battery. Connect the other end of the wrapped wire to one end of the knife switch. Open the switch.
3. Connect one end of the four-inch wire to the other end of the switch. Tighten the screws with the screwdriver. Tape the other end of the four-inch wire to the opposite end of the battery.
4. Close the switch to complete the circuit. See how many paper clips the electromagnet can pick up. Record this number in the chart.
5. Wrap the wire ten more times around the nail. Then repeat Step 4.
6. Repeat Step 5 as many times as possible, each time adding ten more coils.
7. Disconnect the wires from the battery. Tape two batteries end to end. Then reconnect the wires and repeat Steps 4–6.
8. Write your observations on the lines.

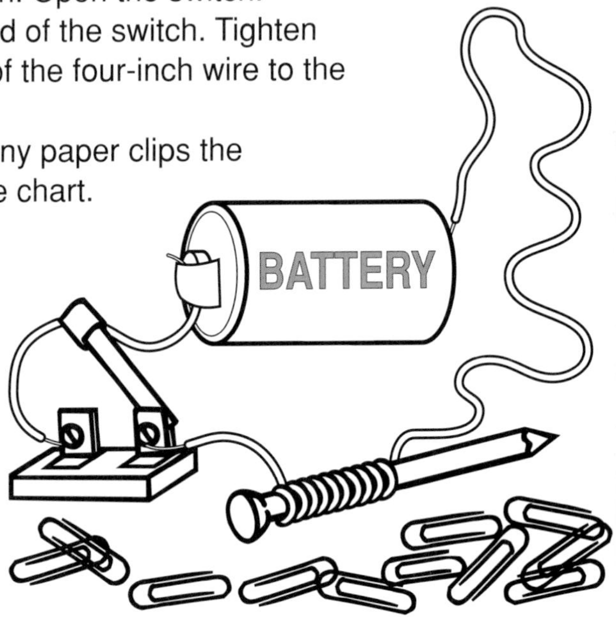

One Battery		Two Batteries	
Number of Coils	Clips Picked Up	Number of Coils	Clips Picked Up
10		10	

What I observed: _____

_____

_____

_____

_____

_____

_____

_____

Bonus Box: Do you think your test results would differ if you used three D batteries? Explain.

Shedding Light on Color

Light up your science curriculum with these bright ideas on investigating the relationship between light and color!

by Dr. Barbara B. Leonard,
Winston-Salem, NC

Fascinating Facts About Light and Color

- Sir Isaac Newton discovered that white light forms when all the colors of the spectrum are mixed together.
- A *spectrum* is produced when white light is broken into a band of different colors: red, orange, yellow, green, blue, indigo (bluish purple), and violet.
- Water droplets, bubbles, and other curved or angled surfaces bend, or *refract,* white light, separating the white light into bands of colors.
- When an object absorbs all the colors in the spectrum, it reflects the light it absorbed and appears black.

Spin Those Colors!

Concept: Blending colors to make white light

Put a new spin on your students' understanding of color with this hands-on activity. First, explain that Sir Isaac Newton discovered that sunlight is made of different colors: red, orange, yellow, green, blue, indigo (bluish purple), and violet. These colors form a band called a *spectrum.* To help students see how the colors of the spectrum create white light, give each child a copy of the color wheel pattern on page 134 and crayons or markers in the following colors: red, orange, yellow, green, blue, indigo, and violet. Have the student color the wheel's parts as labeled. Then have him spin the wheel using a method listed below and describe what happens. *(The colors blend into a creamy color because the human eye cannot detect different colors at this speed.)* Follow up by having students make more color wheels to see what happens when they spin a wheel that is half red and half yellow, half red and half blue, or half blue and half yellow.

Spinning Methods
- Poke a short, sharpened pencil (such as a golf pencil) through the center of the wheel. Spin the pencil like a top.
- Punch a hole in the center of the wheel; then place it on a record player's turntable. Play the record player at its highest speed.
- Remove one of the two beaters from a handheld electric mixer. Tape the wheel to the bottom of the remaining beater. With your teacher's help, operate the mixer at its highest speed.

To find out more about color, visit **www.crayola.com**!
(Current as of March 2006)

Spotlighting Great Light and Color Books

Janice VanCleave's Physics for Every Kid: 101 Easy Experiments in Motion, Heat, Light, Machines, and Sound by Janice VanCleave

Light & Color by Frank Millson

Color Is in the Eye of the Beholder!

Concept: How cones in the human eye detect light

Open students' eyes to the workings of *cones,* the light-sensitive cells in the center of the retina. Explain to students that each of three kinds of cones responds most strongly to a different color: blue, green, or red. If overused, cones can get tired and stop working briefly. When this happens, other cones help out, producing an interesting effect called an *afterimage.* After this discussion, guide students through the steps below.

Materials for each student: blue, green, yellow, and black crayons or markers; scissors; sheet of white paper; copy of the heart, flag, and square patterns on page 134; stopwatch or clock with a second hand

Steps:
1. Cut out the patterns.
2. Color the heart pattern green and place it next to the white paper. Stare at the heart's black dot for 30 seconds while a partner times you. Then look directly at the white paper. *(After several seconds, a fuzzy red heart should appear on the white paper.)*
3. Color yellow the area on the flag that normally includes stars. Color green every other stripe on the flag, beginning with the first stripe and ending with the last. Color the remaining stripes black. Place the flag next to the white paper. Stare at the flag's black dot for 30 seconds; then look at the white paper. *(Old Glory should show its true colors of red, white, and blue.)*
4. Color the diamond in the small square yellow. Color the remaining area blue. Place the small square next to the white paper. Stare at the dot on the yellow diamond for 30 seconds. Then look at the white paper. *(The colors should be reversed, with the diamond being blue and the remaining area yellow.)*

Check out this interesting site for more exciting activities and experiments with color! *(Current as of March 2006)*
www.exploratorium.edu/snacks/iconcolor.html

Your Order, Please

Concept: Food color and appetite

If your students could have blue, green, red, or yellow mashed potatoes, which would they pick and why? Turn your classroom into a cafeteria to find out! Ask parent volunteers to prepare bowls of instant mashed potatoes and elbow macaroni, each cooked in water heavily tinted with a different color of food coloring. Have other volunteers provide pitchers of different-colored juices or drink mixes, plus plasticware, paper plates, cups, and napkins. Arrange everything on a table; then have students go through cafeteria-style to choose what they want to eat. While students eat, have each child write a paragraph explaining why she chose the colors of foods that she did. Allow students to share their paragraphs. Then give each child a small bag of M&M's candies and direct her to record the order in which she eats the candies. Is there a color connection? *(Color and food appeal are closely related. For example, blue is an appetite suppressant. Greens, browns, reds, and several other colors are generally thought to be more appealing in terms of appetite.)*

Mixing the Light Fantastic
Concept: Mixing the primary colors of light

It's a trade secret known by lighting technicians everywhere: when all three *primary additive colors of light* (red, green, and blue) are mixed together, white light is produced. Mixing only two primary colors of light produces a different color. For example, mixing red and blue produces magenta (purplish red), mixing blue and green makes cyan (bluish green), and mixing red and green makes yellow. After discussing this information with the class, have students conduct the following experiment on mixing colors of light.

Materials: 3 heavy-duty flashlights; 8-inch squares of red, blue, and green cellophane (two of each color); 3 wide rubber bands; Ping-Pong® ball; sheet of white paper

Steps:

1. Use a rubber band to cover the light on each flashlight with two same-colored squares of cellophane.
2. Darken the room. Shine all three flashlights onto the white paper so that their beams mix. What do you see? *(You should see white light.)*
3. Shine only the red and green lights on the white paper so that their beams mix. What do you see? *(You should see yellow light, a secondary color.)*
4. Place the Ping-Pong ball in the center of the white paper. Shine one light on the ball. Next, shine two different lights simultaneously on the ball. Then shine all three lights on the ball and record your observations. *(The ball should be white with three vibrant shadows of green, blue, and red around it.)*

Putting Pigments Together
Concept: Mixing the primary colors of paints and dyes

Does mixing colors in paints and dyes produce the same results as mixing colors of light? Pose this question to students; then have them find out for themselves with this activity. First, share that the primary colors of the pigments in paints and dyes are magenta (purplish red), cyan (bluish green), and yellow. These colors are different from the primary colors of light (red, blue, and green). Mixing the primary colors of light produces white light, while mixing the primary colors of pigments produces black.

After discussing this information with the class, allow students to examine a color cartridge from a printer (or a page featuring a color printer from an office supply catalog). Point out its colors: black, magenta, cyan, and yellow. Print a picture from a color printer; then have students use a magnifying glass to look for the small colorful dots that form the images. If possible, allow students to examine a section of the picture under a microscope to see how these four colors produce different shades of color. Follow up by having pairs of students complete a copy of page 135 as directed to experiment with mixing primary colors of pigments.

Looking Through Rose-Colored Glasses

Concept: The effect of color on emotions

To investigate the psychology of color, cut a supply of 1¼-inch squares from different colors of cellophane (two same-colored squares per student). Give each student two cellophane squares, two 4" x 6" index cards, scissors, tape, and a copy of the glasses pattern below. Have each student trace the pattern on each card and cut out the tracings. Then have him tape the cutouts together at the nose piece and tape a cellophane square in place for each lens. Next, have the student put on his glasses, look at an object that matches his lens color, and record what he sees and how it makes him feel. Then direct him to look at other objects (both the same as and different from the color of his glasses) and record his observations. Afterward, have students trade glasses or change one lens to a different color and repeat the activity. Discuss students' observations; then share the chart shown. For an experiment with color, see "What's Hot to Wear?" on page 136.

Common Reactions to Different Colors		
Category	Colors	Feelings Evoked
warm	red, orange, yellow	excited, stimulated, energetic
cool	green, blue, violet	calm, peaceful
neutral	brown, gray	neither excited nor calm

Patterns

Use the flag, heart, and square patterns with "Color Is in the Eye of the Beholder!" on page 132.

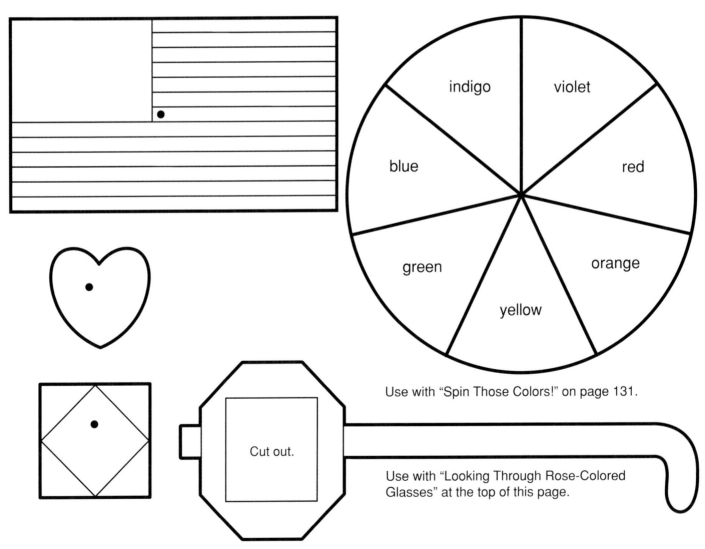

Use with "Spin Those Colors!" on page 131.

Cut out.

Use with "Looking Through Rose-Colored Glasses" at the top of this page.

Conjuring Up Colors!

If you mix together two colors of paint, will you get the same result if you mix the same two colors of markers? To find out, make a spot of color in each box below for each color or color combination in the chart. Then answer the questions.

Materials: paintbrush; water; paper towels; watercolors, tempera paints, water-based markers, crayons, and colored pencils, each in red, blue, and yellow

Color/Color Combinations

Medium	Red	Blue	Yellow	Red and blue	Red and yellow	Blue and yellow	Red, blue, and yellow
Watercolors							
Tempera paints							
Colored pencils							
Crayons							
Markers							

1. Which medium do you think is the easiest to use for mixing colors? _____
2. Which medium do you think produces the most intense colors? _____
3. Which medium do you think produces the faintest colors? _____
4. What color do you think would result if you mixed together all seven colors and color combinations in the chart? _____

©The Mailbox® • *Science* • TEC60859 • Key p. 160

Mixing It Up!

What colors do you get when you mix different colors of food coloring? Follow the steps below to find out!

Materials: 3 bottles of food coloring (red, blue, yellow), 3 bathroom-sized plastic cups, water, medicine dropper, spoon, bottom half of white Styrofoam egg carton

Steps:

1. Half-fill each cup with water.
2. Add five drops of red food coloring to one cup, five drops of blue food coloring to the second cup, and five drops of yellow food coloring to the third cup. Stir each cup.
3. Place five drops of the red solution in one well of the egg carton. To the same well, add five more drops of the red solution. Stir. Place a drop of the resulting mixture in the corresponding spot on the art palette.
4. Repeat Step 3 for each remaining combination of colors listed.
5. Allow the drops to dry.

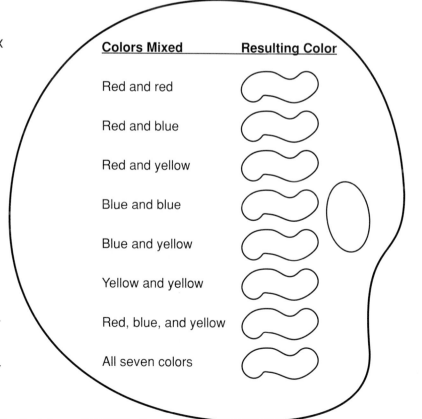

Colors Mixed	Resulting Color
Red and red	
Red and blue	
Red and yellow	
Blue and blue	
Blue and yellow	
Yellow and yellow	
Red, blue, and yellow	
All seven colors	

©The Mailbox® • *Science* • TEC60859 • Key p. 160

Note to the teacher: Use with "Putting Pigments Together" on page 133.

What's Hot to Wear?

Does the color of your clothing affect how hot or cold you feel? Conduct the following experiment to find out!

Materials for each group: 3 different-colored items of clothing (light-colored, medium-colored, and dark-colored), 3 thermometers, sheet of paper, clock or watch

Whew!

Procedure:

1. Have each group member predict the color of clothing she thinks would make her feel warmer and another color that would make her feel cooler.
2. Place the thermometers in direct sunlight. Record the starting temperature of each thermometer in the chart (one per piece of clothing).
3. Position each thermometer inside one layer of a different item of clothing so that the top of the thermometer sticks out.
4. Wait ten minutes. Then record the ending temperature of each thermometer in the chart.
5. Subtract the starting and ending temperatures of each thermometer. Record each difference in the chart.
6. On the sheet of paper, make a graph that shows the change in temperature (use the numbers in the last column of the chart).

Color of Clothing	Starting Temperature	Ending Temperature	Difference in Temperature

Observations and conclusions:

1. Which color of clothing absorbed the most radiant energy (had the greatest increase in temperature)? _____

2. Which color of clothing absorbed the least radiant energy (had the smallest increase in temperature)? _____

3. Were you surprised by any of the results? If so, what surprised you? _____
   _____

4. What variables other than color could have affected the temperature of each item of clothing?
   _____
   _____

5. What could be changed to make this experiment better? _____
   _____
   _____

Bonus Box: If you lived in the Arizona desert, what car color would keep you cooler? Why? If you lived in Maine during the winter months, what roof color would keep you warmer? Why?

©The Mailbox® • *Science* • TEC60859 • Key p. 160

136 **Note to the teacher:** Use with "Looking Through Rose-Colored Glasses" on page 134.

Getting Down With Sound
Hands-On Activities to Amplify a Study of Sound

From boom boxes and surround sound to ringing cell phones and friends' laughter, kids today are surrounded by all kinds of sounds. But do they understand what sound is? Explore this fascinating form of energy with the following hands-on teaching activities.

by Debi Kilmartin, Thomas M. Ryan Intermediate School, Hickory Corners, MI

Tinkling Tines
Concept: How vibrations create sounds

Fork up a great lesson on sound with the help of a little silverware and string! First, review with students that sound is created by an object's rapid back-and-forth movements called *vibrations.* Then divide the class into pairs and distribute the materials listed. Guide students through the steps shown. Afterward, have each twosome take this experiment a step further by completing the activity that follows.

Materials for each pair of students: 60" length of string, metal fork, pencil

Steps:
1. Decide who will be the listener and who will be the tapper.
2. The tapper ties the fork's handle to the middle of the string as shown.
3. The listener wraps one end of the string around one of his index fingers and the other end around the other index finger. There should be an equal amount of string on both sides of the fork.
4. The listener carefully places the tip of one index finger in each ear.
5. As the listener listens, the tapper gently taps the end of the fork's handle once with the pencil. If the listener requests it, the tapper taps the fork a second time.
6. The partners trade places, repeat Steps 3–5, and discuss what happened. *(Each student should hear a bell-like sound. When the pencil taps the metal fork, it causes the fork to vibrate. These vibrations travel through the string to the listener's ears where the vibrations are amplified, stimulating the nerve cells to send signals along the auditory nerve to the brain for interpretation.)*

The Ups and Downs of Sound
Concept: How pitch is the degree of highness or lowness of a sound

Extend "Tinkling Tines" above by adding an extra step that explores *pitch,* the degree of highness or lowness of a sound. After Step 5, have the listener shorten the string by wrapping it twice more around each index finger, making sure the length of the string is equal on both sides of the fork. Next, have the listener place the tips of his index fingers in his ears and signal the tapper to tap the fork. Have the listener continue to shorten the string and listen to the tap—and the changes in the sounds he hears—until the string is too short to wrap again without touching his chin. Then instruct the partners to trade places, repeat the steps, and discuss what happened. *(Pitch is determined by* frequency, *the number of vibrations made by a vibrating object in one second. The pitch is lower when the string is longer and higher when the string is shorter. A longer string vibrates more slowly than a shorter one and produces a lower pitch because fewer vibrations are able to reach the ear in one second. A shorter string vibrates more quickly and produces a higher pitch because more vibrations reach the ear in one second.)*

Gift Box Guitar
Concept: How pitch is related to how fast an object vibrates

Looking for a fun way to "strum" up an interest in sound? Then invite students to pluck on their own handmade guitars! First, ask students what makes sounds different from each other. After some discussion, pair students. Give each pair a copy of page 140 and the materials listed. Have each pair complete the page as directed to find out how different variables affect pitch. To extend the activity, have each pair place the rubber bands in its box and trade boxes and copies of page 140 with another twosome. Challenge each pair to arrange its new set of rubber bands from lowest to highest pitch and compare the arrangement with the other twosome's diagram. If results differ, help students conclude that it may be due to the over-stretching of the bands or pitches that were too similar to differentiate.

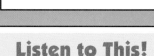

Listen to This!
Concept: How sound travels faster through solids and liquids than through air

Does sound travel faster through a solid than it does through air? Have students find out by doing this simple experiment!

Materials for each student: regular-sized rubber band, 8 oz. sturdy plastic cup

Directions:
1. Wrap the rubber band around the tip of your thumb and the third finger of one hand (see the illustration).
2. Stretch the rubber band between the two fingers as far apart as possible.
3. Pluck the rubber band with a finger of your other hand. Listen to the sound produced.
4. Wrap the same rubber band around the plastic cup from top to bottom. Make sure the rubber band is not twisted.
5. Hold the cup in one hand and pluck the rubber band with the other. Listen to the sound produced.
6. Hold the bottom of the cup next to your ear with one hand and pluck the rubber band with the other hand. Listen to the sound produced. How is it different from the sound produced in Step 3? *(Sound travels slowest through gases like air because its molecules are not close together. Therefore, the sound made when the rubber band is held between the fingers is low and soft because the band can only push a small amount of air. Holding the bottom of the cup next to the ear makes the sound easier to hear because the sound travels through a solid material—plastic. Sound travels fastest through solids because their molecules are close together.)*

Surrounded by Sound
Concept: Awareness of surrounding sounds

A field trip for a sound unit? Sure, and you don't even have to leave school to take it! Take students on a field trip around the school, challenging them to list all the sounds they hear in each location. Visit different spots on campus, such as the playground, cafeteria, and office. At each stop, have students record phrases that describe the sounds they hear. End the trip by returning to class to listen for sounds there. Then have each student use crayons or colored pencils, scissors, and her list of phrases to complete the poetry activity on a copy of page 141. Display the resulting sound poems on a bulletin board titled "Sounds Like Poetry!"

"Sound-sational" Sound Waves
Concept: How sound can be reflected

Help students discover that sound can be reflected with the following easy experiment.

Materials for each group of three students: 2 cardboard paper towel tubes, 4" x 12" piece of smooth cardboard, ruler

Steps:

1. Have one group member use one hand to hold the cardboard in an upright position on a desk or table. Have him use his other hand to angle the paper towel tubes, as shown, so that the front ends of the tubes are about an inch apart and an inch from the cardboard.
2. Have a second group member whisper a sentence into one tube while the third group member listens at the end of the other tube. (Tell the whisperer not to reveal the sentence beforehand.)
3. Have group members repeat the experiment two more times so that each student can perform all three roles. *(The listener can hear the whispered sentence even though the tubes are not connected. The whisper travels in a straight line through the paper towel tube, bounces off the piece of cardboard into the second tube, and continues in a straight line to the listener's ear. This happens because sound travels in a straight line through a medium of uniform density until it meets a surface [smooth, hard ones are best] and is reflected. For this reason, some concert halls are designed with suspended ceilings and angled boxes to help reflect sound from the stage to the audience and create the best possible sound.)*

Discriminating Sounds
Concept: How the human brain can interpret and distinguish different sounds

Demonstrate the brain's ability to make sense of sound with this fun "eggs-periment"! Gather 16 same-colored, plastic, snap-together eggs. Also gather eight pairs of objects small enough to fit inside the eggs, such as pieces of macaroni, grains of rice, dice, marbles, cotton balls, beans, safety pins, and thumbtacks. List the eight objects on a sheet of paper. Then place one object in each egg and put the eggs in a box or basket. Place the container at your science center along with the list of objects and a copy of the directions below.

Directions (for two players):

1. The players remove the eggs from the container and arrange them in rows.
2. Player 1 picks up any two eggs, shakes one egg at a time, and listens to the sound (or lack of sound) it makes.
3. If Player 1 thinks the sounds match, he looks at the list of objects and guesses which item is in that pair of eggs. Then he opens the eggs to see if he is correct. If he's correct, he keeps the eggs and takes another turn. If the objects don't match or he identified the wrong object, he returns the eggs to their original positions and Player 2 takes a turn.
4. The players continue taking turns until all the eggs are matched.
5. The winner is the player with more pairs of eggs.

Twang It High, Twang It Low

What makes sounds different from each other? Construct a box guitar to find out!

Materials: small, sturdy gift box (4" x 5" x $1\frac{1}{2}$" or slightly larger); rubber bands of different lengths, widths, and colors; crayons or markers

Steps:

1. Choose five to six different rubber bands. Make sure each one is a different length and width.
2. Remove the box's lid. Then stretch each rubber band around the box bottom. Arrange the rubber bands with an equal amount of space between them. Make sure they're not twisted.
3. Pluck one rubber band at a time and listen to see if it makes a high or a low sound.
4. Rearrange the rubber bands on the box so they're in order from lowest to highest pitch.
5. Show how the rubber bands are arranged on your box by drawing wide and narrow bands of color on the diagram at the right.
6. Answer the questions below in complete sentences.

Questions:

1. How are your rubber bands different from each other? _____
   _____

2. Does the length of the rubber bands make a difference in the sounds they make? Explain.
   _____

3. Does the width of the rubber bands make a difference in the sounds they make? Explain.
   _____

4. Does the color of the rubber bands make a difference in the sounds they make? Explain.
   _____

5. Do some rubber bands fit more tightly around the box than others? If so, do they make a different sound than those that fit more loosely? Explain. _____
   _____
   _____

6. Based on your arrangement of rubber bands, which strings on an acoustic guitar would play higher notes? _____
   Lower notes? _____

> **Bonus Box:** Which would have a lower pitch: a long, wide rubber band or a short, wide rubber band? Write your answer on the back of this page.

©The Mailbox® • *Science* • TEC60859 • Key p. 160

140   **Note to the teacher:** Use with "Gift Box Guitar" on page 138.

Name _____

Sounds Like Poetry!

RAT-A-TAT!

Clocks tick, water drips, pencils fall to the floor, phones ring, horns honk, radios blare, people talk—sounds are all around us! Capture some of these sounds in a poem by following the directions below.

Directions: Read the sample poems below. Choose the type of poem you'd like to write. Then write your poem on another sheet of paper. Include as many descriptive phrases collected from your sound field trip as possible. After editing your poem, copy it neatly inside the frame. Then color and cut out the frame.

Acrostic: a poem whose lines begin with letters that spell a word vertically

Baton tapping on the director's stand
A flute trilling a high note
Numerous feet tapping the beat
Drums beating a fast rhythm

Free Verse: a poem that doesn't follow a specific form and doesn't have to rhyme

Lunchtime

I walk into the cafeteria.
I hear…
    Milk slurping through straws,
    Paper bags rustling,
    Containers popping open and
        snapping shut,
    Clinking silverware,
    Chairs scraping against the
        floor,
    Trays dragging along a rail, and
    Trash dropping into cans—
    The sounds of lunchtime.

Definition Poem: a poem that defines a word or an idea in a creative way

Basketball

What is basketball?
bouncing leather balls
shrieking referees' whistles
squeaking shoes on a gym floor
the swish of a free throw
voices yelling, "We won!"
That's basketball!!

List Poem: a poem made from a list; the title often names the list

Things That Are Loud!

Booming bass drums
Teachers' whistles
Pans clanging in the cafeteria
Kids' voices in the hallway
The slamming of locker doors
Voices leaving at the end of the day

©The Mailbox® • *Science* • TEC60859

141

Note to the teacher: Use with "Surrounded by Sound" on page 138.

Bullish 'bout ENERGY

Energy exists in different forms, including potential, kinetic, thermal, radiant, chemical, and electrical. Charge right in and energize your forms of energy unit with this hands-on collection of easy-to-do activities!

by Debi Kilmartin, Thomas M. Ryan Intermediate School, Hickory Corners, MI

Toys on the Move
Topics: Potential and kinetic energy

All energy is either potential or kinetic. *Potential energy* is stored energy, while *kinetic energy* is active or moving energy. To introduce students to these two kinds of energy, ask them to bring in toys that move or have moving parts—such as windup, pullback, flywheel, and pop-up toys—as well as toy cars and trucks. Allow time for students to explore the toys' movements on tables, wooden or cardboard ramps, and carpeted and uncarpeted floor space. Then discuss with students how the toys are alike and different.

Next, have students group like toys together. Then divide the class into teams, one per toy type. Give each team a different grouping of toys, a 12" x 18" sheet of white construction paper, and markers. Have each team experiment with its toys. Then have the team draw illustrations of one toy, including labels that identify the toy's potential and kinetic energy. After each team shares its work, ask students to explain when each toy's potential energy changes to kinetic energy *(when it starts to move)*. Also ask students to identify what is needed for the toy's potential energy to become kinetic energy *(force from a built-in mechanism or a physical push or pull)*.

Keep Me From Melting!
Topic: Thermal energy

Thermal energy, or heat, is always on the move! One way it moves is by *conduction,* the movement of heat through one object into another. Insulators, such as ice coolers and drink-can holders, can suppress this flow of heat. After reviewing this information with students, challenge them to design insulators that can slow down the melting of an ice cube. Set out a collection of materials such as those listed, and divide students into small groups. Then provide time for each group to design an insulator using the materials.

On testing day, give each group one ice cube in a paper cup. At your signal, have each group place the cube in its insulator and write the starting time on the board. Have another child in the group periodically check the cube, but not too often since opening the insulator will allow warm air to enter and melt the ice. When the student sees that his group's cube has melted, have him write the ending time on the board. Declare the group with the longest-lasting ice cube the winner. Conclude by asking students to identify the materials that seemed to be the best insulators. *(A foam cup combined with another material—such as aluminum foil, thick paper towels, or a wool cloth—will work well as an insulator.)*

My ice cube hasn't melted yet!

Materials:
aluminum foil
waxed paper
thick paper towels
plastic wrap
wool and cotton fabric
lidded plastic containers
foam or bubble wrap
small cardboard boxes
tape
string
plastic, foam, and aluminum cups

What's the Flap About Friction?
Topic: Thermal energy

What does walking on slippery ice have to do with adding a quart of oil to your car's engine? They both involve *friction,* a source of heat energy produced when objects rub together. Help students explore friction with a fun experiment. At the end of the experiment, discuss the questions provided.

Materials for each group: small paperback book, 45" length of string, eight ⅝" flat metal washers, large paper clip, strip of masking tape, ruler, desk, 8 plastic straws, 4 hexagonal pencils, fabric placemat, copy of the chart on page 145, pencil

Steps:
1. Knot the ends of the string together to form a loop. Insert the loop through the middle of the book, aligning it with the spine.
2. Place the masking tape 12 inches from the desk's edge as shown. Align the book's spine with the tape.
3. Open the paper clip into an S shape and hook the smaller end on the string as shown.
4. Add one washer to the hook at a time until the book slides to the edge of the desk. Record in the chart the number of washers used. Then remove the washers.
5. Return the book to the 12-inch marker. Place eight straws at equal distances under the book and between the book and the desk's edge (positioning them so they are parallel to the book's spine). Repeat Step 4.
6. Return the book to the marker. Repeat Step 4 using the pencils and then the placemat to replace the straws.

Questions:
- When did the book show potential energy? *(when it was lying still)* Kinetic energy? *(when it began to move)*
- Which setup created the most friction? How do you know? *(the one with the placemat because it required the greatest number of washers to move the book)*
- Which setup created the least friction? How do you know? *(the one with the straws because it required the fewest washers to move the book)*

Name _Alex_ _____ Thermal Energy

What's the Flap About Friction?

Setup	Number of Washers Used
desktop only	
straws	
pencils	
placemat	

I Get a Charge out of You!
Topic: Electrical energy

What would we do without electricity? It lights our homes, runs our televisions, and powers our computers. But just what is electricity? It is energy formed by the movement of *electrons,* or negatively charged particles found in atoms. When lots of atoms in an object lose or gain electrons, the object becomes electrically charged, creating static electricity.

To demonstrate static electricity, turn on the water in a classroom or cafeteria sink to produce a smooth, slow trickle. Rub an inflated balloon with a piece of wool. Then slowly move the balloon toward the running water and observe what happens *(the water stream angles toward the balloon).* Point out that the friction produced by the rubbing caused electrons to move from the wool to the balloon, giving the balloon a negative charge that attracted the water. Repeat the experiment three more times, replacing the balloon with a plastic drink bottle, a plastic spoon, and a metal spoon. Have students observe the results. *(The drink bottle and plastic spoon will attract the water, but not as much as the balloon. The metal spoon will have almost no effect on the water.)* Follow up this activity with the group experiment on page 146.

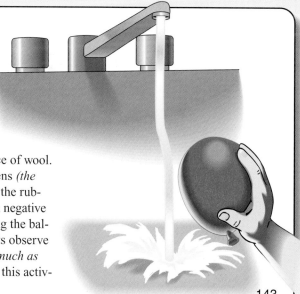

143

Bouncing Beams
Topic: Radiant energy

Investigate the energy of light, known as *radiant energy,* with this cool experiment on reflection. Line adjacent sides of a large box with aluminum foil. Then layer a piece of shiny white poster board and then a piece of matte black poster board in front of the foil. Place two small flat mirrors in front of the black layer as shown. Also place a small flashlight in the box.

Next, show students the inside of the box. Explain that they will test the four surfaces—the mirrors, the black poster board, the white poster board, and the foil—to determine which ones best reflect radiant energy. Demonstrate for students how to bounce the flashlight's beam from one side of the box to the other. Then model how to remove each layer to test the next surface. After students understand the procedure, place the box in a center. Then schedule pairs of students to complete the experiment. Afterward, ask students which surfaces were the best reflectors. *(The mirrors were the best reflectors, followed by the aluminum foil and white poster board. The black poster board absorbs rather than reflects most of the light.)* Conclude by having students suggest situations in which having reflective surfaces would be helpful. For another activity on radiant energy, see the reproducible on page 147.

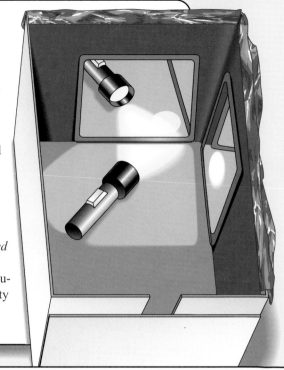

Wow! The flame went out, and I didn't even blow on it!

Pour It On!
Topic: Chemical energy

Show students how one form of energy can cause a surprising chemical change in another with this eye-popping demonstration! First, explain to students that some chemical changes can produce energy. Then slowly add two teaspoons of baking soda to a large, clear plastic cup that contains an inch of vinegar. Have students observe and hypothesize reasons for the reaction. *(The mixture bubbles, showing a chemical change that produces carbon dioxide.)* When the bubbling stops, light a votive candle and announce that you're going to put out the flame without blowing on it. As students look at you in surprise, tilt the cup above the flame, but do not pour the solution onto the candle. Carbon dioxide gas will flow from the cup and extinguish the flame. Point out to students that the chemical energy of the CO_2 converted both radiant energy (the flame) and thermal energy (the flame's heat) into potential energy (the wick). If desired, continue to relight the candle and pour carbon dioxide onto the flame until the gas is completely gone.

"Moo-velous" Energy Resources

Books:
Energy (Eyewitness Books) by Jack Challoner
Heat and Energy (Fascinating Science Projects) by Bobbi Searle

Web site *(current as of March 2006):*
National Energy Education Development Project: www.need.org/index.htm

What's the Flap About Friction?

Setup	Number of Washers Used
desktop only	
straws	
pencils	
placemat	

What's the Flap About Friction?

Setup	Number of Washers Used
desktop only	
straws	
pencils	
placemat	

Charge It Up!

What is *static electricity?* It's the result of two items being rubbed together. During rubbing, items lose or gain electrons. If an item gains electrons, it becomes negatively charged. If an item loses electrons, it becomes positively charged. Items with the same charge repel each other, while those with opposite charges attract each other. Items that don't attract or repel each other are neutral.

Find out more about static electricity by completing the steps below. Write your answers to the questions on the back of this page.

Materials for each group: 2 inflated balloons, piece of wool cloth, 2 small plastic soda bottles, plastic comb, small pieces of paper

Steps:

1. Place one balloon on a table and move the other near it. Record what happens in the chart.
2. Place one bottle on its side. Then repeat Step 1, using the two bottles in place of the balloons.
3. Vigorously rub one balloon with the wool. Then move it near the other balloon and record what happens. Repeat, replacing the balloons with the bottles.
4. Vigorously rub both balloons with the wool. Then move one balloon near the other and record your observations. Repeat, replacing the balloons with the bottles.
5. Place the paper pieces on a table. Bring the comb near the paper and record your observations.
6. Vigorously rub the comb with the wool. Bring the comb near the paper and record what happens.
7. Rub your hands all over a balloon. Record what happens as you do this. (Hint: Listen closely.)

Items	Observations
unrubbed balloon + unrubbed balloon	
unrubbed bottle + unrubbed bottle	
rubbed balloon + unrubbed balloon	
rubbed bottle + unrubbed bottle	
rubbed balloon + rubbed balloon	
rubbed bottle + rubbed bottle	
unrubbed comb + paper	
rubbed comb + paper	
balloon being rubbed by hands	

Questions

1. Which items attract each other? Repel each other? Neither attract nor repel?

2. Describe the sounds you hear when you rub your hands over the balloon. What causes the sounds?

3. Where else can you see or hear static electricity?

Bonus Box: Based on your observations, decide whether the following pairs would attract each other, repel each other, or do neither: rubbed bottle + rubbed balloon, unrubbed bottle + unrubbed balloon, rubbed bottle + unrubbed balloon, unrubbed bottle + rubbed balloon, rubbed balloon + paper, unrubbed balloon + paper.

Peering Through Paper

Did you know that early colonial homes rarely had glass for their windows? Glass was expensive to import from England, so many colonists covered their windows with oiled parchment instead. This oiled paper allowed sunlight, or radiant energy, to pass through. The oil also waterproofed the paper, thus providing protection from harsh weather.

Directions: Make a stained glass version of an oiled-paper window by completing the steps below. Then answer the questions on another sheet of paper.

Materials: colored markers, scissors, 2 thick paper towels, 5 oz. plastic cup of vegetable oil, clear tape

Steps:

1. Use markers to color the picture at the right. Then outline each section in black.
2. Cut out the picture and place it on a folded paper towel.
3. Moisten another paper towel with oil. Gently rub the oiled towel on both sides of the picture until it is shiny.
4. Allow the picture to dry overnight.
5. Tape the stained glass picture to a window.

Questions:

1. Materials through which you can see clearly are *transparent* because almost all of the light passes through them. Materials through which you can see, but not clearly, are *translucent* because only some of the light passes through them. Materials through which you cannot see at all are *opaque* because none of the light passes through them. Which type of material does your stained glass paper window represent: transparent, translucent, or opaque? Explain.

2. List other objects that are in the same category (transparent, translucent, or opaque) as your paper window.

3. How is your paper window the same as a glass window? Different?

©The Mailbox® • *Science* • TEC60859 • Key p. 160

147

Note to the teacher: Use with "Bouncing Beams" on page 144.

Soapy Science

"Bubble" the fun of your end-of-the-year lessons with the following soapy science and art activities!

by Cynthia Wurmnest

Water acts as if it is covered with skin, an effect called *surface tension.*

Water molecules at the surface are attracted to each other more than to the air above, making the molecules stick together. This causes surface tension.

A free-floating bubble will always be shaped like a sphere, regardless of the shape of the bubble wand used to form it.

Don't Burst My Bubble!

Can students learn important science concepts while blowing bubbles? You bet! Make Solutions A and B on page 149, allowing them to sit for several days. Gather the remaining materials listed. Next, give each pair of students a copy of page 149 and the materials. Have each twosome complete the lab as directed; then discuss the results as a class. During the discussion, refer to the facts inside the bubbles on this page (list them on the board or a sheet of chart paper). Then have students experiment with other unique bubble blowers, such as plastic lids in which holes have been cut, paper clips, plastic bracelets, cookie cutters, etc. Follow up this soapy session with the "blew-tiful" art activity on this page.

Soap molecules on the bubble's surface reduce evaporation, making the bubble last longer.

Adding glycerin to a bubble solution makes it more difficult for soap film to evaporate, which lengthens a bubble's life span.

"Blew-tiful" Bubble Prints

For that Friday afternoon when students seem to be bubbling over with energy, this activity can't be beat! Place three small plastic cups several feet apart on a newspaper-covered workspace. In each cup, place two heaping teaspoons of powdered tempera paint: red in the first cup, blue in the second, green in the third. Stir one teaspoon of Joy® dishwashing liquid into each cup; then add enough distilled water to fill the cups three-fourths full. Next, give each student a plastic straw and a sheet of white paper. Direct the student to put her straw into one cup of bubble solution at a time and blow until bubbles spill over the cup's rim. Then have her quickly touch her paper to the bubbles, popping them to create circular imprints on the paper. Instruct her to repeat this step until the paper is filled with abstract designs. After the papers dry, have students cut out a variety of shapes from them (butterflies, flowers, etc.) and use the cutouts to create a "bubble-rrific" bulletin board mural.

148

The Big Bubble Battle

Which bubble solution makes the longest-lasting bubble? Find out who will win the Battle of the Bubble by following the steps below.

Solution A	Solution B	Solution C
1 part Joy® dishwashing liquid	1 part Joy® dishwashing liquid	commercial bubble solution
3 parts distilled water	3 parts distilled water	
	1 part glycerin	

Materials: newspapers, three aluminum pans (each filled with a different bubble solution: A, B, or C), timepiece with a second hand, sheet of loose-leaf paper, plastic bubble wand

Hypothesis: I think that Solution _____ will make the longest-lasting bubble.

Procedure:

1. Cover a workspace with newspaper.
2. Fold the loose-leaf paper into a fan.
3. Using Solution A and the bubble wand, practice making same-sized bubbles and keeping them aloft (and away from other objects) by fanning them from underneath.
4. Have one partner blow a new bubble. Have your partner time the number of seconds that elapse from when the bubble is made until it pops on its own. Record the seconds in the chart. Then trade jobs with your partner.
5. Repeat Step 4 to record the life spans of bubbles 2–5. Try to keep the size of the bubbles the same each time.
6. Find the average life span of Solution A's bubbles by adding the times together and dividing by five. Round the average to the nearest whole number.
7. Repeat Steps 3–6 using Solution B.
8. Repeat Steps 3–6 using Solution C.

Life span in seconds

Bubble	A	B	C
1			
2			
3			
4			
5			
Average life span			

Conclusion:

1. Based on the data, Solution _____ produced bubbles with the longest life span.
2. Compare the ingredients of the three bubble solutions. Ask your teacher to tell you the ingredients on the commercial bubble solution's label (if printed). What effect do you think the ingredients had on the outcome of this experiment? _____

_____

Note to the teacher: Use with "Don't Burst My Bubble!" on page 148. Make one copy for each pair of students. Answers may vary depending on the brand of commercial bubble solution used. Explain to students that glycerin is typically added to bubble solutions because it keeps water from evaporating, resulting in long-lasting bubbles.

Things Are Heating Up!
Hands-On Investigations for Studying Heat Energy

It's heating up outside, making it the perfect time to investigate the transfer of heat by conduction, convection, and radiation!

> Heat energy travels from hot objects to cold ones until there is no difference in temperature.

Getting ready: Enlist parents to help provide the materials needed for each experiment. Also gather two sheets of white paper for each student. Divide students into groups of four and distribute the paper. Have each group member make a booklet by folding her two sheets of paper in half, stapling them along the fold, and labeling the top sheet "How Does Heat Travel?" Before conducting each experiment below, have the student copy the corresponding question at the top of a different page and write her hypothesis. Then guide students through the experiments, having each child record her observations and conclusions.

What's the Best Spoon for Ice Cream?
Topic: Conduction

Materials for each group: three 3 oz. paper cups, each filled with ¼ c. ice cream into which a different item (craft stick, metal spoon, plastic spoon) has been frozen upright overnight to create a handle as shown; stopwatch; paper towels

Procedure: Choose a timekeeper and three "cup-sicle" holders. Have the holders pick up the cups by their handles at the same time and hold them over the paper towels. Begin timing. Notice what happens to the ice cream around each handle. *(The metal spoon will conduct the most heat, causing the cup of ice cream to drop from the spoon within minutes. The craft stick will conduct the least heat and hold the ice cream the longest.)*

How Can a Frozen Treat Create a Current?
Topic: Convection

Materials for each group: fruit-flavored frozen treat, clear container of very warm water

Procedure: Set the container of water carefully on your work surface. Slide the frozen treat into the water and let it lean against the side of the container. Observe what happens to the water around the frozen treat. *(The warm water rises and the cooler liquid from the melted treat fills that space, forming swirling, colored currents.)*

How Can a Hot Dog Get a Tan?
Topic: Radiation

Materials: toaster oven with a broiling element; hot dog, craft stick, and paper towels for each group

Procedure: Put the hot dog on the stick. Describe the hot dog's appearance. Then have your teacher broil one side of the hot dog for three minutes. Record your observations, comparing how the hot dog looked before and after it was broiled. *(The top will be dark and sweaty with small blisters. The bottom of the broiled hot dog will be significantly cooler than the top because the heat traveled from the broiler downward in radiating waves.)*

Science Specials

SPOTLIGHT ON SCIENTIFIC INQUIRY

Lights! Camera! Action! Time to turn the spotlight on teaching science as a process of inquiry and discovery and on getting kids to think like scientists. How? Just use the following terrific ideas as your script!

ideas by Dan Kriesberg, Bayville, NY

Questions, Questions, Questions!
Skills: Observation, asking and recording questions

Try this simple-to-do activity to help students understand that asking questions is an important part of being a scientist. Take students outside and gather them at the base of a tree. Challenge the observers to look at the tree and call out any questions that come to mind. Record the questions on chart paper, guiding students to discover that one child's question can cause someone else to think of another. Continue until there is an exhaustive list. Conclude by helping students understand that—like scientists—the more they question, the more questions they'll have!

1. What kind of tree is it?
2. How old is the tree?
3. Is it a deciduous tree?
4. Are there any birds' nests in the tree?
5. Do squirrels live in the tree?
6. How deep do its roots go?
7. Do the leaves on the tree change color in the fall?
8. How tall is the tree?
9. How big around is the tree?
10. How did this tree get its name?

What's So Special About...a Thumb?
Skill: Observation

Being a keen observer can be critical to being a good scientist. Motivate students to sharpen their observation skills with this easy activity. Without elaborating, direct each student to study his own thumb and record his observations on a sheet of paper. After ten minutes, give each student a magnifying glass (or lens) and have him continue making and recording his observations. If students only list the obvious, lead them to dig deeper by asking the following questions: How many lines are on your knuckle? At how many places does your thumb bend? How long is your thumbnail? Wrap up the activity by having students share their observations round-robin style. Use this activity again to introduce other science units, such as insects, water, or plants.

Books to Inspire Inquiring Minds

Encourage students to think like scientists with these books, which feature real-life examples of scientific inquiry at its best.

- *Birds in the Bushes: A Story About Margaret Morse Nice* by Julie Dunlap
- *Digging Up Tyrannosaurus Rex* by John R. Horner and Don Lessem
- *Dinosaur Ghosts: The Mystery of Coelophysis* by J. Lynett Gillette
- *Monarchs* by Kathryn Lasky
- *On the Trail of the Komodo Dragon and Other Explorations of Science in Action* by Jack Myers
- *To Space and Back* by Sally Ride with Susan Okie

What Are You Wondering About?
Skill: Research

Wondering, asking questions, observing, searching for answers—such are the steps a scientist can take in the quest for knowledge. Inspire students to think like scientists and learn on their own with this activity. First, review with students some methods that scientists can use to find answers:

1. **Observation:** Carefully watching the subject in action
2. **Asking others:** Talking or writing to others who have studied the same topic or related questions
3. **Research:** Using reference materials, including the Internet, to research what others have learned about a topic

Next, have each student list on paper some things she has wondered about. Then have her pick one question from her list, such as "How much weight can an ant lift?" Direct her to use any two of the three methods above to find the answer to this question. When she has found the answer, have her write the information at the right on another sheet of paper and share it with the class. The result? Students who discover that they can learn for themselves!

- My question:
- What I learned:
- How I learned it:
- How it felt to find the answer on my own:

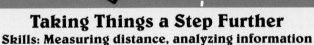

Taking Things a Step Further
Skills: Measuring distance, analyzing information

Are scientists silly for not being satisfied with their first answer to a question? Help students understand that when scientists analyze their own (or other scientists') findings, it can cause them to ask *more* questions, which can eventually result in findings that are even more reliable and conclusive. Simulate this inquiry process by following the steps below to challenge students to a paper airplane–flying contest. Conclude the contest by having students use their experience to respond to the writing prompts below.

Steps:
1. Gather several yardsticks (or metersticks).
2. Give each pair of students three sheets of paper and a copy of the recording sheet on page 155.
3. Have the pair fold one sheet of paper into an airplane.
4. Direct one student in each pair to stand behind a line in an open space and fly the plane. Have the other measure and record the distance the plane travels.
5. Have students think about their plane's design and the distance it traveled compared to the other planes. Suggest that the pairs talk with one another to share information. Then have each twosome decide how to alter its plane's design to increase its flying distance and record those changes on its sheet.
6. Repeat Steps 3–5 two more times.
7. Have students complete the rest of the recording sheet as directed.

Writing Prompts
- Scientists can learn from their mistakes.
- Even though every change may not be an improvement, new ideas would never be developed if people were not willing to take risks.

What Happened Here?
Skill: Distinguishing between fact and theory

Challenge students to put what they've learned about scientific inquiry to the test with this critical-thinking activity. Divide students into groups of three. Explain that an animal's tracks can provide scientists with facts about its movements and activities. Then give each group a copy of the bottom half of page 155 to study. Have the groups call out facts about the tracks, such as those shown, for you to list on the board. (Students may tend to suggest theories about what happened, but remind them that for now, only the facts are important.)

Once you have a good list, explain that scientists can use facts to form theories in which they speculate about what could (or did) happen. To practice this skill, have students study the facts on the board, paying close attention to the tracks' direction, spacing, and frequency. Ask the groups to suggest theories about what the animals could have been doing to create that set of tracks. Be sure to question their theories to find out how they are using the facts. Record students' responses on the board. Wrap up the activity by challenging your young scientists to think of other natural signs that might help them develop a theory about what happened.

Facts
- There are three different animals.
- The bird tracks come to a stop.
- The fox's tracks begin to spread out.
- The tracks of the rabbit and fox eventually meet.
- The rabbit's tracks stop. The fox's tracks continue.

Theories
- The fox begins to run.
- The bird flies away when it sees the fox.
- The fox stops to sniff the bird's tracks before moving on.
- The rabbit is hopping along looking for food.
- The fox chases and catches the rabbit.

Class Museum
Skills: Observation, research

Given permission, kids won't hesitate to show you the natural stuff they've found. Encourage your students to share their discoveries (and keep their eyes open to all the wonders that surround them) by opening your own class museum. Ask students to bring in natural objects to stock the museum, such as feathers, nests, and leaves. Once you have a good assortment of objects, ask each child to pick a different item to read about. After the research is done, have each child write two or three interesting facts she learned about her object on an index card. Have her share the facts and object with the class before placing both items in a corner of the room that has been designated as the museum.

If desired, have the class vote on the most interesting items to feature in a traveling museum. Arrange the selected objects on the shelves of a rolling cart. Have students tape an attractive sign to the front of the cart along with a class sign-up sheet. Then spread the word that your students want to share their hands-on museum with other classes. Once the cart has made its rounds, have students replace the objects with different ones—just as real museums do—and send it around again!

Hawks
- Female hawks are larger than male hawks.
- Swainson's hawk has dark brown flight feathers.

154

Designed for Distance

How can you fold a paper airplane to make it fly a great distance? A greater distance? The greatest distance? Find out! Working with a partner, follow your teacher's directions to design a paper airplane that travels farther than those made by your classmates.

1. Distance flown by plane #1: _____
   Change(s) to make: _____
   _____

2. Distance flown by plane #2: _____
   Did the change(s) make the plane fly farther? Explain. _____
   _____
   New change(s) to make: _____
   _____

3. Distance flown by plane #3: _____
   Did the change(s) make the plane fly farther? Explain. _____
   _____

4. If you had time to design a fourth plane, what change(s) would you make? _____
   _____

5. Based on your findings, what design do you think helps a paper airplane fly the greatest distance? _____
   _____

©The Mailbox® • *Science* • TEC60859

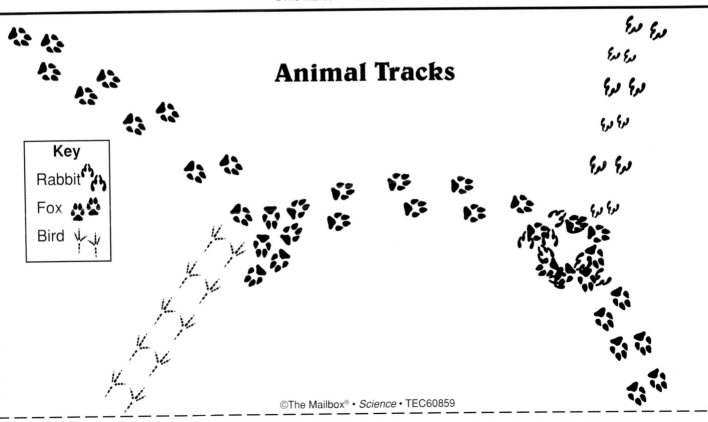

Animal Tracks

Key
Rabbit
Fox
Bird

©The Mailbox® • *Science* • TEC60859

Note to the teacher: Use the top half of this page with "Taking Things a Step Further" on page 153. Use the bottom half with "What Happened Here?" on page 154.

WHO KIDNAPPED TED E. BEAR?
SOLVING A SCIENTIFIC MYSTERY USING CHROMATOGRAPHY

A young bear has been kidnapped, and students will need to observe and experiment in order to nab the nefarious kidnapper! Try this ready-to-use lesson plan about the science of chromatography to help students solve this puzzling case.

by Terry Healy

Materials:
4 coffee filters
3 black, water-based markers, each one manufactured by a different company
1 clear plastic cup of water for each group of four students
paper towels
scissors
rulers

STEP 1: TEACHER PREPARATION

1. Gather the materials on the list.
2. Label the markers "A," "B," and "C."
3. Use one of the markers (A, B, or C) to write the following ransom note on the first filter:

> **Dear Students,**
> **I have taken Ted E. Bear. If you are sly enough to discover who I am, you'll get your bear back.**
> **The Kidnapper**

4. Label the three remaining filters "A," "B," and "C."
5. Use marker A to color a dot in each section of filter A, leaving about ½ inch between each dot and the edge of the filter. (See the illustration.)
6. Repeat Step 5 with markers B and C and the corresponding filters.
7. Make one copy of page 157 for each group of four students.

STEP 2: DEFINING CHROMATOGRAPHY

Share the definition of *chromatography* from the reproducible on page 157 with students. Explain that chromatography will help them identify which marker matches the ransom note's ink.

STEP 3: SHARING THE SCENARIO

Read the following to your class: *A terrible thing has happened! Mr. Ted E. Bear has been kidnapped. The three suspects are Mr. Squirre Ell, Miss P. Q. Pine, and Master Kyle Otey. We've received a ransom note from the kidnapper.* (Read the ransom note to the class.) *By comparing the dyes used in each of the suspect's markers against the ink of the ransom note, we should be able to discover the kidnapper's identity.*

STEP 4: PERFORMING THE EXPERIMENT

Divide your class into groups of four. Direct each group to cut a 2" x 1" ink sample from filters A, B, and C, labeling each sample appropriately. Provide each group with a same-size sample cut from the ransom note and a small cup of water. Direct each group to carefully dip the lower edge of filter A's sample into the water for 10 seconds, making sure that the ink dot stays above the water level. Then have the group lay the sample in its correct place on the chart on page 157 to dry. Students should observe the water spreading through the sample. Have them repeat this process for each of the other samples.

STEP 5: DRAWING A CONCLUSION

Guide the groups in recording their observations on their reproducibles. Have the group members write down the colors seen on each filter sample. Then have them identify the kidnapper by comparing the ransom-note ink to each sample.

A

Dear Students,
I have taken Ted E. Bear. If you are sly enough to discover who I am, you'll get your bear back.

The Kidnapper

WHO KIDNAPPED TED E. BEAR?

Chromatography is the process that lets scientists separate a mixture into its different parts by their colors. The color record that results is called a *chromatogram*. This experiment will help you see what colors are mixed together to make each marker's ink.

Directions: Carefully dip just the lower edge of one sample into the water, **making sure that the ink dot stays above the water level**. Then lay the sample in its correct place on the chart to dry. Repeat this process for each of the other samples, including the ransom note.

Marker A	Marker B	Marker C	Ransom Note
Squirre Ell	P. Q. Pine	Kyle Otey	–?–

Conclusions: What colors were added together to make each ink mixture?

Marker A: _____

Marker B: _____

Marker C: _____

Which one best matches the ransom note: A, B, or C? _____

Who kidnapped Ted E. Bear? _____

Bonus Box: Pretend you are Ted E. Bear. On another sheet of paper, write a story describing how you were kidnapped and the feelings you experienced.

Answer Keys

Page 8
1. outside walls
2. mall entrance
3. hallways
4. mall office
5. mall office walls and door
6. mall office director
7. supply carts
8. vendors
9. electrical system
10. water tank and pipes
11. mall food court

Page 10
Step 1: Predictions will vary.

Step 2:

Day	1	2	3	4	5	6	7
Number of Cells	2	4	8	16	32	64	128

Cells formed in 1 week: 128

Step 3:

Day	8	9	10	11	12	13	14
Number of Cells	256	512	1,024	2,048	4,096	8,192	16,384

Cells formed in 2 weeks: 16,384

Step 4: The pattern is to double the number or multiply by 2.

Day	15	16	17	18	19	20	21
Number of Cells	32,768	65,536	131,072	262,144	524,288	1,048,576	2,097,152

Day	22	23	24	25	26	27	28	29	30
Number of Cells	4,194,304	8,388,608	16,777,216	33,554,432	67,108,864	134,217,728	268,435,456	536,870,912	1,073,741,824

Cells formed in 30 days: 1,073,741,824

Bonus Box: 16,384 cells

Day	1	2	3	4	5	6	7
Number of Cells	4	16	64	256	1,024	4,096	16,384

Page 27

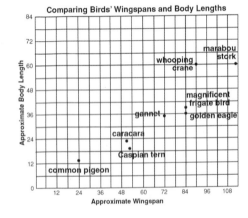

Comparing Birds' Wingspans and Body Lengths

1. marabou stork
2. common pigeon
3. whooping crane and Caspian tern, magnificent frigate bird and golden eagle, caracara and whooping crane, Caspian tern and gannet
4. 89 in., 47 in.
5. 71.3 in.
6. 35.9 in.
7. yes, 60 for the body lengths and 84 for the wingspans
8. According to this set of data, a bird's wingspan increases as its body length increases.

Bonus Box: Body lengths from least to greatest: common pigeon (1 ft. 1 in.), Caspian tern (1 ft. 8 in.), caracara (1 ft. 11 in.), gannet (2 ft. 11 in.), magnificent frigate bird (3 ft. 4 in.), marabou stork and whooping crane (5 ft.). Wingspans from greatest to least: marabou stork (9 ft. 5 in.), whooping crane (7 ft. 6 in.), golden eagle and magnificent frigate bird (7 ft.), gannet (6 ft.), Caspian tern (4 ft. 5 in.), caracara (4 ft. 2 in.), common pigeon (2 ft.).

Page 28
1. horse
2. flea
3. dragonfly
4. cocklebur
5. dandelion
6. maple
7. peregrine falcon
8. swan
9. tumbleweed
10. flatworm
11. earthworm
12. squid

Bonus Box: cheetah, hare, greyhound, African elephant, camel

Page 38
Instructor Aves Birdy's Class
- vertebrate
- warm-blooded
- hatch from eggs
- breathe with lungs
- have a beak or bill
- have feathers

Professor Reptilia's Class
- vertebrate
- cold-blooded
- breathe with lungs
- hatch from eggs (some bear live young)
- have scales

Mr. Mammalia's Class
- vertebrate
- warm-blooded
- feed young with milk
- breathe with lungs
- most have hair or fur
- most bear live young

Dr. Amphibia's Class
- vertebrate
- cold-blooded
- breathe with gills or lungs
- hatch from eggs
- live part of life in water, part on land

Ms. Four-Fish's Class
- vertebrate
- cold-blooded
- breathe mainly with gills
- live in water
- hatch from eggs

Page 39
The bar on the graph for each mammal should correspond as follows:

- giraffe at 450 days = 15 months
- rabbit = about one month
- tiger at about 100 days = about three months
- pig = four months
- African lion at about 98 days = about three months
- black rhinoceros = 15 months
- African elephant = about 22 months
- koala at 35 days = about one month
- spotted hyena at about 110 days = about four months
- vampire bat at 200 days = about seven months

Bonus Box: Yes, the giraffe and black rhinoceros (15 months), the rabbit and koala (one month), the pig and the spotted hyena (four months), and the African lion and tiger (three months). The average gestation period for all the mammals is 7½ months.

Page 44

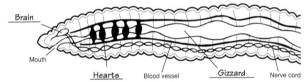

Labels: Brain, Mouth, Hearts, Blood vessel, Gizzard, Nerve cord

Page 45
If left undisturbed, an invertebrate will choose the environment most like the natural habitat from which it was removed. Roly-polies and earthworms usually prefer dark, damp homes.

Page 52
Explanations may vary. Possible responses are provided.
1. Out. The fire could destroy the rabbits' food supply. If the rabbits' food supply is threatened, the coyotes would have fewer rabbits to eat. The fire must be put out.
2. In.
3. Out. The company should be stopped from dumping waste into the stream, and the water in the stream and river should be cleaned up.
4. Out. The hunters should be allowed to kill foxes until the number of mice has increased enough to control the grasshopper population.
5. Out. The souvenir hunters must be stopped from taking coral skeletons. Also, the number of animals that prey upon starfish needs to be increased temporarily.
6. Out. If possible, try to build the highway somewhere else.
7. In.
8. Out. Farmers need to kill fewer coyotes so the coyotes can control the deer population.
9. In.
10. Out. If possible, treat the diseased trees or replace them with new ones so the kangaroo rats and Gila monsters in this area won't die out.

Page 57
1. The Dust Bowl was the result of the earth being weathered by strong wind, dust storms, and a lack of rain over a long period of time.
2. Answers will vary. However, students should mention that the soil began to dry out and blow away.
3. Answers will vary.
4. Answers will vary.

Bonus Box: Answers will vary. A possible disaster could be a tornado, flood, hurricane, or earthquake.

Page 58

Answers will vary. Possible answers include the following:

Material	Appearance Before Shaking	Appearance After Shaking
chalk	smooth, round	pitted
sugar cubes	flat sides	smaller and rounder in shape
cinnamon sticks	long, smooth	little or no change
all three items together	chalk is pitted, sugar cube is small and rounded, cinnamon stick appears to be intact	cinnamon stick has white patches, small particles of chalk and sugar on jar bottom; chalk more pitted; sugar cube even smaller and rounder

1. Unless the chalk was extremely soft, the sugar cube lost the most material.
2. The sugar cube and the chalk lost more material, so they represent softer rocks that weather at a faster rate.
3. Since the cinnamon stick has white specks of chalk and sugar sticking to it, it represents harder rocks that weather at a slower rate.

Bonus Box: Answers will vary but should mention that the calcite would scratch the gypsum since gypsum is the softer material.

Page 63

1. 45,000 thunderstorms
2. 54,000 degrees
3. 10,000,000 times a day
4. 60,000 miles per second
5. 79 degrees
6. 74 miles per hour
7. 300 miles per hour
8. 10,000 water droplets
9. 141 tornadoes
10. 27 inches of rain
11. 689 people
12. 7,000,000,000 dollars

Page 64

Answers may vary. Suggested answers:
Tornado Safety: 1, 2, 4, 5, 7, 8, 9, 11, 12, 16, 18, 19
Hurricane Safety: 2, 3, 6, 8, 9, 11, 12, 17, 18, 19, 20
Thunderstorm Safety: 8, 9, 11, 12, 13, 14, 17, 19, 20
Blizzard Safety: 8, 10, 11, 12, 15

Page 65

1. …it was named David.
2. …so we knew it was a cumulonimbus cloud.
3. …we made sure we had blankets and food in the car before driving to town.
4. …I knew that it wasn't located in the United States.
5. …so we evacuated the island.
6. …they are called earth's "air-conditioning system."
7. …my family gathers in the bathroom in the center of our house during a tornado warning.
8. …that name will never be used again.
9. …I know there has been lightning.
10. …so we stopped and took cover in a deep ditch.
11. …we knew houses and cars had been blown away.
12. …so I knew the storm was three miles away.

Page 70

A and J: Water is made up of tiny particles called *molecules.*
C and F: Water is the only substance that can exist as a solid, liquid, and gas at temperatures normally found on the earth.
H and E: Most substances contract as they become colder, but water expands when it is colder than 39°F.
D and I: The freshwater available to humans from groundwater, lakes, and rivers is only about ¹/₅₀ of 1% of the world's total water supply.
B and G: Because water dissolves more substances than any other liquid, it is known as the "universal solvent."
K and Q: Water freezes at 32°F, and it boils at 212°F.
T and M: The average ten-minute bath or shower uses 25–50 gallons of water.
N and R: A water molecule is made up of one atom of oxygen and two atoms of hydrogen.
O and S: A drop of water would be the shape of a perfect sphere if it were not for gravity and other forces.
L and P: Because water is sticky and elastic, it can move through tiny blood vessels and roots.

Bonus Box: tomato 95 percent, potato 80 percent, elephant 70 percent, human 65 percent

Page 81

1. stingray
2. skate
3. lantern fish
4. lionfish
5. stonefish
6. electric eel
7. porcupine fish
8. angelfish
9. anglerfish

Bonus Box: Questions will vary.

Page 89

A. One string should be 6 cm long; the other string should be 50 cm long.
B.

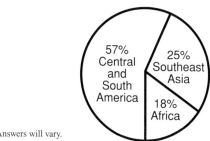

C. Answers will vary.
D.

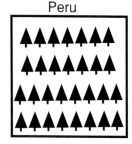
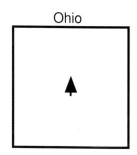

Page 93

Car traveling at 60 mph: 1,550,000 hours; 64,583 days; 2,153 months; 179 years
Plane traveling at 550 mph: 169,091 hours; 7,045 days; 235 months; 20 years
Space shuttle traveling at 25,000 mph: 3,720 hours; 155 days; 5 months; .43 years

Bonus Box: 2,360,000 hours; 98,333 days; 3,278 months; 273 years

Page 97

Assignment I: Mercury, 0.4 AU; Venus, 0.7 AU; Earth, 1 AU; Mars, 1.5 AU; Jupiter, 5.2 AU; Saturn, 9.5 AU; Uranus, 19.2 AU; Neptune, 30.1 AU; Pluto, 39.5 AU

Assignment II: Points representing each planet should be plotted as follows: Mercury, 4 mm; Venus, 7 mm; Earth, 1 cm; Mars, 1.5 cm; Jupiter, 5.2 cm; Saturn, 9.5 cm; Uranus, 19.2 cm; Neptune, 30.1 cm; Pluto, 39.5 cm.

Assignment III: The poppy seeds should represent Mercury, Mars, and Pluto. The grape should represent Jupiter. The mustard seeds should represent Venus and Earth. The peppercorns should represent Uranus and Neptune. The piece of M&M's or Skittles candy should represent Saturn.

Page 98

The objects' masses may vary. Approximate masses—tennis ball: 50 grams, Ping-Pong ball: less than 5 grams, golf ball: 45 grams, marble: less than 5 grams, grape: less than 5 grams

The craters' widths and depths may vary. Crater width should not change much unless the height increases greatly. Crater depth should increase proportionally with the height of the drop.

8. a. ejecta, b. wall, c. rays, d. rim, e. floor

Bonus Box: Students should conclude that the higher the drop, the deeper the crater.

Page 101

Students' predictions and answers will vary. Suggested answers include the following:
1. The model represents how wastes are handled in a real landfill. The materials are the same types found in a real landfill: paper, plastics, cans, food scraps, yard waste, glass, etc. Some materials are covered with soil. Others are uncovered. The plastic box prevents the leaking of *leachate,* fluid that comes from garbage. Placing the box in a sunny area and adding water as needed makes it similar to the environment of a real landfill.
2. Students' options will vary.
3. When people recycle, there is less waste to put into a landfill, meaning that these areas fill at a slower rate. It also decreases the severity of the problems caused by landfills.
4. Microorganisms in the soil cause biodegradable materials like paper and food substances to decay in just a few days. Plastics and aluminum cans (which are not biodegradable) can take hundreds of years or more to decompose.
5. If leachate seeped from a landfill, it could poison the groundwater (often used as drinking water) and the surrounding soil.

Page 109
  a. Not all of the substances will absorb the same amount of solar energy. If performed correctly, students should see the following results:
      Most efficient: water; Second most efficient: soil; Third most efficient: beans; Least efficient: paper
  b. Water would be the best substance to fill the barrels.

Bonus Box: Answers will vary. In some places, the sun does not shine enough to make using solar energy worthwhile. Solar energy is expensive to convert.

Page 110
"Which Waterwheel Works Wonderfully?"
The overshot waterwheel would generate the most power.

"Yesterday and Today"
Answers may vary.
  1. horse-drawn carriages   cars and trucks
  2. fireplace, wood-burning stove electric stove
  3. horse-drawn plow   tractor and plow
  4. broom   vacuum cleaner
  5. washtub   washing machine
  6. clothesline   clothes dryer
  7. candles   lamps
  8. mixing spoon   electric mixer
  9. abacus, paper and pencil   calculator
Students' answers for 10–12 will vary.

Page 117
Answers for 1–2 will vary.
  3. When you sip through a straw, you lower the air pressure in your mouth. The greater air pressure of the atmosphere pushes down on the outside of the straw. The liquid is pushed up the straw by this greater pressure.

Page 119
Answers for 1–3 will vary.   4. Diagrams will vary.

Conclusion: The reason that a roller coaster car doesn't need an engine is that the car is driven by the conversion of potential energy to kinetic energy. All of the kinetic energy that the car needs to make it through the coaster is present once the car descends the first hill.

Page 124
Student answers may vary slightly. Possible answers follow:
• Solids:
Solids are visible. All solid matter takes up space. Solids do not change their shapes easily and do not allow another solid object to be passed through them easily.
• Liquids:
Liquids are visible. All liquid matter takes up space. Liquids change their shapes easily. A liquid will usually take the shape of the container it is in. Liquids allow a solid object to be moved through them easily.
• Gases:
Most gases are not visible. All gaseous matter takes up space. Gases change their shapes very easily. A gas takes the shape of its container and will also expand to fill its container. Gases allow a solid object to pass through them easily.

Page 125
"And the Race Is On!"
The length of time for each jar will vary, but the food coloring should spread more rapidly in the hot water jar. As the temperature of matter increases, the molecules within that matter move faster.

"A Mixture Mix-Up"
The mixture of sand and water is a suspension. The sand will not dissolve in the water and can be easily separated. The mixture of salt and water is a solution. The salt dissolves in the water and cannot be easily separated.

Page 129
Good conductors: aluminum foil, metal spoon, copper penny, quarter
Poor conductors: cloth, plastic spoon, paper, cotton ball, Styrofoam cup, rubber band

Students' messages to Duke should include the list of good conductors.

Bonus Box: Answers will vary but should mention that the insulators keep electric current from passing through the electricians' bodies.

Page 130
Students should observe that increasing the number of coils and using two batteries instead of one increases the electromagnet's strength.

Bonus Box: Each D battery has 1.5 volts of power, so using three D batteries increases the electromagnet's strength more than the two D batteries combined. (Be careful not to use more than six volts for an experiment like this one.)

Page 135
"Conjuring Up Colors!"
Mixing together any two primary colors of pigment-containing media produces another color.
Red + blue = purple
Red + yellow = orange
Blue + yellow = green
Red + blue + yellow = brown

Answers to questions 1–3 will vary.
  4. Mixing all seven colors and color combinations will result in black (or a nearly black color).

"Mixing It Up!"
Red + red = deep red
Red + blue = purple
Red + yellow = orange
Blue + blue = deep blue
Blue + yellow = green
Yellow + yellow = deep yellow
Red + blue + yellow = brown
All seven colors = black (or nearly black)

Page 136
Predictions and recorded temperatures will vary.
  1. Darker colors absorb more heat (radiant energy) and should have the highest temperatures.
  2. Lighter colors absorb the least heat (radiant energy) and should have the lowest temperatures.
  3. Answers will vary. Some light-colored materials could have a greater increase in temperature due to the thickness of the fabric.
  4. Answers will vary. Possible variables include the thickness of the materials, the content of the fabric, or the type of weave.
  5. Answers will vary, depending on the items chosen. Students could note that the only difference in the items should be color.

Bonus Box: A light-colored car would keep a person cooler in the Arizona desert because light colors absorb less heat (radiant energy). A dark-colored roof on a house in Maine would keep it warmer because dark colors absorb more heat (radiant energy).

Page 140
  1. Answers will vary.
  2. Yes, length makes a difference. The shorter rubber bands will have a higher pitch than the longer ones.
  3. Yes, width makes a difference. The wider rubber bands will have a lower pitch than the narrow ones.
  4. No, color does not affect the sound at all.
  5. Yes, some rubber bands fit more tightly around the box than others. The tight-fitting rubber bands will have a higher pitch than the looser-fitting ones.
  6. The thinner, tight-fitting strings would play the higher notes. The thicker, looser-fitting strings would play the lower notes.

Bonus Box: A long, wide rubber band has a lower pitch than a short, wide rubber band.

Page 146
  1. Attract: rubbed balloon + unrubbed balloon, rubbed bottle + unrubbed bottle, rubbed comb + paper
      Repel: rubbed bottle + rubbed bottle, rubbed balloon + rubbed balloon
      Neither: unrubbed balloon + unrubbed balloon, unrubbed bottle + unrubbed bottle, unrubbed comb + paper
  2. Answers may vary depending on the noise level of the testing area. Students should be able to hear the popping or crackling sounds of static electricity when rubbing the balloon.
  3. Answers may vary. Possible answers include the following: combing hair, removing a nylon sweater, walking in rubber-soled shoes across a carpet and then touching a metal doorknob, watching flashes of lightning during a thunderstorm.

Bonus Box:
Attract: rubbed bottle + unrubbed balloon, unrubbed bottle + rubbed balloon, rubbed balloon+ paper
Repel: rubbed bottle + rubbed balloon
Neither: unrubbed bottle + unrubbed balloon, unrubbed balloon + paper

Page 147
  1. translucent; Light passes through the stained glass paper window, but you cannot see through it clearly.
  2. Answers will vary. Possible answers include the following: waxed paper, tissue paper, some lampshades, frosted glass, some sheer fabrics.
  3. Answers may vary. Possible answers include the following:
      Similarities:
        • They are both smooth.
        • They both allow light to pass through.
        • They both provide some protection against the weather.
      Differences:
        • A glass window is transparent, while the paper window is translucent.
        • A glass window is more expensive than the paper window.
        • A glass window will provide better protection against the weather.
        • A glass window would probably last longer than the paper window.